Treatment Techniques for Common Mental Disorders

Treatment Techniques for Common Mental Disorders

Joan D. Atwood, Ph.D., C.S.W.
Robert Chester, M.S.W., C.S.W.

Jason Aronson Inc.
Northvale, New Jersey
London

10 9 8 7 6 5 4 3 2 1

Library of Congress Cataloging-in-Publication Data

Atwood, Joan D.
  Treatment techniques for common mental disorders.

  Includes bibliographies and index.
    1. Mental illness — Treatment.   I. Chester,
Robert.   II. Title.   [DNLM: 1. Mental Disorders — therapy.
WM 400 A887t]
RC454.A89   1987   616.89′1   87-17471
ISBN 0-87668-962-4

*To the many clients and students
whose problems, questions, and struggles
initiated the writing of this book*

Contents

Preface

This book will acquaint the beginning practitioner with the most commonly encountered mental disorders in practice. It is a primer for mental health and human services professionals — graduate students in social work, counseling, psychology, clinical sociology, nursing, guidance, vocational counseling, and the criminal justice system. It is also for service practitioners who are already counseling patients and clients in human resources (welfare) agencies, community support professionals, and educators who counsel adults.

The book imparts technical knowledge in nontechnical language. It is based on many years of clinical practice. The disorders are viewed as part of the individual's struggle with self (the person's dilemma) and environment. The treatment strategies and interviewing techniques described are those that the practitioner would use while working with people suffering from each disorder, whether it be in its mild form or its more serious manifestations. The treat-

ment techniques used are educational, supportive, and ego enhancing in their scope, aimed at helping individuals improve their
learning ability and coping mechanisms. We have attempted to help
each of our clients view themselves and their environment in a different, constructive, healthier way. The techniques used, then, were
not meant to reconstruct personality, although some clients did derive that benefit. All case material is real but disguised, originating
either from our clinical practice or from that of our colleagues. Our
discussions of theory and etiology are selective, as are the techniques and practices, which were also selectively chosen to highlight
certain issues. The problems and issues related, however, are relevant and important for the beginning practitioner.

Each chapter includes (1) a section on the incidence of the disorder and how to recognize it, including a listing of some of the DSM-
III symptoms and a description of how the client presents himself to
the practitioner, (2) actual case histories of the disorder, (3) a description of how the client feels, (4) an account of the accompanying intrapsychic and social dilemmas, (5) a brief explanation of
the various theories of the etiology of the disorder, (6) specific practice techniques to help the professional treat the disorder, and (7) a
section on when to refer clients for psychiatric evaluation.

Thus, it is a book appropriate for those who are learning about or
beginning psychotherapy as well as those who have some experience
with clinical populations. Although there are many books that describe the symptoms of behavior disorder and others that list the
various categories of the mental health disorders, few proceed to
explain how to treat the specific disorder. This book not only
teaches practice techniques but also reviews the current theories, research, and practice issues relevant to treating the disorder—
theories and techniques that a serious practitioner should consider
before entering into a long-term relationship with a disturbed
client.

It also bridges the gap between cognitive-behavioral techniques
on the one hand and those of ego psychology on the other. The authors, trained in different schools of thought, did not find these different theories to be mutually exclusive. The cognitive-behavioral
view provides a practical, concrete approach to clients that in many
ways helps to alleviate painful symptoms. However, it sometimes

lacks a view of clients' internal and affective experiences, which would enhance our understanding of how they experience themselves and their world. This deeper understanding of the client's motivational base was often provided by ego-psychological interpretations. A psychodynamic view increases the capacity for empathy and understanding of the client's difficulties and emotionally conflicted life tasks.

In some ways this is a how-to book: It shows the practitioner how to recognize a specific disorder and how to treat the client who suffers from it. Although the book by no means covers all the disorders listed in the DSM-III, it is a start, a beginning.

It should be noted that while this book was in press, the DSM-III-R was published. It is the authors' belief that the diagnostic criteria put forth in the new edition does not essentially alter the substantive content of the disorders discussed in this book.

Acknowledgments

Writing a book is a very time-consuming enterprise. Almost everyone with whom the author comes in contact is affected in one way or another by this endeavor. Thus, in many ways, the book represents a combination of talents, insights, and ideas that extend far beyond those of the authors.

We would like to thank everyone who has contributed to the book. We are particularly indebted to Joan Langs, our Editorial Director, for her contributions, and to Lori Williams, Production Editor, for her painstaking attention to detail and her professionalism. We would like to thank the following people for reviewing parts of the book: William R. Atwood, Fran Chester, Robin Alloy, and Herbert Schwarz. A particular note of gratitude must go to Donna Hanlon, a research assistant at Hofstra University, who aided the development of the book by researching materials and bibliographies. We are also indebted to Dr. Joseph Vigilante for his initial encouragement of this endeavor.

Finally, we are deeply grateful to our families and friends for their loving support and encouragement. Their patience often gave us the impetus to continue.

Chapter 1

The Depressive Disorders: The Sad and Hopeless Client

WHAT IS DEPRESSION AND HOW DO YOU RECOGNIZE IT?

Depression is a mood or affect that involves subjective feelings, thoughts, fantasies, or wishes. It usually has physical components and behavioral consequences. One type of depression appears to be precipitated by *external* stress. The individual may become depressed because of stress at work, the loss of a loved one, or a psychosocial crisis such as divorce or unemployment. This type of depression is called *exogenous depression*. It is caused by something outside the individual, arising from the social environment. The stressful event contributes to the individual's feelings of worthlessness and guilt, and thus precipitates a depressive episode.

In a second type of depression, the causes are unrelated to external factors; they arise from *within* the individual, as the result of a biochemical or hormonal imbalance. This type is called an *endoge-*

nous depression. The bipolar disorders, involutional depression, and postpartum depressive psychosis are believed to be of an endogenous nature. Early developmental difficulties, later inabilities to cope with stress, preexisting ego deficiencies, and cognitive problems may contribute to this major depressive disorder. Psychotherapy is usually the treatment for exogenous depression. For endogenous depression, medical intervention is often essential. For example, lithium carbonate is a drug that is used to stabilize the highs and lows of manic-depression. The tricyclic antidepressants and the monoamine oxidase (MAO) inhibitors are effective for major depressive episodes.

In endogenous depression, the physical dysfunction and biochemical disharmony occur first, and social factors further contribute to the downward trend. Even in the most severe cases, there may be some identifiable environmental factors contributing to, or at least reinforcing, the endogenous problem. An example is the family that needs an ill member in order to divert its attention from problems within the family system.

The distinction between endogenous and exogenous depression, although helpful, tends to create an artificial dichotomy between biological and social stressors. It is only in an artificial sense that biochemical depression or psychological losses and psychosocial stressors cause the depression. It is probably more accurate to see depression as an interaction of factors, with a prominence of one set of causal factors over the other.

Depression can be categorized as *primary* or *secondary*. In *primary* depression, the depressive disorder exists first; there is no history of psychiatric or physical disorder. Throughout this section, we will be discussing depression basically as a primary disturbance. However, it can also be a *secondary* disturbance. For example, an individual can become depressed if he or she is continuously anxious, is an alcoholic, or has a nervous system disorder. In such cases, the anxiety, the alcoholism, or the nervous disorder is the primary dysfunction, and the depression follows as a consequence. Thus, secondary depression results from other psychological or physical disorders.

Primary depression is characterized by an episode of illness or mood change lasting at least two weeks. Dysphoric mood, anorexia, loss of energy, lack of joy (anhedonia), lowered self-esteem, and poor concentration are other important symptoms to look for.

The *Diagnostic and Statistical Manual of Mental Disorders* (DSM-III, 1980) lists two categories of primary depression: unipolar and bipolar. In *unipolar depression*, there is no history of mania. Episodes may be singular or recurring. In *bipolar depression,* there is also a single or recurrent episode, but there is a history of mania and/or hypomania. In order for a person to be diagnosed as having one of the depressive disorders, according to the DSM-III, they must exhibit certain of the following symptoms. (For a more detailed listing of the diagnostic criteria, please refer to the DSM-III.)

DSM-III SYMPTOMS

The DSM-III has estimated, based on studies in Europe and the United States, that 18 to 23 percent of women and 8 to 11 percent of men have at one time or another had a depressive episode; these episodes had been severe enough to require hospitalization in about 6 percent of the cases for females and 3 percent for males. Depression also frequently occurs among young people. Some 75 percent of a large sample of college students reported experiencing at least mild depression at some time during their freshman year; 41 percent reported moderate to severe depression during the same time period (Bosse et al. 1975).

Many of these individuals will seek professional help at some point. It is therefore important to understand the symptoms, etiology, and treatment of clinical depression. Following is a list of the symptoms of depression, compared with those of mania.

Depression	Mania
1. insomnia or hypersomnia	1. decreased need for sleep
2. low energy or chronic fatigue	2. more energy than usual
3. pervasive feelings of inadequacy	3. inflated self-esteem

4. decreased effectiveness or productivity at school, work, or home

4. increased productivity, often associated with unusual and self-imposed working hours

5. decreased attention, concentration, or ability to think clearly

5. sharpened and unusually creative thinking

6. social withdrawal

6. uninhibited people-seeking (extreme gregariousness)

7. loss of interest in or enjoyment of sex

7. hypersexuality without recognition of possibility of painful consequences

8. restriction of involvement in activities that were previously pleasurable; guilt over past activities

8. excessive involvement in pleasurable activities with lack of concern about the potential for painful consequences (examples are buying sprees, foolish business ventures, reckless driving)

9. feeling slowed down

9. physical restlessness

10. less talkative than usual

10. more talkative than usual

11. pessimistic attitude toward the future or brooding about past events

11. overoptimism about the future or exaggeration of past achievements

12. open tearfulness or crying

12. inappropriate laughing, joking, or punning

CASE DESCRIPTIONS

Case 1

Leslie S. was a 38-year-old woman, married to Philip, a 40-year-old service manager for a department store. When Leslie began therapy, she was about 30 pounds overweight. While she was attractive, her demeanor was not. Her facial expression was sad and pained, her eyes were lifeless, and the corners of her mouth turned down as if she were in constant anguish. There was a joyless expression in her eyes, and her hair was limp and oily.

Her presenting problem was indecisiveness about getting a divorce. Although she was unhappy in her marital situation, she was not sure that she would be able to take care of herself if she were to live alone. She cited as reasons for her unhappiness in her marriage infrequent and unfulfilling sexual intercourse, Philip's lack of ambition, too little money for their needs, and the fact that they had no children. She believed that she led a miserable existence because her husband did not make enough money to support the life-style she wanted.

Case 2

Henry B. was an inpatient in a psychiatric hospital. His first psychiatric admission had occurred at the age of 22. At a height of 6 feet 3 inches, he was extremely overweight, somewhere close to 450 pounds. His tremendous size was threatening to patients and staff alike. He frequently seemed on the brink of losing control and, indeed, would periodically have an explosive episode during which he would damage property. Fortunately he vented his destructive anger on property and not people, for he had incredible physical strength. He was verbally abusive to his mother, however, and the staff worried that he might hurt her.

His behavior on his first admission to the hospital had been far from menancing, though, and he had seemed passive, tearful, depressed, and hopeless. He appeared much younger than his age and acted like a pathetic young child. His family brought him to the hospital because he had been sleeping and "hiding" in his room for almost two months.

In the first case history, Leslie was diagnosed as having a primary depression. Her depression was primary because it was a consequence of her inability to deal with herself and her external stress. She viewed the world in negative terms and, although she tended to focus on superficial external causes for her depression, such as her inadequate husband, she was merely blaming him for her negative internal state. If he were not there to bear the brunt of her negative internal view of self, she would have found some other person or reason for her unhappiness. In other words, the source of her view of self and the world was generated from within, probably due to a genetic predisposition and to unresolved early developmental problems, possibly resulting in biochemical dysfunction. Her unhappy marriage contributed further to these problems. If one had listened superficially to Leslie, however, one would have believed that correction of the marriage alone would change the depression, without Leslie's ever having to alter her self-view.

In Henry's case, the diagnosis was bipolar disorder. While at times he was passive, tearful, and depressed, there were other times when he vented his anger destructively. He vacillated between periods of depression and periods of mania. In his states of mania, he operated as if the depression never existed.

WHAT DOES THE DEPRESSED PERSON LOOK LIKE?

Depressed individuals *look* sad. Everything about them seems unhappy. They *speak* slowly, as though every word is a tremendous effort. Their bodies droop and lack tone. Their clothes seem to hang limply on their bodies. Their shoulders seem to sag, as though they carry the worries of the world on their shoulders. In Leslie's case, every facial feature seemed anguished and sad. Her shoulders, her mouth, every facial expression, and every body action indicated sadness and loss of tone. She walked slowly, sighing frequently. To her, every aspect of her life seemed sad and listless.

HOW DOES THE DEPRESSED PERSON FEEL?

Depressed persons feel sad. They believe their lives are hopeless and futile. No one cares about them. No one can help them. They sometimes say that they would just like to be left alone to die. They have no energy reserves to draw upon. They often preface sentences with "I can't." Although seemingly preoccupied with themselves and events in their own lives, they actually do very little and often accomplish nothing all day long. Sometimes they are so depressed that they cannot energize themselves to get dressed in the morning or take care of their personal hygiene. Every activity seems insurmountable. Taking a shower drains all their energy. Leslie would often report that she didn't get dressed all week because it would just have taken too much energy. Why bother? She had no place to go and no one to see. And, even if she did, no one would care anyway.

THE CLIENT'S DILEMMA

Leslie's affective state of well-being was solely dependent upon others' responses to her. If her husband was tired when he came home from work and fell asleep on the couch, Leslie would become depressed. She would think, "Poor me, I'm married to such a boring, useless person. Other women are married to romantic, interesting men." In this way, she devalued the very person on whom she wanted to depend and from whom she needed help. She discounted most, if not all, of his efforts. In so doing, she set up the expectation on his part that he could do nothing to satisfy her, that nothing he could do was right, and that he was generally a useless person.

Because there was a part of Philip that believed Leslie's definition of their situation, he often acted as she expected him to. In this manner, a mutually self-fulfilling prophecy was set up by Leslie with Philip, who cooperated to ensure the accuracy of her definition of both him and their situation. Feeling unable to achieve her goals and unable to get her husband to achieve these goals for her, Leslie felt useless and helpless. She experienced this as a blow to her view of herself as an achieving, accomplishing person. Thus, if Philip was not able to meet some of her needs, or if she had difficulty gratifying herself, he was perceived by her as similar to her emotionally depriving parent.

From Philip's point of view, he could never satisfy Leslie anyway, so after a while, he stopped trying. In so doing, he reinforced her negative perception and feelings. And so the dysfunctional cycle persisted, each reenacting the emotional psychodrama of childhood, redoing in adulthood an early childhood script that seemed fixed in its outcome.

According to Leslie, her husband did not earn enough money to buy her the house she desired. They would never be able to afford the material possessions that would make her feel happy and fulfilled. She believed that if she had a more dynamic husband who could give her more in terms of romantic attention and material possessions, she would then be happy and fulfilled.

For Leslie, life weighed her down. By comparison, her friends and acquaintances had life situations that were far happier than hers. She was not as charming, not as smart, did not have as fine a house, was not as pretty as the women around her. Leslie believed she had many physical flaws. She was overweight, she thought her nose was too large, and she had a slight imperfection in her left eye which she was convinced spoiled her appearance because she believed everyone noticed it.

She felt incapacitated by persons in her life. She had always wanted to go to college, but her mother never gave her the support she needed in order to complete her degree. She felt burdened and trapped by people around her who failed to fulfill her expectations. The self-fulfilling prophecy was realized. Philip failed to provide her with the life-style she felt she deserved. She saw no way out of her situation except to leave her marriage in the hope of finding another man who would fulfill her needs and wishes.

She saw Philip as the cause of her problems, blind to the part *she* played. For example, Philip did not want children. They had discussed, and supposedly settled, this issue before they married. Leslie had agreed to go through with the marriage anyway. She never hesitated to remind him, though, that it was his fault that she was deprived of children. She ignored the fact that she had agreed to remain childless. Leslie continually complained about the frequency and quality of their sex life. They managed to have sex once a year; after they did, she would bitterly deride him for his inadequacy as a lover and blame him for depriving her of an active sex life. Leslie's critical attacks made Philip hesitate to approach her again. They thus colluded in maintaining a sexless, joyless marriage. The fact was that Philip had strong desires for sex, but he kept them from Leslie.

Henry's dilemma was somewhat different. Although he also had a negative view of himself and the world, he tended to be phobic and avoidant. His interpersonal skills were extremely poor, and he felt that others would reject and humiliate him if he tried to approach them. He thereby controlled their impact on him. He often said to himself, "They can't frighten me; I will intimidate them." By allowing himself to reach such a socially unacceptable body size, he felt he had magically disengaged himself from the world; instead, he had created a course of action for his own self-destruction, a negative self-fulfilling prophecy. He believed that people did not like him and he set it up so that they would not. This fed the rage within him, which he in turn acted out during the manic phases of the cycle, when he felt capable of overcoming the negative course of events in his life.

During his manic phases, Henry often held responsible jobs, seemed successful and ambitious, and at one point had even moved out of his parents' home into his own apartment. He convinced his employers that he was an asset that the company could not do without. During the manic phases, Henry was out of touch with the sorrowful little boy who needed constant nurturance, protection, and even institutional support to help him deal with the overwhelming, powerful, and fear-inducing world. It was usually at this point in the cycle that Henry required hospitalization.

After hospitalization, things went well for about six months before the uncontrollable anger surfaced again, directed toward his mother and family. He experienced paranoid feelings, overwhelming anxiety, feelings that he was about to lose control. He began to function poorly at work and was often late or absent. He also stopped his outpatient treatment and became pessimistic about his potential for improvement. He continued to decompensate and soon had to be hospitalized for the second time. During this depressive stage, he was out of touch with the energy, ambition, initiative, and tremendously invigorating feeling that had made him believe he could do anything.

THEORIES AND EXPLANATIONS OF DEPRESSION

Depression is affected by many factors. To assume that it is unicausal is an oversimplification. Thus, the theories presented in this section are not necessarily mutually exclusive. Psychoanalytic, social-learning, and biological theories of depression are briefly considered and are viewed as interacting causal factors contributing to what seems to constitute an uninterruptable chain of events.

Psychoanalytic

Freud (1917) drew a parallel between bereavement and depression. He believed that the depressed individual was communicating a sense of grief similar to the feelings associated with bereavement. Depression, according to Freud, represents the unconscious and symbolic loss of a love relationship. Depressives feel just as unloved and bereft as they would if someone close to them had died or abandoned them. They experience feelings of dependence and vulnerability.

According to Freud, children ambivalently both love and hate their parents. This same unresolved ambivalence is present in depression. The individual feels abandoned and at the same time feels enormously angry and frustrated about the abandonment. Yet for some unconscious reason, depressives cannot express this hostility openly. They preserve their dependent attachment to the powerful parent and fear losing control over their own murderous rage. The rage is then directed inward and turned against the self. It becomes the source of their own terrible self-accusations. Since they have been unable to verbally acknowledge and attack the person who has disappointed them, they attack themselves. Freud's position on the causality of depression is depicted in Figure 1.

As the figure shows, unresolved feelings of loss and deprivation lead to increased feelings of unconscious hostility and guilt, which, in turn, increase the dependency on the depriving or abandoning love object. The depriving object is primitively incapacitated and unconsciously fused to such an extent that the cruel and sadistic feelings of the love object become part of the ego and result in feelings of self-derogation and worthlessness.

Bibring (1953) pays less attention to object loss and its impact on the ego. For him, depression is a product of the ego state itself and its inability to self-gratify, which is not necessarily connected to the aggressive drive. Helplessness in obtaining what the person desires and finds valuable is the key issue. The ego is aware of certain goals and may also be unconsciously aware of the unattainableness of

Unresolved ambivalent⟶ Deprivation ⟶ Hostility ⟶ Guilt⟶ Melancholia and
love feelings　　　　　⟵　　　　　　⟵　　　　⟵　　　　⟵depression

| | | | | |

Unconscious feelings
of symbiotic fusion
with the sadistic love
object

(This can lead to regres-
sion to childhood fanta-
sies or a desire to join
the object through
suicide.)

Grieving the loss of the love object (unconsciously identifying with the love
object).

Feeling that one can start anew (and
resolution of the difficulty).

Fig. 1. The causality of depression according to Freud.

these goals. It therefore suffers narcissistic injury and collapse of
self-esteem. The individual cannot live up to such unconscious,
unrealistic, and unattainable ideals, so conscious depression and
self-blame occur.

Hostility is not the primary cause of depression, according to
Bibring. He believes that feelings of inability to achieve desired
goals are a more important factor. Depressed individuals, because
they cannot obtain the valuable things they desire, often feel like
small children, completely vulnerable and defenseless in a world
they cannot control, and in an inner world on which they cannot depend for supplies of self-esteem.

Social Learning

Liberman and Raskin (1971) assert that people become, and remain, depressed because of the social rewards they obtain when
they appear to be dejected. They elicit sympathy and concern from
others. However, the well-meaning people surrounding the depressive only sustain the client's symptoms. Although focusing on
the present interacting world of the adult person, this model somewhat resembles the previous analytic model, which also emphasizes
the helplessness and depletion of the childish ego.

Lewinsohn and colleagues (1979) argue that people are depressed
because of the reinforcement contingencies they experience, but

these theorists focus instead on the *lack* of reinforcement in the client's environment. Many depressives may never have acquired the social skills they need to ensure themselves of a high possibility of positive reinforcement. This deprivation helps account for their depressive behaviors.

Seligman (1972) states that individuals become depressed when they are confronted by an uncontrollable and painful series of events that leads them to believe that they will continue to suffer regardless of what they do. Thus, he believes that depression occurs, not so much because of early loss and its traumatic early influence, but rather through the reinforcement of "learned helplessness." Depressed individuals are not assertive. They have not learned to cope. Learned helplessness is a way of life. Seligman argues that when we are children, we are indeed helpless; consequently, we feel overwhelmed. As adults, we return to those feelings. Depressives have a pervasive negative self-view. Life becomes overwhelming and traumatic due to their inability to change that negative self-view.

Beck (1972, 1976) focuses instead on the "faulty logic" and "selective abstractions" of depressives. They easily misinterpret events so that they fit into their negatively distorted belief pattern that they are worthless, unlovable, and incompetent. Their impressions are largely negative and selectively distorted. They define their future as bleak and grim. Beck's position on depression is summarized in Figure 2.

Biological

In order for the brain to function properly, neurotransmitters must be released at certain rates. It is believed that if too much or too lit-

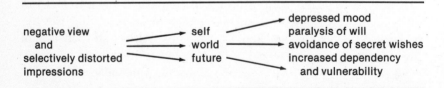

Fig. 2. The causality of depression according to Beck.

tle of the chemical serotonin is released, the individual may exhibit the psychological symptoms of depression (Barchas et al. 1977, Schildkraut 1977). Other theorists (Post et al. 1977, Sweeney et al. 1979, Weiss et al. 1979) believe that the chemical involved is noradrenaline or norepinephrine.

Women are twice as likely as men to experience depression (see Weissman and Klerman 1977). These theorists report that the changes in hormone levels which occur in women as a result of the menstrual cycle is a possible cause of depression in at least some cases. However, to assume that depression is unicausal even on a

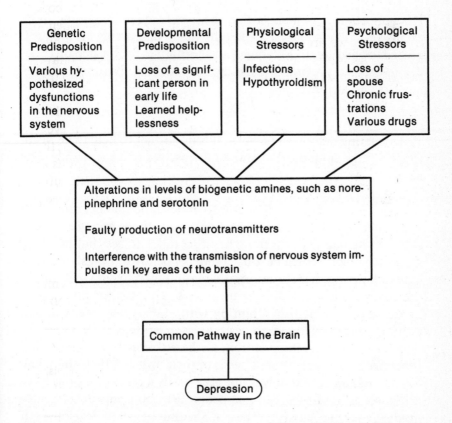

Fig. 3. Comprehensive model of depression. Based on Akiskal and McKinney, 1975, p. 300.

biological level is an oversimplification. A comprehensive model is presented in Figure 3. As the figure shows, several precursors are involved in depression, including genetic, developmental, physiological, and psychological factors. It would appear that the potentially reversible state of neurophysiological hyperarousal may be based on disordered biogenetic amine or electrolyte disturbance, which coexists with environmental stressors that signal impending decompensation, hopelessness, and negative self-perception.

PRACTICE TECHNIQUES

It is important to remember that these techniques are not mutually exclusive. They should be thought of as interacting techniques, geared toward creating change and alternatives for the person in order to replace previously existing, interlocking dysfunctional behaviors and attitudes.

1. In treating depressed persons, it is important to help them begin to clarify the boundaries between themselves and the people they need.

Leslie, for example, was unable to understand that her husband's needs were different from hers. She was at times appalled by the fact that he had his own thoughts. She failed to see that he was a separate person. When he did act independently of her, she considered him wrong, bad, or unreasonable and tried to convince him of the error of his ways. She set up rules of conduct for him, and if he deviated, she punished him by withdrawing her affection and pouting. She wanted him to desire the same things she wanted.

With therapeutic intervention, Leslie was able to recognize that other people have rights and needs of their own and that Philip had a separate existence that was not necessarily a reflection of hers. In other words, Leslie learned that people are not machines that automatically see and satisfy her needs. She thus began to develop a self separated from her husband. She was no longer symbiotically tied to him out of ambivalent caring, nor was she solely dependent on his nurturance and positive responses. She could plan, think, and wish on her own. She was no longer tied to controlling him or punishing him should he not respond as she wished. She also did not feel compelled to set up a prearranged dependent hostile relationship as the only outcome of their marriage.

2. Help depressed persons to see their active part in their own gratification.

At one point during her therapy, Leslie decided that she could not live another day without having the bathroom redecorated. This, according to Leslie, was Philip's responsibility because it was the type of thing that "men were supposed to do." According to her, he was responsible for financing the plan and for doing the actual work. Leslie's part in this project was to choose colors, curtains, and wallpaper. Philip wanted to delay beginning the project until there was a slow period at work so he could give it more time. He also wanted to wait until he had more money.

While Philip was willing to redecorate the bathroom, he felt some resentment because he was compelled to live up to Leslie's role expectations and to be responsible for the major part of the project. Although Leslie was earning money at the time, she could not accept responsibility for any household financial matters. She thereby avoided taking responsibility for meeting her own needs. When this was brought to her attention, she complained that she *did* assert herself with Philip (which she defined as evidence of her psychological growth). It never occurred to her that *she* did not have to depend on Philip to begin the project, or that she could fulfill some of her own needs. A part of the therapeutic intervention was important to help Leslie see that she had a part in her own destiny and that she could in fact positively affect her environment. The therapist helped her understand that some of her anger and unresolved ambivalence was a need to see herself as a victim of Philip's deprivation rather than of her own self-deprivation and guilt. In this negative way, she had believed that she was controlling her own life. This only led to feelings of helplessness and self-deprivation.

3. Help depressed persons to see that there are alternatives to their negative view of self and the world.

Leslie focused on the negative side of most situations. She was unable to see the positive aspects of her house or positive traits in her husband and generally considered most people in her world to be lacking in some way. The therapy often focused on teaching her to see that there were alternatives to her negative self-definitions. If Leslie verbalized that Philip was totally useless, the therapist would ask, "*Totally,* Leslie?" Leslie then started to consider some of Philip's positive traits. The therapist then asked her to elaborate on some of Philip's more positive aspects. In other words, she was encouraged to generate some positive attributes of her husband and not to see him or other aspects of her world in dreary, dismal terms.

Leslie also saw *herself* in negative and unfulfilling ways. She felt that she excelled at nothing and would never be able to be a professional person, a goal that was very important to her. Because of this self-definition, she felt guilty and became increasingly dependent on Philip to fulfill her every self-desire. In therapy, Leslie learned that she did in fact have office skills, which were then utilized to help her find a job. She learned also that she had academic skills, which she later used to acquire a bachelor's degree. Her new definitions of her situations were thus broadened to include alternatives to her negative and distorted view of self and the world. In so doing, Leslie was able to bring some personal and social rewards and satisfactions into her life, which in turn helped her to recast her depression and hopelessness. She discovered that she was in charge of those rewards and gratifications and that she could even initiate some ideas and rewards of her own.

4. Help depressed persons to partialize their needs and wishes.

When Leslie began therapy, she was overwhelmed with depression. *Everything* in her life felt hopeless. She defined herself and her life situation in persistent, global terms. *Nothing* in her life was going right. There was *no* part of her that was at all useful. She was *completely* stupid and *totally* unhappy. Her husband was a *complete* jerk—unable to be successful in even the most minor endeavor. As long as she continued to see the world in these bleak, global terms, Leslie would, of course, remain depressed.

In therapy, Leslie learned to partialize her problems. Was she *completely* stupid? Or were there times when she was minimally intelligent? Was Philip *always* boring? Or were there times when she felt that he was somewhat interesting? Was there *never* a time when she felt happy? Or did she sometimes enjoy being alive? Leslie would usually answer affirmatively to a few of the second questions in each pair. The therapist would then ask her to elaborate on the tiny bit of positive potential in her life. Leslie was then taught to *create* positive situations of her own. In therapy, Leslie learned to enhance, always in small increments, any positive moments in her life; she thereby decreased her overwhelming feeling of depression and her internalized negative view of herself and the world.

WHEN DO YOU REFER THE CLIENT?

When evaluating the depressed client's progress, it is important to ask the following questions:

1. Has the treatment progressed?
2. Has the client reached some of his/her self-defined goals?
3. Does the client feel better?
4. Does the client feel as though s/he has achieved more control over the environment, and has s/he taken on some of the responsibility for his/her own well-being?
5. Does the client have control over internal reinforcers and satisfactions? Is s/he able to provide some positive experiences for himself/herself?
6. Is the client sabotaging treatment in any way? For example, is s/he blaming the therapist for lack of progress in treatment or for ongoing unhappiness?
7. Is the client becoming increasingly depressed? Does s/he have suicidal thoughts?

If after answering these questions, you decide that the client either is not progressing or sinking into a more serious depression, it would be wise to refer the client for further psychiatric evaluation, hospitalization, medication, or any appropriate combination. If you feel the client is expressing suicidal ideation, it is crucial that s/he be referred for psychiatric evaluation. At this time also involuntary hospitalization should be considered.

Chapter 2

Anxiety Disorders and Related Problems: The Tense, Fearful Client

WHAT IS ANXIETY AND HOW DO YOU RECOGNIZE IT?

Anxiety is a difficult term to define fully and precisely because it actually refers to a complex set of events involving all the dimensions of behavior, particularly the affective, motivational, cognitive, biological, and interpersonal dimensions. Moreover, the pattern of anxiety may vary considerably from person to person and from time to time. What one person experiences as anxiety may be very different from what another experiences, and different yet again from what either of them would experience at another point in time. With these limitations in mind, we will now attempt to define anxiety.

This chapter focuses on two types of anxiety reaction: (1) generalized anxiety disorder and (2) panic disorder. *Generalized anxiety disorder* is characterized by chronic (of at least a month's duration), diffuse anxiety and apprehensiveness, which may be interspersed with recurring episodes of more acute, disabling anxiety. Thus, the most prominent affective or emotional component of generalized anxiety is an unpleasant sense of apprehensiveness and impending calamity. Because this pervasive type of anxiety may be a vague, diffuse feeling, not seeming to stem from any particular threat, it is said to be *free-floating anxiety*. These anxiety episodes do not occur in the presence of specific stimuli and can occur at any time.

The individual with generalized, free-floating anxiety experiences combinations of the following symptoms: rapid heart rate, shortness of breath, diarrhea, loss of appetite, fainting, dizziness, sweating, sleeplessness, urinary frequency, and tremors. These individuals tend to experience these symptoms on a day-to-day basis, thus living their lives in a relatively constant state of tension, worry, and diffuse uneasiness. They tend to be oversensitive in their interpersonal relationships and very often feel socially and emotionally inadequate and depressed. They usually have difficulty concentrating and rendering decisions; they dread making a mistake. The high level of tension they experience is often reflected in strained, tense postural movements, overreaction to sudden or unexpected stimuli, and continual nervous movements. Typically they will complain of muscular tension, especially in the neck and shoulder region, pains in the chest, chronic mild diarrhea or the opposite, constipation, and sleep disturbances, possibly including insomnia and nightmares. They generally perspire profusely, their palms are often clammy, and their hands are frequently cold; they may show cardiovascular changes such as elevated blood pressure, increased pulse rate, breathlessness, and heart palpitations.

Regardless of how well things seem to be going, individuals with generalized anxiety disorder are apprehensive and anxious. Their vague fears and fantasies, combined with their generalized sensitivity, keep them in a continuously upset, uneasy, discouraged frame of mind. Not only are they indecisive, but after they have finally made a decision, they worry excessively over errors and unforeseen consequences that may eventually lead to disaster. The lengths to which they go to find things to worry about are remarkable, for as fast as one cause for worry is removed, they find another, until most of their friends and relatives lose patience with them.

Even after going to bed, people who suffer from generalized anxiety disorder are not likely to find relief from their worries. They seem to be unable to relax, often spending hours reviewing every mistake, real or imagined, recent or remote. When they are not reviewing and regretting the events of the past, they are anticipating all the potential difficulties they may have to face in the future. After they finally manage to fall asleep, they frequently have anxiety dreams. They dream of being choked or shot, of their teeth falling out, of falling from high places, or of being chased by murderers, with the horrible sensation that their legs will move only in slow motion.

Panic disorders, on the other hand, are characterized by sudden, brief attacks of acute anxiety and extreme autonomic arousal. The individual experiences *intense* apprehensiveness and terror, and a sense that something dreadful is about to happen. Panic attacks usually come on suddenly, lasting anywhere from a few seconds to an hour or more. These attacks mount to high intensity and then subside—all in the absence of any obvious cause.

Symptoms vary from one person to another, but they usually include palpitations, a choking feeling, bounding heart beat, chest pains, shortness of breath, trembling, profuse sweating, faintness and dizziness, coldness and pallor of the face and extremities, urinary urgency, gastrointestinal sensations, and a terrifying feeling of imminent death. The individual feels that he or she is losing control. The physiological symptoms, together with the sense of impending death or catastrophe, make an anxiety attack a truly terrifying experience. It is an experience not to be underestimated, dismissed, laughed at, or even objectively perceived by the therapist or the patient at the height of its intensity. It is crucial that the therapist recognize the intensity and the irrationality of the feeling. These clients believe that their lives are out of control, and the therapist must acknowledge these feelings.

The panic attack generally subsides within a few minutes, but it may last longer, even up to a few hours. If it continues, the individual may frantically implore someone to summon a doctor or beg to be taken to a hospital emergency room. After medical treatment has been administered, commonly in the form of verbal reassurance and a minor tranquilizer, the person usually feels better and quiets down. In fact, these individuals often calm down by the time they arrive at the hospital, and feel rather ridiculous when the physician or nurse attempts to ascertain the presenting problem.

Such attacks vary in frequency of occurrence from several times a day to once a month or even less often. They may occur during the day, or the person may awaken from a sound sleep with a strong feeling of dread or apprehensiveness, which rapidly develops into a full blown attack. Between attacks the individual may be relatively unperturbed; sometimes, though, mild anxiety and tension persist. In some cases, excessive use of tranquilizers, hypnotics, and alcohol complicate the situation. Since these individuals do not know when a panic attack will occur and anticipate disastrous events, they tend to become reluctant to venture far from home, fearing that they might be seized with panic while walking on the streets or while driving. Clinicians often misdiagnose such cases of anxiety disorder as agoraphobia—the fear of open places. However, the real fear here is not of going out of the house; rather, these individuals fear that the panic symptoms will occur if they do go out. In this case, while agoraphobia may be complicating the picture, the primary problem is panic disorder. Once these individuals learn how to control the panic attacks, they typically resume their normal life-style.

Since anxiety reactions rarely require hospitalization, statistics on the incidence of the disorder are difficult to compile. Using the percentages that are available from practitioners and physicians, and keeping in mind the methodological problems associated with this type of data collection, one can conclude that anxiety disorders are fairly common. It is estimated that approximately 2 to 4 percent of the population have at some time in their lives been diagnosed as having an anxiety disturbance. As has been stated, the DSM-III recognizes two basic types of anxiety disorders: anxiety states and phobic disorders. Chapter 3 addresses the general area of phobic disorders. This chapter deals specifically with the anxiety states, which include generalized anxiety disorder and panic disorder.

In order for individuals to be diagnosed as having generalized anxiety or panic disorder according to the DSM-III, they must exhibit certain of the following symptoms. (For a more detailed listing of the diagnostic criteria, please refer to that source.)

DSM-III SYMPTOMS

Generalized Anxiety Disorder

Generalized anxiety disorder is manifested by the presence of three of the following categories:

1. motor tension: shakiness, jitteriness, trembling, fatigability, eyelid twitch, strained face, furrowed brow, startle pattern
2. autonomic hyperactivity: sweating, heart pounding or racing, cold clammy hands, dry mouth, dizziness, light headedness, hot and cold spells, frequent urination, diarrhea, high resting pulse and respiration, flushed pallor
3. apprehensive expectations: anxiety, worry, fear, ruminations, and anticipation of misfortune to self or others
4. vigilance or scanning: hyperattentiveness, difficulty in concentrating, feeling on edge, impatience, resting indistractibility

Panic Disorder

This diagnosis is characterized by the occurrence of at least three panic attacks within a three-week period (not in a life-threatening situation). They are manifested by discrete periods of apprehensiveness or fear and at least four of the following symptoms:

1. dyspnea
2. palpitations
3. chest pain
4. choking or smothering sensation
5. dizziness, vertigo, or unsteady feelings
6. feelings of unreality
7. paresthesia
8. hot and cold flashes
9. sweating
10. faintness
11. trembling or shaking

CASE DESCRIPTION

Peggy B. was a 38-year-old single parent of two boys, ages 7 and 10. She had been divorced for about 5 years, after having been married to a heroine addict for about the same number of years. She was employed as a legal secretary for a large law firm not too far from her home. She first came in for therapy because she was suffering severe anxiety attacks. Whenever she would experience an attack—and she could not predict when they would occur—she would feel as though her legs were going to cave in and as if she could not breathe. She would also become preoccupied with the pounding of her heart, and she believed her throat was closing up. Often she thought that she was going to have a heart attack. She felt terrified, but she did not know what was causing her terror. She initially thought she had some terrible physical disease, and she had consulted many physicians, desperately seeking the source of her problem.

She was especially terrified in the car. Since she could not predict when her "illness" was going to appear, she was constantly on the alert for manifestations of the symptoms. She reported that the attacks most often began when she was in the car, where she always felt on the verge of passing out. She thought that if she did, she would get into a fatal accident. She would drive to work each morning with a thermos of ice water and cold facecloths, which she would place on her neck whenever she started to feel weak. While driving, she would sip the cold water and hold the cold facecloth on her neck and face; this seemed to make her feel somewhat better. One day she forgot the facecloths. When she realized this, she began to panic. So desperate was she to alleviate her terror that she grabbed some old rags from the floor of the car, poured some of the thermos water on them, and placed them on her neck, whereupon she felt better.

She had stopped going out socially. She was afraid that if she went anywhere, the symptoms would surface. In order to avoid the symptoms, then, she would go straight home from work and get into bed, where she felt somewhat safe. Her days consisted of work and bed.

She had developed elaborate systems for ordering things over the phone and having them delivered. This enabled her to keep the family intact while hardly ever having to go out. She had not been in a department store for over a year. When the children needed new school clothes, she called a department store and ordered their clothes over the phone. She would not go into a supermarket, so the family's diet consisted mainly of pizza and various macaroni dishes, all of which could be delivered. A pharmacy nearby also delivered to her. She would pay a teenager who lived next door to take her clothes to the cleaners and pick them up. She mailed her check to the bank so she would not have to wait on the bank line. She paid for everything with a check or credit card. She would occasionally force herself to go to the bank, but it always took great preparation and courage. She went only during off hours, and only if she was armed with her thermos and magical facecloths. If there was a line she would go home, drained of energy for the rest of the day.

At the point when Peggy began therapy, she had been to about ten physicians, most of whom had suggested psychological counseling. She still believed, though, that she had an undiscovered physical ailment which was responsible for her symptoms. If only her mysterious ailment could be diagnosed, she could take medication to cure it. She was unaware that she was having rather common anxiety attacks.

Because of Peggy's refusal to leave the house, her friends were beginning to dwindle, tiring of her inability to take hold of herself and her life. This added to Peggy's depression, and she felt very alone. She had not had a boyfriend in over a year and felt that she would be alone for the rest of her life. She believed that she was a failure as a mother because she could not go on family outings with her children. Her life was bleak and she could see no hope for the future. She wished that she could feel like she did before she got "sick." This was the picture Peggy presented during her first therapy session.

WHAT DOES THE ANXIOUS PERSON LOOK LIKE?

The anxious person appears tense, as though in a constant state of agitation. They seem continuously on the alert, energized to meet the impending calamity, whatever it may be. If they are sitting, their knuckles may be white because they are grasping the arm of the chair so tightly. Or they may be twisting their fingers or wringing their hands. If they are standing, they may pace back and forth. Their facial muscles are strained, so that they often appear frozen. Often, they will clench their jaws, biting down hard on their back molars. A person in the middle of a panic attack may pace rapidly. They are terrified and fearful for their lives, believing that they may die at any moment or that they will lose control over themselves and their feelings.

When Peggy first came in for therapy, her lips were quivering. She was so nervous, she could barely talk. Her whole body was trembling. She was afraid that she wouldn't make it up the stairs to the office, that her legs would cave in before she got there. Once in the office, she clutched her purse, twisting the handle. She could concentrate only on herself, barely focusing on the therapist's questions. She seemed to be reading from a script of symptoms and feelings that she needed to report to the therapist; she was unable to focus on anything else.

Although Peggy was in a state of high anxiety during that first session, she was not having a panic attack. A panic attack is dramatic, frightening. The individual seems to be losing control of his/her body and his/her life. During a later session, Peggy did in fact have a panic attack and, although it lasted only a few minutes, it seemed to drain her of all energy. In the throes of the attack, she hyperventilated and paced rapidly back and forth in the office. Believing that she was choking to death, she begged the therapist to call an ambulance. When the episode passed, she sat on the couch and for the remainder of the session seemed to be on the verge of falling asleep. Such a relaxed state could not have been predicted from the agitated one that she had been in just a few minutes earlier.

HOW DOES THE ANXIOUS PERSON FEEL?

Anxious persons are scared to death. They feel like they have no control over what is happening to them. They feel terrified, and if asked what they are frightened of, they say, "I don't know." This is the most frustrating aspect of the disorder. They feel an impending sense of doom, but they don't know what form the doom will take. They feel that they are "terrified out of their minds," but they cannot isolate the cause. Peggy initially thought that some physical disease was the cause of her distress. Even though many physicians had found nothing physically wrong with her, she insisted that they just had not given her the right diagnostic test. She desperately hoped that they would find an illness to which her symptoms could be attributed, and that a rational explanation for her dreadful condition could be found.

THE CLIENT'S DILEMMA

Peggy was overwhelmed with the many responsibilities in her life. Since her ex-husband was unable to hold a job for more than a few weeks at a time because of his drug problem, Peggy was the sole support of her two young sons for many years. When she began treatment, she was barely able to survive; after she paid the bills, there was little money left over to buy food, never mind luxuries. Peggy constantly compared herself to her two sisters, who had married very wealthy men. They had beautiful homes and were more than able to buy their children anything they wanted. Peggy had a modest home and felt guilty about the quality of care she gave her children. Her sisters had very expensive cars, while Peggy's was barely able to get her back and forth to work.

Whenever Peggy would fall behind on her bills, she would ask her parents for money. They lived in Florida, having retired early in order to travel and enjoy the rest of their lives in a warm climate. Both had been successful professionals and were now financially secure. When Peggy was first contemplating the divorce, they had encouraged her, promising to help her financially for as long as she needed it. They had disapproved of Michael, her ex-husband, from the beginning, feeling that he was not good enough for Peggy. This was nothing new for Peggy; they had disapproved of all her boyfriends. Peggy's parents agreed to send her a set amount of money every month in order to help her pay her bills. This arrangement went smoothly for only a few months. Then they began sending the money late, and Peggy worried about when and if she was going to be able to pay the mortgage on her house. Peggy eventually began to have to call them each month and ask them for money in order to survive. They sent the money in response to her request, but the price she paid for their financial help was high. Every time she called to "beg" them for the money, they would barrage her with questions: What had she fed the children for supper? What did they wear to school that day? What did she wear to work? Had she lost any weight that month? Had she made any efforts to meet a man? Their questions undermined her ability as a parent and her functioning as an autonomous person. Peggy had fainted in the middle of one of these barrages, perhaps the only way that she could turn her mother off and shut out her anger, anxiety, and humiliation.

Peggy had never firmly established herself in the first stage of separation/individuation (Mahler 1975). Her emotional separation from her husband had forced her to be solely responsible for the care of her children before she felt ready and required her to be financially and emotionally dependent on her parents once again. A diagnostic appraisal of her ego functioning indicates that upright locomotion, or "standing on one's two feet," was again recathected with anxiety and unconscious conflict. This manifested itself in the trembling in her legs and the fear that she would not be able to seek help or physically complete the tasks necessary to care for herself and her children. Her automobile terror unconsciously pictured for her the state of entrapment, morbid helplessness, and dependency that would ensue should she not reach her desired destination.

Peggy's mother was both critical and intrusive, and felt free to question her daughter's ability to adequately take care of herself and to make appropriate decisions. Peggy's mother was unable to help her child clearly differentiate between the child's internal self-representation and that of an internalized adequate mother who protected Peggy from an overwhelming, disastrous world. As an adult, Peggy no longer saw the world as her oyster, and even her ritualistic verbal recitations of her symptoms and feelings for the therapist only elaborated her internal self-representation as that of a deprived, humiliated child who sought the approval of the idealized parent. Her present life events reactivated separation anxiety and fear of engulfment by the internalized aggressive mother who was out of tune with her child's needs for self-gratification at her own psychological level of maturation (Mahler 1976).

On the positive side, Peggy never completely regressed to a point of losing ego functions, and she enlisted help by unconsciously coercing others in her plight to cope. On the one hand, she saw people as a source of help; on the other hand, she felt like a dependent child who needed to coerce them into helping her. She tried to comfort herself by using cold cloths to dampen her anxiety and temporary dizziness. She also had a beginning awareness of her own separateness from her mother.

Not only did Peggy feel financially responsible for the children; she also felt solely responsible for all their needs, which frightened and overwhelmed her. She would often say, "If anything happened to me, what would happen to the boys? There would be no one to take care of them. They have no one but me."

When Peggy began therapy, her entire life was being run by her parents. She felt that there was little she could do or say to them because they were being kind enough to give her money each month. Any time she did verbalize any discontent, she would quickly negate it by saying, "Yes, but they're so good to me. If it weren't for them, I don't know what I'd do. I would be lost." She psychologically pictured both herself and her sons in the same situation, both dependent upon their parents for survival.

THEORIES AND EXPLANATIONS OF ANXIETY

Psychoanalytic

Freud believed that the motivation to avoid both awareness and overt expression of unacceptable impulses centered around the concept of anxiety, a powerful and unpleasant emotion that he believed to have primitive beginnings. He distinguished between two kinds of anxiety-provoking situations. In the first kind, which birth may be taken as the prototype, the infant's initial experience is that of being overwhelmed by uncontrollable stimulation. In this case, the anxiety is caused by excessive stimulation which the organism does not possess the capacity to handle.

In the second kind of anxiety-provoking situation, which occurs later in the child's psychosexual development, there is an accumulation of instinctual energy, which is blocked from expression by internalized inhibitions and taboos. A traumatic state ensues, which mobilizes the ego's defenses. In pathological situations, the ego becomes overwhelmed, but the defenses do not help the person to cope and ego functions begin to break down, accompanied by symptoms of panic and terror. In other words, according to Freud, many common anxiety-provoking situations occur after the ego has matured somewhat. As the child matures, anxiety takes on a new role: It begins to serve as a warning of impending danger. In these situations the ego is using anxiety as a way of helping it to avoid a panic or traumatic state. The danger that the ego perceives may be *internal*, in the form of some disturbing instinctual impulses that threaten to break into conscious awareness and may be expressed in overt behavior. In these cases, the anxiety may arise because the individual has learned to recognize it at a preconscious level; or, the anxiety may serve the ego as a signal that unconscious derivatives from earlier, once-traumatic situations threaten the ego boundaries.

The perceived danger may also be *external*, such as a threat, or loss, or withdrawal of love, or a physical injury. This is sometimes referred to in analytic literature as *objective reality anxiety*. The child, as a result, learns various defense mechanisms to prevent these anxiety-arousing impulses from entering awareness or being overtly expressed in ways that might evoke negative consequences from significant others (Freud 1953).

Repression was the defense mechanism on which Freud focused in his early writing. He believed that repression was the unconscious but intentional forgetting of memories associated with anxiety-arousing impulses and conflicts. In Freudian theory of neurosis, then, anxiety played a central role, especially anxiety associated with an unresolved oedipal conflict. The oedipal conflict is an assumed inevitable sexual attraction that a young child will have toward the opposite-sex parent and the resulting competition with, and fear of, the same-sex parent. In boys, for example, irrational fantasies involving death wishes toward the father and expected retaliation in the form of castration are thought to be the basis for most neurotic anxieties. The oedipal conflict becomes most intense when the child is 4 to 6 years of age; in an effort to reduce the associated anxiety, the entire conflict is repressed at that time. Children deal with this anxiety and conflict by identifying with the parent of the same sex and developing an unconscious guilt and superego which will monitor the actions of the ego at its various levels of functioning. The ego is then supplied with guilt or self-approval to guide it in its reactions to and judgments of others.

As was pointed out earlier, the overt tension and turmoil in anxiety states is seen as a failure of ego defenses to control anxiety. Overt anxiety reactions, then, represent behavior in search of more adaptive ego responses and better-functioning defenses. An anxiety reaction or attack represents an effort by the individual to rid himself of excessive tension by direct discharge, for example, in autonomic dysfunctioning. The person with an anxiety disorder has not developed more adequate methods for dealing with threatening affect and overwhelming tension. While psychodynamic theorists assume that infantile conflicts underlie anxiety reactions in later life, the conflicts themselves usually are not apparent in the person's conscious experiences. Defense mechanisms succeed in repressing conflicts and unacceptable impulses and fantasies. Only the indirect derivatives of this unconscious material, together with indirect derivatives of unconscious defenses and the superego, get through to the preconscious mind. Thus, according to Freud, poorly repressed unconscious forces introduce strange contradictions in adult attitudes and lead to sustained fruitless, self-defeating behavior.

Some of the more modern neo-Freudians and the ego psychologists mention the following as causes of anxiety: perception of oneself as helpless in coping with environmental pressures; separation, or the anticipation of separation or abandonment; privation and loss of emotional supports as a result of sudden environmental changes; unacceptable or dangerous impulses that are close to the point of breaking into consciousness; threats or anticipation of disapproval and withdrawal of love (Blanck and Blanck 1974).

Social Learning

Social-learning theorists have tended to argue that there is no reason to attribute neurotic disorders to complex and elusive unconscious processes. Many have long insisted that symptoms are merely learned behaviors and that, like any other learned response, symptoms can be acquired through simple conditioning and stimulus generalization. As this chapter emphasized in the analysis of the case interventions, however, a combination of both ego psychology and behavioral theory can lead to a more comprehensive understanding of what is happening at an internal subjective level as well as an external objective behavioral level.

Social-learning theorists believe that, as a response that is susceptible to learning, fear can be treated like any other response and studied in terms of classical conditioning, operant conditioning, and observational learning. From a social-learning point of view, then, most defense mechanisms are learned behavior patterns by which we try to avoid or escape circumstances that produce fear or anxiety. This kind of learning, known as *avoidance* or *escape learning,* has the following characteristics: If persons are exposed to some intensely unpleasant stimulation, they will usually learn to make some response that will reduce the unpleasant situation or permit them to escape it entirely. When such a response is made, it is reinforced by the cessation of the aversive stimulation. In many instances the person eventually learns to avoid the unpleasant experience altogether by making an avoidance response before the unpleasant stimulation begins.

With regard to panic disorders, behaviorists believe that by classical conditioning, at some point in a person's life, an association is formed between a particular stimulus and anxiety. The two variables involved could have initially been paired randomly. After the initial pairing, this anxiety reaction is elicited in the presence of other similar stimuli in the person's environment. At a later point, the stimuli that once elicited the anxiety response may bear no resemblance to the original traumatic association. Thus, the behavioral explanation for panic disorders centers around the notion of classical conditioning and stimulus generalization.

Cognitive

Cognitive theorists believe that any emotion can be influenced by what an individual believes (or does not believe) about a particular situation. These emotions and beliefs can then generalize to a great many other situations. If an individual has learned a particular negative belief about a given situation, more negative emotions and reactions can therefore generalize to many situations. In other words, given the same objective situation, the magnitude of the negative emotion can be greatly influenced by what a person "tells" oneself about the situation. Covert thought processes, such as beliefs, interpretations, and consequent expectations, can have a negative or positive effect, depending on whether one is thinking negatively or positively about the situation. When one makes a covert interpretive response to a situation that reduces negative emotions and anxiety, the response is then positively reinforced and hence is more likely to occur in the future in similar situations. Cognitive therapy attempts to modify the individual's cognitive interpretation of environmental events, rather than to alter the environment or behavior.

Rational emotive therapy typifies the cognitive approach to anxiety. This approach is a broad system of therapy developed by psychologist Albert Ellis (1962, 1970) based on the following assumption: When individuals are faced with stressful situations, they interpret the situation in terms of pairs of declarative sentences. For example, a person who fears rejection and humiliation might react to meeting an attractive woman with the following two sentences: (1) "She may not like me enough to go out on a date." (2) "That would mean that I am hopeless and no good." Ellis suggests that individuals with anxiety disorders are creating their own anxiety and negative evaluations through the second type of sentence. Treatment, therefore, is aimed at teaching the anxious individual to reinterpret stressful situations in more adaptive ways; for example, "If she doesn't like me, that's okay, because someone else will." "It also does not mean that I am not a good person."

Biological

Is anxiety, as an affective state, the same regardless of the person experiencing it, and is the affect only qualitatively different? Recent psychopharmacological findings indicate that differential diagnosis varies according to the person's ego state. For example, anxiety suffered by neurotics is not the same as anxiety suffered by schizophrenics. Antianxiety drugs such as chlordiazepoxide hydrochloride (Librium) and diazepam (Valium) are very effective when administered to neurotics. However, the antipsychotic phenothiazines are poor agents for neurotic anxiety. The antipsychotic drugs affect different biochemical systems and in psychotics prevent the pervasive kind of primitive anxiety that may break down certain ego functions (Sahakian 1979).

PRACTICE TECHNIQUES

1. When treating anxious clients, it is crucial to first neutralize some of their intense anxiety.

Peggy's psychotherapy could not proceed until some of her anxiety was dissipated. She was too focused on her physiological responses to the anxiety to think about anything else. Various methods can be used to help clients relax. First, speak in a soft voice, slowing down your own verbal pace. This helps to set the tempo and climate for the client, helping him/her pace himself/herself with tolerable levels of anxiety. Second, universalize the client's experience. Tell him/her about your other clients who have had panic disorders. Describe some of their symptoms. Often the client will say, "Yes! That's it! That's what I have." Reassure the client that there are successful techniques for dealing with this disorder. This helps the client selectively identify with the helpful, empathic feelings and attitudes of the therapist and thus neutralizes the anxiety.

If anxious, catastrophic feelings can be infused with care and some confident predictability, they become less overwhelming, and the client feels ministered to in a time of dreadful anticipation. Repeated moments of feeling cared about need to be internalized by the client instead of defended against (denied, projected, and displaced). Of course, helping the client own up to these more comfortable moments becomes the continual struggle of the therapeutic process. In the initial therapeutic intervention, Peggy realized that she was not alone in her anxiety — that other people had not only experienced anxiety as severe as hers, but had also overcome it.

Generally, after these initial techniques are used, the client noticeably relaxes. This relaxation may be short-lived, however, and the client may call in a few days in the same state of terror as s/he was in initially. This is why it is sometimes wise to start off by seeing the client twice or three times a week until the anxiety subsides substantially. In the more severe cases, it may be useful to refer the client to a psychiatrist for prescription of an antianxiety agent. Once the anxiety is more manageable, psychotherapy can proceed. The therapist thus establishes, by actual deed as well as verbal example, comforting and caring events for the client to cathect, creating positive memories and hopeful experiences which later will aid the client in coping on his/her own.

2. Teach the client deep muscle relaxation techniques and thus gain mastery over overwhelming affect and an uncontrolled physiological state.

Clients who are experiencing panic attacks feel as though they are losing control over their affect and over their own physiological reactions. It is very useful to teach them a technique that will enable them to dissipate some of their anxiety and thereby give them some sense of control. The deep muscle relaxation exercise is one such technique. Explain some of the theory behind the procedure — that a person cannot be in a state of anxiety and relaxation at the same time. Demonstrate the exercises and tell the client how often to practice them and when to use them.

Peggy was taught the exercises during the second session, when, due to her agitated state, she was very motivated to learn. It was explained to her that the relaxation exercises were a technique that would help her gain control over what her body was doing. She was told that once she mastered them, she would be able to put herself into a state of deep relaxation within seconds. Peggy's therapist explained that her anxiety might disappear initially once she started the exercises, but that it would probably return a few more times before it finally disappeared. Peggy was thus prepared for any further bouts of anxiety, which lessened the potential for feelings of failure and helped prevent her from becoming overwhelmed by future stirrings of anxiety. After Peggy had mastered the exercises, she learned how to proceed quickly from an anxious state to a relaxed one, and to use the exercises whenever she felt a panic attack coming on. At this point, Peggy finally began to believe that she could control her panic attacks; therefore she no longer had to fear becoming overwhelmed by anxiety or by her own helpless self-representation. As a consequence, she experienced fewer and fewer attacks and began to feel better about her deprived internal self. The fear aroused by the panic attack may awaken in clients the earlier infantile ego state in which they possessed no defenses or coping ability.

3. Help these clients realize that they can effect positive changes in the environment. Help them test their internal subjective experiences and fantasies against objective reality.

Anxious clients feel as though they have no control over their lives. Outside forces seem to dictate what course their lives take. Peggy felt that everyone had control over her life — and that she had none. This was partly due to her experience of her internal self as a helpless, deprived child who was unable to manage without the idealized parent who could give her constant nurturance and approval. During the course of therapy, she learned that she could tell her parents to stop criticizing her and intruding in her life, and that even if she did this, they could still love her. She learned that it was all right if she did not conduct her life exactly the way her parents dictated. If she did not feel like washing the dinner dishes, she learned that she did not have to — that she was not a bad person or a failure for not being the flawless housekeeper that she thought her mother was.

Once Peggy developed some self-respect, her identity was no longer tied up in an externally defined self, dictated by her mother. She began to master both her internal self-representation and her environment. Once she believed that her house did not always have to be as spotless as her mother's, it became less overwhelming for her to maintain it with some semblance of order. She also learned that her children did not have to be above reproach, and she was therefore able to feel better about her own unique maternal abilities. When she learned that her clothing and hair did not have to be beyond criticism, it became easier for her to take care of herself in a conflict-free way. She began to become her own person and establish her own identity when she ceased to live by her mother's definitions and standards. She became free of the depriving, critical internalized parent and learned that she did not have to fear abandonment by her parents if she did not behave properly. She was on the road to bridging the dichotomy between the good and bad parent, between the critical, depriving one and the benevolent, approving one. Stated another way, the chasm between the internalized angel and the witch mother was no longer as wide.

4. Help the anxious client to establish a support system of peers rather than of relatives.

Clients who are suffering from generalized anxiety or panic disorders tend to gradually isolate themselves from their friends, mainly because they fear suffering an anxiety attack if they go out. After a while, their support systems begin to dwindle, and they are soon left friendless. By this time, the only people who will tolerate their behavior are their relatives — the very people who are generally involved in precipitating their anxiety.

Peggy had isolated herself from her friends, and at the point when she entered therapy, she socialized only with her sisters. Unfortunately, her sisters reminded her of all the things she thought she failed at. They often acted as spokespersons for her mother, reminding her of all the things she needed to do or all the things she hadn't done. When Peggy learned that she could tell her sisters to mind their own business without fearing retaliation, she felt freer. Her declaration of independence and emotional separation somehow made it a reality. She then began to seek out old friends and make new ones, encouraged in this pursuit by her therapist, who also encouraged her to begin dating.

When Peggy terminated therapy, she was relatively free of anxiety attacks. She would occasionally begin to feel an attack coming on, but she would do her relaxation exercises and the feelings would disappear. Thus, while the relaxation techniques were not necessarily a cure, they certainly helped Peggy proceed with her life. She eventually developed a support structure that consisted of four or five close girlfriends and a boyfriend whom she had been dating for about six months. She was able to go out at will, and she took her children on more outings. Her family no longer had such a devastating effect on her, and she was able to tell them to "get off her case" if they tried to interfere with her life. Peggy finally felt some sense of mastery over her environment.

WHEN DO YOU REFER THE CLIENT?

When evaluating the anxious client's progress, it is important to ask the following types of questions:

1. Has the client's anxiety subsided to a great degree? If not, it might be necessary to reduce his/her discomfort by referring him/her to a psychiatrist for medication.
2. Has the client been able to establish some awareness of his/her patterns of interaction and of the feelings that threaten to overwhelm him/her?
3. Has the client managed to maintain relative control over the anxiety? If the client's anxiety had initially subsided, only to return and continue at a high level of intensity, it is possible that the initial change was an artificial one and that more frequent and extensive therapy is needed.

Chapter 3

Phobic Disorders: The Socially and Emotionally Inhibited Client

WHAT IS A PHOBIA AND HOW DO YOU RECOGNIZE IT?

A *phobia* is an intense, irrational fear that greatly interferes with a person's life. As a result, phobic individuals begin to structure most, if not all, of their daily activities around the feared object, situation, or event. It is sometimes difficult to distinguish a phobic person from one who is experiencing panic disorder, but there are several distinguishing characteristics. A panic attack seems to appear suddenly, with no obvious precipitating factor; a phobia, by contrast, appears to be much more directed and specific. Phobic people are overcome with anxiety *only* in the presence of what they fear. A woman with a dog phobia may feel quite content until she actually meets up with a dog; only then will she be seized with terror. A man who cannot bear riding in elevators may remain free of anxiety as long as he avoids these conveyances and makes all his journeys between floors by using the stairs. People who turn pale at the very thought of looking down from the top of the Empire State Building may feel safe as long as they stay on the ground.

Phobias sometimes begin with an anxiety attack, but the anxiety becomes crystallized around a particular object or situation. As long as these individuals can avoid the feared object or situation, their anxiety level does not reach disturbing proportions. A phobia, then, is an intense, irrational fear of some object, event, activity, or situation. It is irrational in the sense that the fear greatly exceeds any danger that might be inherent in the feared stimulus. People who suffer from phobias know this on a rational level and will often state that they know they have nothing to be afraid of; yet when in the presence of the feared object, they exhibit severe anxiety symptoms. Phobias involve levels of fear which are not only intense but also interfere with normal living patterns. People who experience such intense specific fears strive to organize their lives in such a way as to minimize their exposure to the fear-arousing stimuli. The most prominent maladaptive features of phobic disorders are the amount of fear experienced, the accompanying autonomic arousal, and the behaviors engaged in to avoid the feared stimulus. The term *phobic disorder* is used only when the fear and avoidance behavior are sufficiently intense to seriously disrupt the individual's life. Although phobias are common among children, they are generally relatively transient before adulthood. DSM-III distinguishes three types of phobias in adults: simple phobias, social phobias, and agoraphobia.

Simple phobias involve maladaptive fear and avoidance of discrete objects or situations. Some of the most common simple phobias are fear of animals and insects; fear of heart attacks, cancer, and other diseases; fear of heights; and fear of closed spaces. These phobias rarely cause a serious problem for the phobic person, unless the feared stimulus happens to be something that is commonly or necessarily encountered, as in the case of a person who fears riding in elevators but works in a high-rise office building. Unlike other phobias, simple phobias usually are not associated with generalized anxiety or other problems. Except for animal phobias, which afflict women 95 percent of the time (Marks 1969), the incidence of simple phobias is approximately equal in males and females.

The individual with a *social phobia* is fearful of and avoids social situations, especially those in which there is potential for public scrutiny and evaluation, such as meeting new people, speaking in public, or going on a date with a new acquaintance. Intense fears of this sort are generally quite maladaptive since they interfere with important areas of normal social functioning. Individuals with social phobias often experience diffuse anxiety, depression, and other phobias, but they generally do not have other serious behavior problems. This diagnosis is usually first assigned in late childhood, adolescence, or early adulthood. Slightly more women than men receive this diagnosis (Marks 1969).

Agoraphobia is defined by intense fear of leaving a familiar setting, and accompanying restriction of activities. *Agoraphobia* literally means fear of open spaces. The agoraphobic individual becomes anxious at the thought of leaving home or when actually outside, particularly when alone. Many phobic persons rarely, if ever, go out in public, but they can often function fairly well within the home. The great majority of agoraphobic individuals also suffer from panic attacks, either preceding the development of the agoraphobic pattern or concurrent with it. Fear of having a panic attack outside the home is often cited as the reason for staying home. The agoraphobic pattern is more closely related to panic attacks than are the other phobias. As with panic disorders, its onset is generally in late adolescence or early adulthood, and it usually follows a course of repeated episodes of anxiety interspersed with periods of mild, diffuse anxiety. Agoraphobia is three times more common in women than in men (Marks 1969). In addition, its onset in most cases is clearly precipitated by stress, particularly marital and interpersonal stress (Goldstein and Chambless 1978).

More than any other phobia, agoraphobia is frequently accompanied by a variety of other behavior problems. The most common of these are social difficulties, depression, the abuse of alcohol and other anxiety-reducing drugs, and other phobias.

Phobias are common at all levels of society, at all ages, and in both sexes. Phobias are generally more common in females than males, but this varies according to the type of phobia. It is difficult to determine the incidence of phobias because people often can deal with phobias simply by avoiding what they fear. It is generally only when the phobia results in a great deal of inconvenience that the person decides to seek therapy. For example, if a person works on the 21st floor of an office building and has an intense fear of elevators, he or she may decide to seek therapy to eliminate the fear because of the degree to which it interferes with his/her life. Based on a survey of a Vermont community, Agras and colleagues (1969) estimated that the overall presence of phobic individuals in the general population was 7.7 percent, though less than 1 percent of the population were bothered by severely disabling phobias.

In order for a person to be diagnosed as having a phobic disorder according to DSM-III, one must exhibit certain of the following symptoms. (For a more detailed listing of the diagnostic criteria, please refer to that source.)

DSM-III SYMPTOMS

Simple Phobia

The individual has a persistent, irrational fear of, and compelling desire to avoid, an object or a situation. This does not include fear of being alone, or in public places away from home (agoraphobia), or of humiliation or embarrassment in certain social situations (social phobia). Phobic objects are often animals, and phobic situations frequently involve heights or closed spaces.

Social Phobia

The individual has a persistent, irrational fear of, and compelling desire to avoid, situations in which she/he will be exposed to possible scrutiny by others and fears acting in a way that will be humiliating or embarrassing. The individual experiences significant distress because of the disturbance and recognizes that his or her fear is excessive or unreasonable. The fear is not due to another mental disorder, such as major depression or avoidant personality disorder.

Agoraphobia

The individual has a marked fear of, and thus avoids, being alone or in public places from which escape might be difficult or in which help might not be available in case of sudden incapacitation. Common fears are of crowds, tunnels, bridges, and public transportation.

Normal activities become increasingly constricted until the fears or avoidance behaviors dominate the individual's life.

The fear is not due to a major depressive episode, obsessive-compulsive disorder, paranoid personality disorder, or schizophrenia.

CASE DESCRIPTION

Pat H. was a 53-year-old woman married to John, a 59-year-old town clerk. She was also mother to Bill, a 33-year-old bachelor who worked in Manhattan as a keypunch operator. Bill lived in his parents' home and traveled to his job every day. Pat had married John when she was 20 years old, and she had been a homemaker and mother all these years. Prior to her marriage, she had been a bookkeeper.

Approximately ten years earlier, Pat had begun feeling anxious; diazepam (Valium) was prescribed for her by her family physician. Since the prescription was refillable, she continued to take it for the next ten years. When she first entered therapy, she was basically addicted to the drug.

Pat was an intelligent, attractive woman who over the years had withdrawn from the outside world. She gradually stopped attending social functions with her husband, who was active in various clubs. Going to the supermarket became more and more difficult for her. About five years before entering therapy, she began to have trouble leaving the house. She simultaneously stopped driving the car, giving the excuse that it made her too anxious because of all the terrible drivers on the road.

As the years went by, she gradually became more and more dependent upon her husband; when she entered therapy, she was basically dependent upon him for her daily survival. She reported that whenever she left the house, she felt as though she were going to faint. She could barely go a block when she went out for a walk, and would do so only if John were there to hold her up. The two appeared as though they were many years older as they walked slowly down the street, holding each other up.

Pat could manage to travel only to her therapist's office and to the office of her family physician. She felt it imperative to visit her family physician at least once a week in order to make sure that there was nothing physically wrong with her. She believed that she had some sort of serious gastrointestinal disorder and spent a good deal of the day monitoring her internal gas levels and physical examples of her evacuation process. She also monitored her food intake because she believed that the food she ate might be responsible for her discomfort. According to all the medical tests, she was in good physical health. Clearly, then, she suffered from hypochondriacal concerns, anxiety about her appearance, and fear of losing control over certain physiological processes.

While Pat's husband was at work during the day, she would roam about the house, refusing to clean or to do much of anything. She would eat the breakfast her husband prepared for her and then pace back and forth waiting for John to come home. When John was at work, he was required to call her every hour to make sure that she was all right. Her greatest fear was that she would lose consciousness as a result of her gastrointestinal disorder and that no one would find her. She begged John to rush home from work, but when he did, he would find her crying and upset, despairing over her supposed physical deterioration. Since her gall bladder operation two years before, she had lost quite a bit of weight, which only served to reinforce her belief that she had a serious disorder; she insisted that the resultant weakness rendered her totally dependent on John.

Their typical interaction proceeded as follows: John would rush home from work and begin cooking supper while he listened to Pat's description of her symptoms and fears of the day. If he asked her to accompany him to one of his club's social functions, she would burst into tears, insisting that he knew she could not endure the pressure of going outside the house. "And besides," she would shout, "nothing fits me anymore. All my clothes are too big." Pat had stopped going shopping for clothing because she could not bear to be in a large building. As a result, she wore old clothes that were much too large for her. This only served to emphasize her pitiful appearance.

Whenever Pat would meet someone she knew, she would describe her ailments in great detail, repeatedly listing her symptoms, until the person found an excuse to leave. Needless to say, her friends and relatives were dwindling, becoming annoyed with Pat's self-preoccupations.

WHAT DOES THE PHOBIC PERSON LOOK LIKE?

Phobic persons look much like the anxious persons, inasmuch as they appear tense and exhibit "nervous" symptoms. If they attempt to approach, rather than avoid, the phobic situation, they will become overwhelmed with anxiety, which can vary from mild feelings of uneasiness and distress to a full-fledged anxiety attack. These individuals also experience a wide range of symptoms in addition to their phobias, including tension headaches, back pains, stomach upsets, dizzy spells, and fear of going mad. During times of more acute panic, these individuals often complain of feelings of unreality, of strangeness, and of not being themselves. Feelings of depression often accompany phobias, and many patients report serious interpersonal difficulties. Some also have serious difficulty making decisions.

At the start of therapy, Pat was unable to leave her home for more than fifteen minutes, unless she was going to visit one of her doctors, in which case she could stay out for extended periods of time. She was constantly anxious, dreading the time when she would have to go outside for her walk down the block. Like Peggy in Chapter 2, who suffered from panic disorder, Pat also was somewhat comforted by drinking cold water, and she carried a thermos with her wherever she went. When in the presence of another person, she spoke of either her fear of going outside or the wide array of physical symptoms she experienced. During her therapy sessions, she was often unable to sit still and would pace back and forth. She lived in a state of constant fear. Most of her day was spent waiting for John to come home so that she could feel somewhat safe, although she never really did. Her speech was rapid and she spoke constantly, describing either her symptoms or her plight in life. Her body movements were fast and jerky rather than gradual and harmonious.

HOW DOES THE PHOBIC PERSON FEEL?

Like the person who experiences panic disorder, the phobic individual is petrified whenever the feared object or situation is close by. Unlike the person with a panic disorder, however, the phobic person can reasonably predict when the anxiety will begin. Severely phobic individuals experience anxiety even when thinking about the feared object. In other words, the phobic anxiety generalizes so that objects, persons, events, or other stimulus patterns that even slightly resemble the feared object elicit the fear response to varying degrees. When Pat even thought about going outside, she began to feel anxious. Phobias can become so severe that the client is forced to lead an exceedingly constricted, inhibited life. As a consequence, they become housebound.

Pat often reported that she felt as though she was out of control—that her physiological processes were taking hold of her and that she did not have any control over them. The feeling of loss of control results when certain feelings and reactions are removed from consciousness and defended against. In another sense, however, Pat had a great deal of control in the household: The entire family structured their lives around her, the "sick one." It is important to examine this pattern from a family-systems perspective because the incapacitated person is often getting needs fulfilled as a "victim" that are not obvious at first glance. In Pat's case, her phobic behavior relieved her of many adult responsibilities, won her a great deal of attention and concern from her husband, and allowed her to control the lives of other family members. It created the necessity for them to structure their lives around her "sickness," to help take care of her, and to see to her former responsibilities and tasks. Thus, Pat received many secondary gains from remaining phobic.

THE CLIENT'S DILEMMA

Regardless of how Pat's phobia initially began, it is crucial to recognize how her phobic behavior was reinforced. By avoiding the feared object (the outside world), she felt somewhat safer (anxiety

reduction). In addition, her phobia was at least partially maintained by secondary gains. In other words, Pat received many rewards by remaining "sick." Some of those gains were increased attention and concern from John, together with some general concern on the part of her relatives and family. By remaining a
dependent, helpless victim, she was also able to give up many of the
responsibilities involved in housekeeping and cooking. She relin-
quished a great many adult responsibilities and remained in the role
of the child, totally helpless and dependent on others.

Pat's agoraphobia was the overriding concern in her life. She had
little enthusiasm or energy for anything else. Her entire illness was
tied up in her self-involved, dependent, helpless role. When Pat's
sister-in-law was dying of cancer, for example, Pat could not bring
herself to visit her in the hospital because she was too afraid to leave
her home. She was completely self-absorbed and had little time for
anyone else. By the time she entered therapy, she was unable to concern herself with any of the needs of others, including those of her
immediate family. The paradox of her behavior was that while the
immediate effect of remaining at home seemed initially to reduce
Pat's anxiety, she was ultimately doomed to a life of misery and
entrapment.

No long-range solution was possible for her, and she was becoming more and more absorbed by her phobic processes. At one point
in the beginning of therapy, Pat was considering wearing adult dia-
pers in order to prevent an accident because of her "intestinal problems." She had thus regressed to almost total dependency, and in
many ways her life was out of control. She experienced a notable
submissiveness and clinging dependency to John, which created in
her another dilemma. While she desperately needed his nurturance
and support, she tremendously resented her dependency on him. It
was not unusual for her to lash out at him, "Why are you so good to
me? Why don't you get a divorce and get away from me?"

In some way, this was Pat's secret wish. When they were first
married, John would occasionally disappear with his friends for
days at a time. There would be no warning, no phone call, nothing.
One day, he would simply fail to come home from work, only to return four days later, having left his young bride and infant son to
fend for themselves. Pat said she learned to adapt to these situa-

tions, but later on in therapy she revealed her fury at his irresponsibility. As John got older, he gradually stopped this behavior.

After she had been married for about four years, Pat began an affair with the husband of a couple with whom she and John had been very friendly. The relationship lasted until the man died about seven years prior to Pat's entering therapy. Throughout the years, the foursome remained good friends, socializing on a regular basis. Pat believed that John knew nothing of this affair. Pat said that on a few occasions she wished that she could leave John for this man but, at the last minute, always decided to stay. As was typical of women who were Pat's age, she said she did "what was expected of her" and stayed with John. Her phobic symptoms worsened after the death of her friend, and it was around this time that she also increased her drug usage. In this way she unconsciously thought she could contain her anxiety and guilt. Her own sense of autonomy was submerged, as was her sexuality, although she must have feared exposure of these painful feelings that she felt made her a bad person.

THEORIES AND EXPLANATIONS OF THE PHOBIC DISORDER

Psychoanalytic

Psychodynamic interpretations of phobias center around the notion that phobias develop when people find themselves in situations that cause them a great deal of internal conflict. In the past, these people had successfully used ego defense mechanisms to deal with this sort of conflict, but at this point the stress is so intense that their defenses start to give way. As a consequence, they start to regress and display various neurotic symptoms. As with the patient's original ego defenses, they represent a way of binding and symbolizing the patient's internal conflict. The symptoms express indirectly what the patient cannot express directly and finds too painful to experience.

According to Freud, the phobic individual not only readily uses the defense of displacement, but he also makes use of projection. These defenses displace an internal danger (eruption of previously unconscious material into preconscious awareness) onto an external danger and a concrete situation. The result is an irrational, but avoidable, fear. The person now gives control over his life to a fear-evoking, overwhelming external situation and forces that to guide his life while simultaneously enabling him to suspend judgment and guilt about the situation.

Phobic symptoms also represent a concretization of thought processes. According to Arieti (1955), this concretization is an active, unconscious process that not only simplifies emotional issues for the client but also makes concrete, focused, and specific that which is often vague and not clearly demonstrable. It undermines conceptual, abstract notions and thought processes, thus making the ego a more fragile and childish psychic structure. This, in turn, undermines the client's ability to perceive and test her internal feelings and resources against what she perceives as an overwhelming, fearful world. It thus hinders the process of separation/individuation and the establishment of an active, aggressive, autonomous self.

Many phobic people are characterized by a strong desire to be nurtured. In Pat's case, it could be said that she had a need for a dependent relationship that was similar to an emotional symbiosis. It is not unusual for a phobic person to have a companion or spouse who serves as protection from acting out forbidden impulses and comforts them from anxiety and pain. It is perhaps true that as children, phobic individuals were not adequately protected from excessive internal or external stress, and their present fears are regressions under stress to a more infantile level of psychosexual adjustment. The protector and symbiotic partner appears to be in charge of the "victim's" life, accountable for all the decisions and responsibilities.

Pat had always envied her friends who worked, and she often spoke of wanting to do "something meaningful." She was a very bright woman who quickly became bored with household chores. John refused to agree to her working. He felt that he could adequately support his family, and that Pat's working would only serve to show the world that he was inept as a breadwinner. In a sense, this represented her dilemma: By becoming fearful of leaving home, she was expressing her own conflict — her desire to hold a job coupled with the unspoken knowledge of her husband's insecurities. Thus, her symptoms were protecting her from having to make a choice that could at some point jeopardize her marriage.

Pat's fear communicated a wish — a wish not to have to examine her marriage, which might prove to be ultimately very painful and for which she felt unprepared. Thus, the symptoms carried secondary gains. By holding on to the symptoms, Pat did not have to face the painful unconscious conflict underneath. The symptoms themselves represented an outlet — a way of expressing the conflict in a disguised fashion. Her helplessness and demanding behavior enabled Pat to partially express her anger and blame John for her life situation. She was the good girl who saved him and the marriage from her sexual feelings, her accusations of his wrong doings, and her wish to leave this uncaring man.

Social Learning

Wolpe (1952, 1953) noted that if an animal was fed in the presence of an object that it had come to fear, the fear would gradually diminish. He decided to put this technique to use with humans in a procedure that came to be called *systematic desensitization*. As a first step he asked his clients to describe a "graded hierarchy" of fears, moving from objects or situations that terrified them to those that evoked only mild anxiety. Then, starting with the least feared item on the list, Wolpe encouraged his patients to relax by using several techniques, the best known being Jacobson's method (1938).

Wolpe believed that phobias can be explained, not by complexes and unconscious conflicts, but by concepts like conditioning, generalization, and drive reduction. People acquire irrational fears merely because they have undergone a traumatic experience. Once they have suffered this sort of overwhelming anxiety, they will try to avoid similar situations — including perfectly harmless objects that happened to have been present at the time of the trauma.

Another behaviorist explanation is put forth by Skinner (see Sidman 1960). The key concepts for Skinnerians are reinforcement and punishment. Pat's phobia, as was stated earlier, enabled her in many ways to be a privileged person. She received a great deal of attention and love for remaining the sick, helpless victim. These "fringe benefits" of her phobia are called *secondary gains*. Unlike the psychoanalysts, who feel that unresolved unconscious conflict is the cause of phobias specifically and neurotic behavior in general, the behaviorists look at the here-and-now environment for the reinforcers. They also look for the secondary gains the person receives as a result of maintaining the dysfunctional behavior. As we saw in Pat's case, however, certain unspoken words and feelings that have been removed from awareness sometimes need to be discovered and verbalized.

Cognitive-Behavioral

Although Beck's cognitive behavioral therapy was developed initially for the treatment of depression (Beck et al. 1979, Hollon and Beck 1978), it can also be used to explain phobic behavior. The main thesis is that problems arise from people's illogical thinking about themselves, the world they live in, and the future. These illogical ideas are maintained even in the face of contradictory evidence, because these individuals typically engage in self-defeating and self-fulfilling behaviors in which they selectively perceive the world as harmful while ignoring evidence to the contrary. They overgeneralize on the basis of limited examples, seeing themselves as totally worthless and magnifying the significance of undesirable events ("This is the end of the world") and engaging in absolute, "all-or-none" thinking — "I am always successful or else a failure."

Beck believes that there is a connection between patients' thoughts and the symptom. He believes that such ideas are the primary source of all neurotic symptoms. He would state that Pat had "morbid fantasies" about the catastrophes that might befall her if she went outside. Pat exhibited symptoms because of what she told herself. She lacked a sense of self-efficacy and was convinced that she could not master a particular situation. She engaged in negative self-talk and was anxiously preoccupied with herself and her impending catastrophe. Thus, her images of the world were entirely negative and her own self-perceptions were faulty.

Biological

More recently, biological theories have put forth the notion of "preparedness" to explain neurotic behavior. A number of behaviorists have noted that symptoms do not appear at random (Seligman and Hager 1972, Marks 1976, Lader 1976). While a good many people are afraid of snakes, heights, driving, and going out alone, very few people are fearful of kittens òr foods. They believe that some objects seem to elicit fears more readily than others. Marks (1976) suggests that there may be a link between "neurotic" behavior and man's "phylogenetic inheritance." Because of our biological constitution, and as an evolutionary adaptive response, we may be more "prepared" to avoid certain situations or objects. Thus, certain phobias may be indicative of some sort of biological predispositions to avoid certain dangers.

PRACTICE TECHNIQUES

1. Train clients to use relaxation techniques.

The first step is to train the client to relax. Try to accomplish this in the first four sessions. The relaxation techniques require the client to first contract and then gradually relax specific muscle groups until a state of complete relaxation is achieved. Instruct the client to start with the right foot, then the left, and gradually work his or her way up the body to the facial muscles. Direct the client to flex the particular muscle until a certain level of tension is achieved and to focus on the tension, and then to relax the muscle and focus on the tension flowing out of the system. Emphasize the shoulder, face, and neck area where tension typically accumulates. (An example of this relaxation procedure is provided in the Appendix.)

It took Pat quite a while to learn to use these exercises; when she first practiced them, she would focus on how much tension was built up in her system and was then unable to focus on the tension *leaving* her system. Initially, she was *increasing* her tension level instead of decreasing it. With practice, however, she was soon able to relax and thereby experience a sense of control over her physiological responses. Her autonomic arousal had precipitated loss of control over these responses. Perhaps she had unconsciously given up control over her body so that she would require constant care.

2. Create a hierarchy of concerns and responses ranging from the least feared activity to the most feared activity.

The least feared activity on Pat's list was walking to the front door. The most feared activity was being in a large department store. Pat was first told to put herself in a deep state of muscle relaxation and then to picture herself at home, all by herself. She was then told to imagine herself walking out of her bedroom to the front door. If at any point during the session she experienced anxiety, she was told to signal the therapist by raising her finger, at which point she would be instructed to resume the exercises in order to maintain the relaxed state.

After one item of the hierarchy had been successfully accomplished, Pat would progress to another, more fear-evoking item. Pat was taught, at each step of the way, to imagine herself in the fearful situation, with the result that she was imagining herself in the situation while still in a relaxed state. The goal, then, was to break the association between the feared situations and the anxiety. Pat progressed slowly up the hierarchy until she was able to go outside for short periods of time and drive the car for a few blocks. She then gradually increased the time she spent outside until she was able to go quite comfortably to the places she had been able to go to in the past.

It should be noted that the therapist and Pat were working together to master the feared external situation. The therapist helped Pat to gain control over her fearful fantasies and responses to them. The client's participation at first is minimal: She has only to raise her finger. The therapist responds by giving the client permission to discontinue, to go back to a more comfortable state. In so doing, the therapist begins by allowing the client to be dependent and ends by encouraging more independence and mastery as the client becomes ready.

3. Help clients put themselves in some "win" situations.

It was crucial for Pat to accomplish something on her own. For all of her adult life, she had been largely incapacitated and dependent on her husband. She had to start to develop a life apart from his. In order to help her accomplish this, she was given homework assignments — very small ones at first because that was all she could handle. She was sent to the store once a day to purchase the newspaper. She was then asked to read one article in the newspaper and report on it to her therapist, under the guise that the therapist was so busy that she did not have time to read the newspaper and that in this way they both would benefit. Later she was sent to the library to take out books.

At one point, during a setback when she was feeling particularly fearful again, Pat decided that she wanted to enter a psychiatric hospital. The therapist agreed that this might be restful for her, but that before she entered the hospital she would have to research the various hospitals on Long Island. So Pat went back to the library. By the time she finished researching psychiatric hospitals, she was feeling better about her abilities. Thus the therapist never challenged her decision to have control over her life, even if it meant being sick and returning to a more dependent and helpless state. Her helpless state would thus be decided by her own actions and decisions, and she made a conscious choice that undermined her own helplessness. She had unconsciously reached a healthier position in her life even if she ultimately chose to be hospitalized.

4. Help clients to express anger about their life situation, and help them to take responsibility for their own guilt.

Pat carried a great deal of unexpressed anger at her husband. She was furious because he used to leave her without warning when they were first married. She was angry because she felt forced into an extramarital affair. She believed that if John had been more attentive to her and fulfilled her sexual needs, she would not have had to resort to extramarital sex. Thus, she never took responsibility for her own sexual feelings; instead, she projected blame onto John, and felt herself to be a victim of his lack of caring. Helping the client become aware of *herself* as a sexually active participant, rather than a sexually disinterested bystander, is the long-range goal toward which the therapist guided the client.

Pat was angry about John's relationship with their son. Bill resented his father because John could have helped him obtain a good position in the town clerk's office. Instead he refused, and Bill had to work for less money at a job which he defined as uninteresting. Pat was also furious at John for this decision, and for his general disinterest in their son. Further, Pat was angry with John for catering to her every whim, for taking her to psychiatrists, dieticians, and every other medical specialist she decided to consult. She was angry with him for having forced her to sell her mother's house and moving them into a much smaller, less expensive house. On many levels Pat was aware that John was enabling her to continue her phobia. She understood that he was helping her to be incompetent. It was crucial for her to express and dissipate some of her anger. During the course of therapy, she learned first how to express her anger to the therapist and then how to express some of her sexual and autonomous needs to her husband in a way that could be constructive.

After the client has faced what initially appeared to be an overwhelming situational fear, with its accompanying threat of loss of ego control, the client is then ready to face other fearful emotions. After the therapist has helped the client build trust and take risks with their environment, the next step of taking risks with feelings does not seem so dreadful. As before, the client can continue at his own pace, temporarily retreating (if necessary) from overwhelming fear and anxiety without "loss of face" or fear of humiliation or inadequacy. The therapist, then, helps the client deal with safe dosages of feeling, working toward the goal of enabling the client to manage his approach–avoidance behavior in the phobic situation.

5. Help the client's family to adjust to the client's "wellness."

When Pat started to take charge of her life, John began feeling insecure. His role of caretaker was disappearing; his role as the only competent one was disintegrating. As Pat became increasingly healthy, John became more unstable. In order to counteract these feelings in John, couple counseling was needed. John had to learn that he could be competent in other areas, and that it was unnecessary for him to cater to Pat's every whim and need. Pat had to learn that she could receive constructive attention and concern from John. They could discuss some of the painful negative feelings that had previously gone unverbalized without the threat of marital dissolution. It is often necessary for the therapist to help the couple see that disruptive and "negative" feelings can be dealt with if they have a commitment to a stable marriage. Differences in feelings and values can be negotiated and resolved if the couple can make compromises within their marital relationship.

WHEN DO YOU REFER THE CLIENT?

It was crucial for Pat to have a psychiatric evaluation upon entering therapy because of her dependence on tranquilizers. After her psychiatric evaluation, it was decided by the psychiatrist and the therapist that Pat should be gradually weaned from the drug. She remained in therapy on a weekly basis and had once-a-month sessions with the psychiatrist to determine the appropriate level of tranquilizer.

Clients must be referred to a psychiatrist for evaluation whenever drugs are involved. A phobia should initially be dealt with from a behavioral perspective, using systematic desensitization techniques and setting up a hierarchy of fears. Once the phobia has successfully been eliminated, it becomes important to examine the client's psychodynamics on a comprehensive level so that long-lasting cure and a stable adjustment to a more rewarding life can be achieved. If, during any point in this process, the phobic behavior remains or returns and becomes entrenched, consultation or referral for more extensive treatment may be necessary.

Phobias also play a part in other mental disorders, such as borderline personality disorders and schizophrenia. In these cases, they serve to stabilize a fragile ego structure, preventing further overwhelming anxiety and decompensation. The phobia thus serves a different purpose for these individuals than it does for the "true" phobic, and treatment therefore involves recognition of the more serious underlying disorder.

Chapter 4

Obsessive-Compulsive Disorder: The Rigid, Indecisive Client

WHAT IS OBSESSIVE-COMPULSIVE BEHAVIOR AND HOW DO YOU RECOGNIZE IT?

An *obsession* is a persistent, recurring preoccupation with an idea or thought. A *compulsion* is an impulse that is experienced as irresistable. Obsessive-compulsive individuals feel compelled to think thoughts that they say they do not want to think or to carry out actions that they say are against their will. These individuals usually realize that their behavior is irrational, but they cannot control it. In the case that will be presented in this chapter, the client's obsession was the fear that she was going to poison her children. The compulsion was the urge to ritualistically wash her hands in order to prevent this from happening.

Most people resort to minor obsessive-compulsive patterns under severe pressure or when trying to achieve goals that they consider critically important. An example is the student who feels that she cannot pass an exam unless she brings her lucky charm with her. People with compulsive disorders, though, feel *compelled* to perform some act that seems absurd to them and that they say they do not want to perform. Such compulsive acts vary from relatively mild ritual-like behavior, such as skipping over every third crack in the sidewalk, to more extreme forms of behavior, like washing one's hands fifty times a day. They can involve actual physical acts or can be essentially cognitive in nature, involving feelings and thoughts. The performance of the compulsive act usually results in reduced anxiety and a feeling of relief. If the person tries to avoid the compulsion, however, tension, anxiety, guilt, and fear usually increase.

An individual who has an obsession or compulsion can be almost as impaired as an agoraphobic; in this case, however, the anxiety is not quite as overt. People who suffer from obsessions and compulsions find their lives extensively governed by strange ideas or rituals. The obsession may take the form of an alarming, disruptive thought that creeps into the client's mind, seemingly of its own accord and not of the person's own volition. Clients claim that they cannot account for the idea and that even though it seems crazy or alien, it continually recurs. A typical example of such a thought is the belief that some harm may befall the client or a relative. An obsessive- compulsive disorder is considered maladaptive both because it is characterized by irrational, exaggerated behavior in the face of stressors that are not upsetting to most people and because such behavior reduces the client's flexibility and capacity for self-direction.

Compulsions complicate obsessions. Here, a persistent fantasy is accompanied by an irrational but irresistible need to perform the same act over and over again. Part of the phenomenon is *obsessive doubting*, which involves the person's inability to tolerate uncertainty about himself and his life situation. While the phobic individual feels compelled to *avoid* certain ideas and activities, the obsessive-compulsive person *must* entertain a particular idea or perform a particular activity. But the underlying concern in both cases is quite similar. People with both types of disorders fear losing control over their own behavior and being humiliated or experiencing inadequacy or helplessness. As Salzman (1968) aptly pointed out, phobias often develop when persons utilizing an obsessive-compulsive defense system face a situation (often set up to be avoidable) in which they can no longer maintain control.

Neurotic obsessive thoughts center around a wide variety of topics, such as bodily functions, committing suicide, immoral acts, or even finding the solution to some seemingly unsolvable world problem. Particularly common are obsessive thoughts about committing some immoral or humiliating act — shouting out obscene remarks in a crowded church, for example. Even though obsessive thoughts are not generally acted upon, they can remain a source of torment. Examples of thoughts or actions designed to counteract these forbidden, distressing thoughts include almost any kind of thought ritual, such as counting to oneself or memorizing license plate numbers; cleanliness rituals; excessive orderliness or neatness; and inordinate attempts to conform one's activities to a precise timetable.

Most people engage in some compulsive behavior — stepping over cracks in sidewalks, not walking under ladders, throwing salt over their shoulders if they break a mirror — but they are generally not compelled to the extent that the neurotic obsessive-compulsive is. Most of us have experienced minor obsessional thoughts, about an upcoming trip, perhaps, or a favorite old song that we cannot seem to get out of our minds. In the case of obsessive-compulsive reactions, however, the thoughts are more persistent, tend to appear irrational even to the individuals involved, and tend to interfere considerably with everyday life.

The precise incidence of obsessive-compulsive reactions is difficult to determine. Scattered anecdotal evidence suggests that the disorder has occurred throughout history. Obsessive-compulsives are often secretive about their neurotic behavior and are frequently able to work effectively in spite of it. Consequently, the problem is probably underestimated. A relatively high proportion of obsessive-compulsives remain unmarried; some surveys report that up to 50 percent are married. Obsessive-compulsive reactions are more commonly found among upper-income, highly intelligent groups

(Nemiah 1967). The incidence of obsessive-compulsive disorder has been estimated to comprise 12 to 20 percent of the anxiety disorders. Age and sex have not been systematically studied.

DSM-III SYMPTOMS

Obsessions are recurrent, persistent ideas, thoughts, images, or impulses that are ego dystonic; that is, they are not experienced as voluntarily produced, but rather as thoughts that invade consciousness and are experienced as senseless and repugnant. Attempts are made to ignore or suppress them.

Compulsions are repetitive and seemingly purposeful behaviors that are performed according to certain rules or in a stereotyped fashion. The behavior is not an end in itself, but is designed to produce or prevent some future event or situation. However, the activity is either not connected in a realistic way with what it is designed to produce or prevent, or may be clearly excessive. The act is performed with a sense of subjective compulsion coupled with a desire to resist the compulsion, at least initially. The individual generally recognizes the senselessness of the behavior (although young children may not) and does not derive pleasure from carrying out the activity, although it provides a release of tension.

The obsessions or compulsions are a significant source of distress to the individual or interfere with social or role functioning. They are not due to another mental or neurological disorder, such as Tourette's disorder, schizophrenia, major depression, or organic mental disorder.

CASE DESCRIPTION

Gail R. was a 29-year-old woman married to Jim, a 34-year-old certified public accountant. This was her second marriage. She was first married when she was 18 to Craig, a repairman for the telephone company. This marriage lasted three years, after which they divorced. Craig, by Gail's definition and description, was an alcoholic. He would go out with his friends after work and drink until about 11:00 PM. He was often abusive and loud when he returned home. Gail reported that she had tried on many occasions to leave him but "just couldn't." Whenever she would tell him that she wanted a separation, he would beg her to stay, promising he would change. One night he knocked her against a wall, and she decided to leave him "once and for all."

Two years later she married Jim. She had become pregnant while they were dating and had had an abortion. She became pregnant again about a year later, but this time they decided to get married. Jim's parents were very upset about her pregnancy and the fact that she was "forcing" their son to marry her. She gave birth to a boy and three years later, to a girl. When she entered therapy, the children's ages were 4 and 1. Between the births of her two children, she had a miscarriage.

Her presenting problem was that she was extremely fearful that she was going to poison her family, especially one of the children. She feared that poisonous chemicals would get on her hands and that she would then unwittingly contaminate her family's food. In order to prevent this from occurring, she felt that she had to wash her hands at least twice an hour.

Gail related a history of events in support of her obsessive fear. She stated that the week before her miscarriage, her cesspool had backed up into the house, and chemicals had to be poured into it to clear it out. She believed that she had somehow ingested these chemicals, causing her to miscarry her baby.

Later there was another episode, this time involving Gail's daughter. Dishwashing liquid had accidentally contaminated their drinking water and the daughter had begun choking on it. Jim corroborated this. Gail thought that she might have had the chemical on her hands and somehow poisoned her daughter. At her mother-in-law's hysterical insistence, she called a poison control center and asked if it was possible for her to have poisoned her child. They, unfortunately, said yes, which only served to reinforce her worst fears.

Prior to this episode, her son drank some of her perfume, necessitating a trip to the hospital, where his stomach was pumped. These events served as "proof" for Gail's belief that she could very easily poison her children. Confirmed for her was the underlying thought that she was a dreadful, dangerous person who had magical powers and could eliminate others just by thinking about it.

WHAT DOES THE OBSESSIVE-COMPULSIVE CLIENT LOOK LIKE?

In general, the person who suffers from obsessive-compulsive disorder feels insecure and inadequate, and has a rigidly developed conscience. There is a tendency toward feelings of guilt and remorse and a high vulnerability to feelings of fallibility. Gail was brought up in a strict Catholic home where thinking about an evil deed was just as morally wrong as doing the deed. Her early background and development did not help her discriminate between the trivial, inconsequential thought and the horrendous deed. Religion had been very important in her life during her childhood. Because of her strict religious upbringing, whenever she felt stressed, she would pray to God or other omnipotent beings to relieve her of her evil thoughts so that she could again be the perfect child. She thought that this would please her frustrating, unpleasable parents.

Unlike most obsessive-compulsive individuals, Gail was very disorganized with her daily activities, often complaining that she accomplished nothing all day. She had trouble getting out of the house and, at times, when her husband returned from work, he would find her in her nightgown playing with the children. He would become angry and helplessly frustrated, shouting that she seemed unable to adequately run the household. She seemed unable to provide them with a predictable, stable life. Procrastinating for most of the day, she often would not find time to go food shopping, complaining that the children took up too much of her time. If she was scheduled to meet her husband, she would invariably be late. In fact, she was chronically late for every appointment she made, including her therapy sessions.

Gail's presentation was usually pleasant and affable. Although she was quite upset during the first session, she was later able to compose herself and articulately present her problems. She was an attractive woman, neatly dressed. She did not appear to be excessively anxious, and it was in this manner that she approached the remainder of the sessions.

HOW DOES THE OBSESSIVE-COMPULSIVE CLIENT FEEL?

Obsessive individuals are preoccupied with ruminations, doubts, and thoughts that maintain for them a low level of well-being (Sullivan 1956). Gail felt that she had to monitor whatever she touched to make sure that she did not come in contact with anything poisonous. Obsessive-compulsive individuals feel as though they are driven by forces they can sometimes (but not always) name but cannot change or ignore, and they find themselves pushing to attain goals that never seem satisfying once they have been achieved. To be mediocre, to err or make mistakes are human foibles to be avoided. To avoid being wrong or mistaken, one must never take a firm stand or advocate only one side of an issue. They cannot allow themselves unbridled participation in life or its projects, other than as a disinterested spectator or uncommitted bystander. Obsessive individuals cannot relax, enjoy, or savor life; instead, they struggle, brood, and worry. Gail constantly worried about poisoning her children. She could not enjoy being their mother.

At times, obsessive persons are able to recognize the absurdity of their actions. They are sometimes even able to laugh about their preoccupations. There were times, in fact, when Gail would laugh at her behavior. Unfortunately, though, after a while, obsessive people generally begin to brood again, this time to begin worrying about why they cannot stop worrying and brooding!

These individuals are constantly evaluating themselves, examining whether they are "doing it right." The obsessive sets up firm expectations of specific reactions and responses from significant others. The obsessive individual may relate more to the expected response than to the person from whom the response is expected. This expected agenda now provides a vehicle for social interaction. The obsessive individual is so preoccupied with her agenda, however, that she often misses the chance for social intimacy and close communication. Anger, hostility, and unfriendliness are more easily recognized and acknowledged because they encourage distance.

The obsessive person often becomes completely preoccupied with details and documentation of experiences with the uncaring and uncommunicative world. This often makes genuine communication and focused, clear thinking quite difficult. For this reason, obsessive individuals often have problematic interpersonal relationships.

Despite the rigid defenses attributed to them, obsessive neurotics often feel very anxious. Beginning in early childhood, Gail had a difficult time coping with problems of everyday life. She mentioned one experience that typified her parents' overprotection and misguided concern for her.

As a child, Gail had had a very close relationship with her parental grandfather. They lived in the same house, and he would often take Gail to the park and play with her. She remembered these as the only moments of genuine tenderness and concern she had ever experienced. When her grandfather died, her parents did not inform her of his death for many months. She could not imagine what had happened to him, and she later doubted whether she really cared. Many years later, as an adult, she still becomes anxious and tearful whenever she thinks about that time in her life, doubting whether she will ever again experience caring and happiness. It is not surprising that the two men Gail later married were also initially overprotective of her and enabled her to avoid coping with everyday reality.

The degree of manifest anxiety in obsessive individuals depends on how successfully they use their defensive systems to maintain feelings of self-worth and effective operation of their ego systems. Doubt and rumination beset obsessive-compulsives because of continuous uncertainty and concern about what they have or have not done, or about the efficacy of their ritualistic behavior. In psychoanalytic terms, their id–ego boundaries are too permeable and their ego–outer world boundaries are too rigid. Insight-oriented psychotherapy is often directed at realigning those boundaries. Investigation of the origin and history of their anxiety and self-doubts may prove fruitless if the day-to-day doubts, ruminations, and overwhelming lack of self-worth is not understood and dealt with in terms of their present-day functioning. As is true of most forms of maladaptive behavior, the longer the history of obsessions and compulsions, the more resistant they are to modification. The behaviors of roughly three-quarters of hospitalized obsessive-compulsives remain unchanged ten to twenty years after admission (Kringlen 1968).

THE CLIENT'S DILEMMA

Significantly, a large proportion of obsessive-compulsive individuals are found to have been unusually preoccupied with issues of control long before their symptoms appeared. These individuals often have histories suggesting marked discomfort in any situation in which they did not have a large measure of control. Obsessive-compulsives need to be in control of all phases of their lives and are typically driven by anxiety about being controlled by other people or events that undermine their security. If the obsessive's ritualistically ordered existence fails to protect him from exploitation by another, he might have to submit to the fearful impulse.

This kind of anxiety is typified by Gail's behavior when she first started having sex. Because she felt that her sexual wishes were dirty and contaminating, she would take three or more showers a day in order to cleanse herself. She felt that she was doing something bad by giving in to her sexual desires, and that God would punish her. This became her preoccupation. Interestingly, when Gail was a child, her father had threatened to wash her with a scrub brush if she did not take a bath. Thus, the importance of cleanliness was coupled with the childish sexual wish for her father's loving care and concern. The compulsion represents the once-feared parental command to "go and wash yourself," now internalized as a super-ego command to prevent dirty thoughts or wishes. It could also have represented a threat to Gail that unless she washed (or omitted a certain act), she might lose parental care and concern (Fenichel 1945).

The extraordinary concern with self-imposed regularity and control in the preobsessive-compulsive individual can take the form of exaggerated perfectionism or concern that one's actions might lead to terrible consequences. Two other characteristics common in obsessive-compulsive disorders are indecisiveness and highly controlled emotions. Indecisiveness results from strong conflicting tendencies; some individuals become almost incapacitated by endless compulsive rituals and immobilize their will and actions with obsessive indecision and doubt. The excessive inhibition of emotion is reflected in the cold, detached, and unemotional fashion in which persons experience their obsessive ideas and compulsive acts. It is also reflected in the lack of spontaneity associated with rigid patterns of orderliness and timetable living, and in highly formalized interpersonal relationships.

THEORIES AND EXPLANATIONS OF OBSESSIVE-COMPULSIVE BEHAVIOR

Psychological theories tend to focus on conditions that would produce the observed conflicts. Since the obsessions and the counteracting responses almost always involve the expression of unacceptable aggressive or sexual impulses, it is natural to look for environmental learning experiences that promote strong conflicts in this area.

Psychoanalytic

The Freudian contention is that three defense mechanisms are especially significant in the development of obsessive-compulsive neurosis: isolation, undoing, and reaction formation. The contention is that *isolation* separates the affect from a thought or act, which then becomes obsessive or compulsive in nature. The affect is usually experienced as an impulse not completely barred from consciousness and constantly threatening to break through the ego controls and defenses that have been imposed on it.

Obsessive persons use the defense mechanism of isolation to separate feelings from intellectual content so that their obsessive thoughts become detached from their emotional roots; an over-intellectualized pattern of life is the result. In their desire to be overly cautious or protective of their loved ones, they often rob them of their affectionate loving care.

Undoing refers to many features of compulsive rituals in which the person attempts to undo the harm, real or imagined, that could result from the unacceptable impulse. Engaging in a certain ritualistic behavior "cancels out" the dangerous impulse. Undoing is illustrated by the individual who, whenever he turns off a light, thinks, "My father will die," which is the unconscious wish. This thought compels him to turn around, touch the switch, turn on the light, and say, "I take back that thought." The compulsive act thus undoes that which he feared would result from the initial thought. The initial thought might have had its roots in an unresolved underlying aggressive or death-wish impulse toward the father.

Reaction formations are also quite common. Obsessive concern with cleanliness may be a defense against sexual wishes or underlying urges to be dirty. Compulsive orderliness may protect the person from the fear of unleashed aggression, from the wish to smash everything in sight. Or, excessive politeness and formality may protect the person from urges to be cruel and sadistic. Reaction formation is illustrated by the mother who is overly solicitous of her children because of her underlying aggressive feelings toward them. Thus, she compulsively checks their room dozens of times a night to make sure they are safe. She thereby undertakes an attitude contradictory to the original thought.

Reaction formations are often used with undoing defenses, except that they are expressed in broad personality styles rather than in highly specific rituals. To protect their loved ones from hostile wishes, compulsive neurotics so rigorously and devoutly guard them from danger that they often torment them with their doubts. They then inadvertently express the unconscious hostility despite their need to prevent it.

From a developmental point of view, the obsessive person has regressed, in the face of an intense oedipal conflict, to the anal stage. Compulsive concerns with cleanliness and orderliness represent reaction formations against anal impulses to be dirty and messy. Compulsive tendencies to inhibit emotion or to be formal or excessively good, on the other hand, reflect reaction formations against anal-sadistic impulses, originating in the child's defiance of parental efforts to force compliance with toilet training.

It is interesting to note that at one point during Gail's therapy, the therapist requested that she question her mother about her toilet training. Gail's mother informed her that she was trained when she was 1 year old because her mother was pregnant with her second child and wanted Gail trained before the baby was born. Her wish for Gail's mastery and control was based on her own needs, not the child's developmental readiness. Unfortunately, her mother had a miscarriage. Her mother was 27 years old at the time, exactly the same age as Gail was when she had her miscarriage, leading the therapist to wonder whether Gail felt incapable of caring for the child, just as she had felt that her mother was incapable of loving and caring for her. In this way she may have unconsciously contributed to aborting her own child.

Interpersonal

In Sullivan's interpersonal and social view, the obsessive social self-system is a crude but stable attempt to deal with the interpersonal world, which never really achieves for them a true sense of a well-defined, competent self. Neither do they have a clear sense of how badly they have dealt with others. This helps them to avoid a great deal of anxiety and self-doubt. Their internal, unconscious self-representation reflects a great need for grandiosity and perfection to exclude or minimize any feelings of inferiority or badness.

In spite of their arrogance and grandiose contempt for others, they feel inferior to others. They invariably make inordinate demands on friends, spouses, and coworkers, not so much out of the need for unconscious hostility, as the Freudians maintain, but due to their need to have others maintain their shaky self-esteem and their grandiose self-expectations. They are often not above a certain amount of cruelty to others if it helps to maintain their own tenuous self-operations. The underlying fear is that despite their rituals and compulsions and expansive self-ideas, they will never quite be capable of being rescued or regenerated from their feelings of badness and evil. Their rather desolate early life experiences do not innoculate them from misunderstanding and future exploitiveness in their relationships with others (Sullivan 1956).

Social Learning

The social-learning explanation holds that most of the strategems of the obsessive-compulsive are responses learned and maintained because they reduce or avoid anxiety and negative emotions. Parents of obsessive-compulsives not only fail to model humor, spontaneity, or fun, but may also actively punish the child's expression of these traits. They seem to have carried to an extreme the conditions thought to promote the internalization of parental admonitions. There is generally a history of clearly repeated rules of expected thought and conduct. These parents typically have themselves modeled conscientious behavior of a compulsive quality. They have also conditioned the child to experience positive emotion upon behaving (or thinking about behaving) in a desirable way and to experience negative emotions such as anxiety, shame, or guilt upon behaving (or thinking of behaving) in an undesirable way. Obsessive children have internalized their parents' rules to such an extreme degree that their whole world is dominated by striving for imagined parental approval by thinking good thoughts and by avoiding imagined parental disapproval by engaging in all manner of magical and ritualistic thoughts and behaviors.

The treatment of obsessions and compulsions has taken directions somewhat different from the treatment of other anxiety disorders. The goal in treating individuals who engage in compulsive behaviors is to stop the behavior long enough for them to discover that the vague dreaded consequence does not happen (Marks 1973). Mills and colleagues (1973) used the *response-prevention method* to treat five individuals with serious compulsive behaviors. In the case of a woman hospitalized for excessive handwashing (over fifty times a day), they removed the handles on the sink so that the woman could not turn on the water. Her handwashing behavior fell to zero; after this period, when the handles were replaced, the frequency of handwashing remained much lower than it had been before intervention. Correspondingly, the client's compulsive urges gradually approached zero. Implementation of this procedure generally involves finding some effective way of temporarily blocking a compulsive behavior, although some clients are able to voluntarily stop the behavior when urged to do so by a therapist.

Turner and co-workers (1979) confirmed the effectiveness of response prevention in the treatment of compulsive disorders; however, they found that this approach did little to reduce the problems that are often associated with obsessive-compulsive behavior, such as depression and interpersonal difficulties. Obsessive thoughts and compulsions also can often be eliminated by mild aversion conditioning (Bandura 1969, Bandura and Bareb 1973, Stern et al. 1973). Here, the conditioning works best when combined with reinforcement of more adaptive alternative behaviors.

PRACTICE TECHNIQUES

1. Be supportive yet firm in your initial approach.

Where there exists better ego functioning and less preoccupation with obsessive thoughts and rituals, the therapist can engage the conflict-free ego in making its own decisions and taking actions (that is, to use judgment). Initially, Gail contacted the therapist three or four times a week. Her reason for calling typically was that she was facing ambivalent feelings, confusion, and doubt and could not decide what to do next. For example, an entire day would go by and she would not have accomplished anything because she could not get out of the bathroom. Washing her hands in the bathroom often took up a good portion of her day. The magical ritual substituted for decision making and leading her own life. Now it was evening and her husband would soon be home. Gail knew that he would be angry when he saw that she had accomplished nothing all day.

At this point, perhaps a half hour before her husband returned home, she would call the therapist, overreacting, upset, and in crisis. Should she just remain in her undressed state and prepare for his screams, or should she make some attempts at organizing herself? The husband in this case became a displacement and projection of the originally loved and yet feared, punitive, frustrating parent (superego figure), complete with commands and cautions. At the same time, he also represented the desired protector against feared impulses, who would guide Gail toward desirable actions. For some reason, Gail never resolved her conflicted and dichotomous feelings about the punitive or loving parent, perhaps because she had never felt enough genuine caring and concern as a child to counteract the punitive, commanding parent with the loving one.

When Gail telephoned with this question, the therapist, always in a supportive manner, would ask Gail what needed to be done in order to avoid the yelling and the feared humiliation. Then the therapist would tell Gail what to do next. The therapist thus became the protective parent who was lacking in Gail's internal ego system. Gail would make a list and follow the therapist's instructions, thereby minimizing her chances of being lectured by her "punitive husband." After a while, Gail was able to compose her own list and deal with her husband more realistically and less as a commanding, punitive protector. This can only be accomplished, though, if the therapist is felt to offer options and beliefs that add to the client's self-esteem, which, in turn, helps to negate some of the evil thoughts.

2. Help the client to gain some control over the obsessive thoughts.

Obsessive thoughts have been successfully treated using a technique known as *thought stopping* (Wolpe 1958). This procedure involves telling the client to focus on the obsessive thought for a moment, after which the therapist shouts, "Stop!" This usually distracts the client and momentarily stops the obsessive thought. The procedure is repeated several times until the client can silently give the command to himself and thereby terminate the obsessive thought.

Rimm, Saunders, and Westell (1975) used a modified version of this method, in which the client also reduced anxiety by repeating positive thoughts to take the place of the obsessional thoughts — "I will keep control of my mind and never hurt anyone!" This study indicated that thought stopping was generally effective, confirming other reports by Hays and Waddell (1976), Marks (1973), and Rimm (1973). The therapist presents the client with reasonable limits to his/her painful suffering and a rational, loving approach to protect him/her from losing control over her/his life and his/her "evil, disordered impulses."

Gail was told during the intial sessions that it would be helpful if she talked to herself. In other words, whenever she started to think of the possibility of her hands being contaminated with chemicals, she was told to tell herself that she was being ridiculous, that she was not going to poison anyone, that there were no poisons on her hands, and that she did not, therefore, have to wash her hands.

Another aspect of this technique was to help Gail to see the unreality of her thoughts. The therapist would encourage Gail to indulge in her secret fantasies, "What would happen if you *did* get the bleach on your hands?" The purpose of this technique was to lead her through the fantasy from beginning to end in order to help her see whether she was going to hurt anyone. By answering questions about what she would do next, Gail was able to rationally explore and "know" that she was not going to hurt anyone.

3. Encourage the expression of anger, frustration, and a host of other feelings that become possible when the client is not preoccupied with loss of control and evil thoughts.

As was stated earlier, Gail was chronically late for appointments. At first, the therapist was supportive, saying it was all right. In so doing, the therapist was colluding with the negativistic child in Gail. As time went on, however, the therapist became less and less understanding. When Gail arrived late with her many excuses, the therapist would say nothing. At one point, the therapist told Gail that when she arrived on time for her appointment, they could indeed have a celebration. Interestingly, this statement led to an important insight for Gail. Shortly thereafter, the therapist was about five minutes late for a session. It happened to be the first time that Gail was there on time! The therapist, after apologizing, asked Gail how she felt about her being late. Gail said that it was all right, that she understood; she was submissive, compliant, and understanding, as was usual for her.

Three weeks later, however, Gail reported during a session that on the day when the therapist had been late, she had been waiting outside, pacing back and forth, feeling frustrated and disappointed. She had dropped her glove in the snow and later became terrified that the glove had gotten contaminated with dog urine and that she would thus poison her children. The therapist asked how Gail felt about the therapist's having disappointed and frustrated her. Finally, Gail started to express her annoyance, disappointment, and anger. She admitted that she actually had been annoyed with the therapist for being late, especially since it was the first time that she was on time and she had wanted to show the therapist that she really could be on time. It was shortly thereafter that Gail realized that whenever she had a negative feeling about something or someone, that she also had an urge to wash her hands. Gail had spent most of her life being an obedient, good child who ritualistically obeyed her mother regardless of her own secret wishes. However, she was also the naughty child who would put on a pleasant face to hide her desire to rebel against her mother's strong, domineering will. If she only secretly rebelled against the frustrating, bad mother, perhaps she did not have to risk losing the loving, protective one. Her passive, disobedient behavior with her husband enabled her to go along with his demands and controls so that she did not have to deal with being a competent, loving mother.

4. Teach these clients to use assertiveness techniques to express their needs, and help them to risk expressing these needs no matter what the feared consequences.

After Gail had the initial insight into why she was washing her hands, the handwashing ritual began to occupy a secondary place in her life. At this point in the therapy, whenever the client began to feel annoyed at her parents or her husband, she talked about it. If she did not want to do something, she was better able to express herself and to define her own desires. She could also discriminate between appropriate and inappropriate behavior. The inappropriate behavior was a false front, needed to convince her mother and husband that she was not a terrible, unlovable person—that she was not a bad person that nobody could love, not even Gail herself.

Soon after Gail started expressing herself, her husband began having trouble at work and wanted Gail to get a job to add to the family finances. The therapist was somewhat concerned about the responsibilities involved and questioned Gail as to whether she felt ready and willing to work. Gail believed that she was ready, and she soon found a job working as a receptionist in an office. Gail functioned very well at this job and found the role gratifying. After a few months she terminated the therapy.

The therapist needs to allow the client to make the decision to terminate treatment, in order to enable him to deal with his own self-doubts. This helps the client to establish an inner self-representation that is competent to make decisions and to deal with the punitive superego, which may try to undermine constructive actions.

It is now two years since Gail terminated therapy. The therapist received a Christmas card from Gail each year. On both occasions, Gail included a short note describing how happy she is with her life.

In reviewing this case, one would have to wonder whether Gail had unresolved feelings of guilt and whether she feared punishment for having an abortion. She must have unconsciously believed that she had indeed killed the child. When she became pregnant again, she felt compelled to marry the father. This absolved her from having to make the decision as a mature adult to marry him and give birth to her child. After all, hadn't her parents led her to believe that she was incapable of leading her own life. Even her future in-laws felt that the marriage was "wrong in the first place." These circumstances and events combined to contribute to Gail's doubt, and her guilt and ambivalence about her children confirmed for her that she did not deserve to be a mother. The message was conveyed that it was better for her to symbolically displace these thoughts and unconsciously eliminate the children altogether. In that way she could be protected from both her evil thoughts and her punitive and guilt-inducing superego. The compliant, helpless child could then feel protected from the powerful, frustrating, depriving parents, and perhaps even gain from them the love and protection that she was so unable to give to herself.

WHEN DO YOU REFER THE CLIENT?

The therapist must ascertain whether the client is able both to render objective judgments and to envision the possibility of engaging in more constructive behavior. With the therapist's help, the client can differentiate between the evil thoughts and the compulsion to act on them. It is difficult to determine whether to refer this type of client because it is sometimes difficult to ascertain when the ritual will take on a secondary, delusional meaning in the client's life. If there is no decrease in the ritualistic behavior after three months of regular (at least once a week) therapy, however, the patient probably should be psychiatrically evaluated. A more severe underlying disorder may be operating, and a second opinion might help the therapist to make this determination. Differential diagnosis is necessary because obsessional thoughts and rituals sometimes operate as a defense against a more serious mental disorder, such as schizophrenia.

Chapter 5

Eating Disorders: Primitive Struggles with Autonomy

WHAT ARE ANOREXIA NERVOSA AND BULIMIA AND HOW DO YOU RECOGNIZE THEM?

The client with *anorexia nervosa* loses so much weight by refusing food or by vomiting shortly after eating, that she risks dying of starvation. Sufferers of this disorder typically envision themselves as "fat," no matter how emaciated they really are. Some theorists consider anorexia nervosa to be related to hysterical conversion disorders. Because of its widespread and often very serious effects on various organ systems, however, it seems fitting to include it within the psychophysiological category.

According to a number of experts (Bruch 1973, 1978; Rosman et al. 1975; Van Buskirk 1977), anorexia nervosa appears to follow a characteristic course. The typical client grows up in a fairly affluent home where food is plentiful and takes on a magical role. The future client has distinguished herself as a "model" child—obedient, cooperative, bright, and very industrious. She is a child who always obeys her parents' commands. She often "empties her plate," to her parents' delight. Such children play this role so well that the parents are indulgently contented with their ritualistic conformity. These children rarely dare to shed this role, possibly for fear that if they were to do so, their parents will be unable to recognize them.

The parents of these children seem to count on them to maintain the system's stability; it is as though if these children were not obedient, conforming, and well fed, the narcissistic security system of the family would be seriously threatened and the parents would become ridden with anxiety. "Aren't you eating today?" "Don't you feel well?" "Is there anything wrong with you?" The parents of the future anorectic appear to be blind to their child's emotional and physical needs for self-validation. The "preanorectic" is too good to be true. There appears to be something ominously "driven" about her desire to please. She cannot be satisfied with being good; she must be perfect. She also seems somewhat anxious and phobic, remaining close to home and giving the impression of being strongly attached to mother.

In addition, the future anorectic often has a history of problems with food. She may always have been a "picky" eater, or (a much more likely possibility) she may always have had trouble controlling her weight and may tend to be slightly plump. In any event, at some point during adolescence (usually between the ages of 12 and 18), she decides that she is too fat and proceeds to go on a diet. Any extra pounds disappear quickly. People compliment her on her altered appearance, telling her how nice and thin she looks. Despite her success, however, the anorectic is convinced that she still is not thin enough and continues to try to lose weight. Gradually and insidiously, her dieting gets completely out of hand, out of control. No matter how gaunt and emaciated she becomes, even if she tips the scales at a meager 70 pounds, the anorectic insists that she is too fat.

At this point her concern with food is an all-consuming obsession. Often she measures out her daily rations in advance. If she happens to take in more than her allowance, she may resort to laxatives or force herself to vomit. She may begin to engage in excessive physical exercise in order to ensure her continued slim state. Strangely enough, until her weight drops dangerously low, the anorectic tends to have enormous energy and adheres to a very active schedule. Even after she has become markedly underweight, she still may be able to maintain a strenuous exercise program.

The typical client, then, is an adolescent female who becomes obsessed with a fear of becoming overweight and who then places herself on a rigidly controlled diet, often accompanied by rigorous exercise routines. She proceeds to lose a substantial amount of weight. As she loses weight, she becomes even more frightened of becoming overweight, so she restricts her diet even more stringently. The client is now obsessed with food and its preparation. She may collect recipes and cookbooks, and may even contemplate a career in nutrition. Bizarre habits of hoarding food, cutting food into small pieces, dawdling and playing with food, and concocting weird food combinations are quite typical behavior of the anorectic female. Although many clients with anorexia also have depressive symptoms and eventually become socially isolated, their thinking, outside of their distorted body perception, is usually not grossly disturbed. They are not suffering from a psychotic disorder.

Bruch (1973) describes three basic symptoms of disordered psychological functioning in primary anorectics. First, there is a disturbance, of delusional proportions, in the individual's body image and self-concept. Even when reduced to a grotesque, pitiful, skeletonlike appearance, the anorectic may deny that she is too thin and indeed continue to worry about being too fat. As Arieti (1974a) and Bruch (1978) observe, the adolescent who suffers from this disturbance appears to be somewhat delusional about her body image and the reality associated with it. She may look like a refugee from a concentration camp. She may have grown so weak that she can barely walk from room to room. Yet she continues to insist that the image she sees reflected back in her mirror is obese. If asked to show the examiner where she is fat, she will point out some excess fold of skin. Her alarmed family, friends, and physician may plead with her to eat — all to no avail. She will eat for no one. The diet she is following utterly dominates her existence, often to the point of threatening her life. It appears as though the diet regimen becomes the instrument through which she can subdue her body and exert some control over her helpless, impotent existence.

Second, there appears to be a disturbance in the accuracy of the perception, or cognitive interpretation, of stimuli arising in the body. Rather than a mere loss of appetite, there is a failure to recognize cues of hunger, a failure similar to that occurring in many obese individuals. The anorectic may also fail to recognize bodily cues indicating fatigue. Despite severe malnutrition, the client may exhibit hyperactivity.

Finally, there is usually a paralyzing sense of ineffectiveness—a feeling of acting only in response to the demands of others, rather than to one's own needs and wishes. This feeling of lack of control is typically masked by a surface negativism and stubborn defiance, which, unfortunately, make treatment difficult. These clients reject their bodies, reject the notion of life through a positive somatic existence, and, finally, reject the notion of death as an inevitable consequence of disregarding their corporal needs.

In anorexia nervosa, eating is reduced to a point at which severe weight loss occurs. Although it was once apparently quite rare, the incidence of this disorder has increased alarmingly in recent years, for reasons that remain obscure. It is estimated that approximately 1 percent of women between the ages of 12 and 25—approximately 260,000 women—suffer from anorexia nervosa. Anorexia nervosa is typically a disease of young women. It occurs in women nine times as frequently as in men, and although it may appear at any age, its onset is typically in adolescence or early adulthood.

Anorexia nervosa can be fatal. In a survey of studies, estimates of the death rate ranged up to 19 percent, with about half of the studies reporting a death rate below 5 percent. Since it can be fatal, anorexia nervosa should always be regarded as a clinical emergency, requiring prompt therapeutic intervention.

Bulimia, the second eating disorder considered in this chapter, is characterized by recurrent episodes of binge eating. These episodes appear uncontrollable. The bulimic consumes large amounts of food in a short period of time, which leads to feelings of shame and revulsion. Following binge eating, most clients attempt to rid themselves of calories by inducing vomiting or abusing laxatives. The use of purgatives is not deemed mandatory in diagnosing bulimia in the present DSM-III criteria, however. Johnson and Larson (1982) found that 74 percent of respondents to his magazine survey met the criteria for the psychiatric diagnosis of bulimia. Of the bulimics, 6 percent were also classifiable as anorectic. The respondents tended to have never married (70 percent), were white (97 percent), had some college education (84 percent), and had a median age of 22 years. Although 62 percent were of normal weight when they responded, 43 percent reported weights during adolescence (at 15 years of age) that were classified as overweight. Binge eating usually began at around 18 years of age.

Of those who binged, almost half reported doing so at least once a day. The average number of calories consumed during a typical binge was estimated at approximately 4,800, usually in the form of sweets (94 percent). Of those who reported purging (71 percent of the respondents), 69 percent vomited, 39 percent used laxatives, and 26 percent used both. These bulimic women reported normal sexual interest and experience but unusually low frequencies of alcohol, drug, and cigarette use. What was surprising about this study was the apparent widespread incidence of bulimia among ostensibly normal young women.

Most individuals with bulimia or binge eating who present themselves for therapy are of normal weight. This pattern of binge eating may also occur in clients who are anorectic and in clients who are substantially overweight. While the dietary habits of the two groups are dissimilar, there is substantial overlap between the two syndromes. About half of the clients currently hospitalized for anorexia nervosa are also bulimic. A significant number of normal-weight bulimics also have histories of anorexia nervosa. Thus, the disorders of excessive food deprivation and consumption appear linked in some way.

Bulimics are usually people who are frightened, lonely, and emotionally unfulfilled. Characteristically, the binge-purge cycle is a substitute method of dealing with poor self-esteem, depression, and a deep sense of inadequacy that they are unable to cope with more directly. It is important to note that in some cases, the purge part of the cycle is the real end sought. The binge eating, in these cases, is associated with shame, guilt, and panic. Purging is associated with the release of these emotions.

Although individuals with anorexia and bulimia frequently report feelings of failure and isolation, it is basically their preoccupation with food and their association with it that often leads to the isolation and loneliness. Their low self-esteem puzzles their friends, family, and teachers since, in other areas, they are often successful in their accomplishments. They harbor overwhelming fears that they will fail or be rejected.

DSM-III SYMPTOMS

The anorectic and bulimic syndromes are characterized by both physical and psychological symptoms. The pathology is interwoven with the drive for thinness and manifestations of starvation.

In DSM-III, *anorexia nervosa* is classified as one of several eating disorders. The diagnostic criteria for anorexia nervosa are as follows:

1. intense fear of becoming obese, which does not diminish as weight loss progresses
2. disturbance of body image, e.g., claiming to "feel fat" even when emaciated
3. weight loss of at least 25 percent of original body weight, or, if under 18 years of age, weight loss from original body weight plus projected weight gain expected from growth charts may be combined to make the 25 percent
4. refusal to maintain weight over a minimal normal weight for age and height
5. no known physical illness that would account for the weight loss

The diagnostic criteria for bulimia include the following:

1. recurrent episodes of binge eating (rapid consumption of a large amount of food in a discrete period of time, usually less than two hours)
2. at least three of the following:
   a. consumption of high-calorie, easily ingested food during a binge
   b. inconspicuous eating during a binge

    c. termination of such eating episodes by abdominal pain, sleep, social interruption, or self-induced vomiting

    d. repeated attempts to lose weight by severely restrictive diets, self-induced vomiting, or the use of cathartics or diuretics

    e. frequent weight fluctuations greater than ten pounds due to alternating binges and fasts

3. awareness that the eating pattern is abnormal and fear of not being able to stop eating voluntarily

4. depressed mood and self-deprecating thoughts following eating binges

5. the bulimic episodes are not due to anorexia nervosa or any known physical disorder

CASE DESCRIPTION: ANOREXIA NERVOSA

Diane W. was an 18-year-old girl who, upon entering therapy, weighed 62 pounds. Originally approximately 20 pounds overweight, she decided to diet. After losing the initial 20 pounds, she decided that she was still too fat and continued to lose weight. Upon entering therapy, the only food she would eat was ice cream, which she would eat only when no one was watching. Her appearance was pitiful. She was a small girl to begin with, only about 5 feet tall. Her small frame combined with her thinness created a look of total fragility, as though even the slightest touch would be dangerous to her.

She was a good student, always getting *A*'s. Her career goal was to be a graphic designer. Throughout the period of her weight loss, she never missed a day of school, insisting that there was nothing wrong with her. If the therapist pressed her about her weight — or the lack of it — she would point to a place on her thigh or buttock where she would find a fold of skin, proof of her "battle of the bulge." Diane had a lot of friends, with whom she seemed to interact appropriately. When asked how they felt about her loss of weight, she said that they accepted it or did not even notice it because she always wore very loose clothing.

Diane's family situation was poor. Her father was a carpet installer who worked long hours. Her mother, who ran his business from home, spent most of the day answering telephones and keeping the books. For the major portion of Diane's early life, she was responsible for taking care of her brother while her mother answered the telephones. The two children were told to go play in the basement, where they would be out of earshot of the phones. They then had to amuse themselves all day, lest they anger their mother. At lunch time, their mother would quickly run downstairs to feed them and then return upstairs to continue answering the phones. Diane had full responsibility for caring for her young brother. At the time Diane was only 4 years old and her brother was 2—an unusually young age for so much responsibility. This pattern continued for many years, until the children were old enough to fend for themselves. So for most of Diane's childhood years, she was responsible for her younger brother, forced to focus on his needs rather than on her own.

When Diane was about 16 years old, she was about 20 pounds overweight and decided to go on a diet. She still felt fat after she lost the initial 20 pounds, so she continued to diet. Early on, she learned to make herself vomit. If she ate more than she felt she should have, she would excuse herself from the table, go into the bathroom, stick her finger down her throat, and vomit. It was difficult the first time, but after that it was quite easy. She used this technique any time she happened to "eat by accident."

It soon became obvious that there was a problem. Diane's parents encouraged her to eat, but she refused. Every time she refused their requests that she eat, she felt a sense of victory—like she had won a major battle. She felt that she had finally gotten even with her mother; on a conscious level, however, she was not aware of the meaning of the battle and its overwhelming intensity. Her parents at one point took her to see a psychiatrist. The psychiatrist asked her many questions, but once again Diane refused to answer. The psychiatrist told her parents that if she would not speak, he could not help her. Once again Diane felt victorious. She had won, and they had lost! She walked through life existing only for these secret little victories, losing more and more weight until finally her life was in danger. However, these small victories seemed to add only temporarily to her feelings of power, resulting eventually in her distorted self-worth.

CASE DESCRIPTION: BULIMIA

Elaine K. is a 29-year-old overweight, drably dressed young woman who came in for therapy accompanied by her mother. She had been binge eating for the last 3 months and had done so episodically for the last 10 years. Elaine had been in and out of treatment with numerous prestigious therapists, without success, for the preceding 5 years. During that time, she had lost three jobs in her career as a registered nurse, usually due to an uncontrollable need to binge.

Elaine's binge eating was followed by induced vomiting. After vomiting, Elaine felt humiliated, shamed, out of control of her life, and "disgustingly fat." Her weight varied from within the normal range to being 50 or 60 pounds in excess. She was using large quantities of syrup of ipecac to induce vomiting in order to rid herself of the calories from the ingested food. She had developed a high tolerance for this emetic drug.

A pattern of behavior typically associated with Elaine's binge-purge pattern was to call her mother and demand help in controlling her need to binge. The help she requested was that her mother place her in a motel room without money or clothing in order to prevent her from compulsively seeking food. In spite of these precautions, however, she would find ways to escape from these external restrictions and would proceed to steal food from nearby stores; her objective was to obtain high-calorie "junk food." Unconsciously, she needed to lose the inner tension from her primitive, rage-filled impulses, which threatened her ego stability. After her secret eating orgies, she would vomit, and then feel guilty, depressed, worthless, and hopeless.

Elaine was brought up in a middle-class Catholic family, the middle child of three girls. She viewed herself as the "ugly duckling" in the family constellation, when compared with a bright, very pretty older sister. She blamed many of her difficulties on her mother, who forced her to transfer from a public school to the parochial school where she worked as a school nurse. She believed that her family and others always drew attention to her unattractiveness and lack of success, and unfavorably compared her with her older sister.

Despite her academic achievement — she had graduated with a *B* average from a respected university school of nursing—Elaine felt inferior in her ability to perform professional tasks when she compared herself with her colleagues. She had obtained employment at several teaching hospitals but had left each without notice. Sometimes she was terminated, usually due to problematic interpersonal relationships with coworkers or roommates in the nursing quarters. She would then feel rejected, unaccepted, and angry, and would seek solace in her binge eating. She would subsequently withdraw from her social milieu.

Elaine attributed her difficulties to her belief that she was not the "star" that her sister was. In fact, during the course of her treatment, her mother had allowed her sister to return home because she was in the process of a difficult divorce and was feeling very depressed. Elaine reacted with intense rage and envy. How could her mother do this to her when she was desperately trying to gain control over herself and her life? She had very little empathy for her sister, nor any real understanding of why her mother might be sympathetic to her sister's plight. Once again, Elaine felt second best to her sister.

WHAT DOES A PERSON WHO HAS AN EATING DISORDER LOOK LIKE?

Several psychological characteristics have been noted among anorectic clients. They are usually from the upper socioeconomic levels. Onset of the disorder is confined largely to the adolescent or young adult years. A history of unusual or bizarre eating habits is quite common. A distorted body image, particularly an overestimation of their physical dimensions, is almost universal. These patients are usually described as sensitive, dependent, introverted, anxious, perfectionistic, selfish, and unusually stubborn. They almost invariably report little or no interest in sex. They have typically been extremely conscientious in regard to conventional duties, such as school work. They sometimes feel that eating blunts their intellectual acuity.

Diane presented the typical case of anorexia nervosa. Her physical sense of herself was so distorted that it was almost delusional. Even when she weighed less than 65 pounds, she truly believed that she was overweight. Her defiance of her mother was remarkable. It was perhaps true that the only way Diane could become a person separate from her mother was to direct all her energy toward not eating — the exact thing that her mother was demanding. By doing the opposite, Diane made a statement: "I can't be you, because you want me to eat. I am not eating; therefore I am separate." Eating meant giving in to passivity and receptivity, the qualities from which Diane needed to dissociate herself in order to free herself from feeling impotent. She had to resort to these drastic measures in order to free herself from her mother's consuming control. In this sense, Diane's anorexia represented a healthy symptom — a drastic attempt to individuate from her intrusive mother.

It is not unusual for anorectic girls to describe their mothers in very unflattering terms. During childhood and latency, the parent's insensitivity, criticism, and interference in all aspects of the child's life prevents her from developing vital feelings of her own that accrue to a self-affirming experience. The girl is therefore not able to differentiate and identify with a loving, appropriate, caring parent.

Diane saw her mother as excessively dominant, intrusive, overbearing, and ambivalent. While it is possible that Diane's mother responded in these ways because of her concern over her daughter's failing health, it is much more likely that her domineering traits contributed to the etiology of anorexia. For the major portion of Diane's life, her behavior was controlled by her mother. All of Diane's life decisions were made by her mother. At age 16, it was time for Diane to begin preparing to go to art college, a dream she had since she was a little girl. Psychologically, though, Diane could not have handled a life that involved independent decision making. She had not achieved a separate identity. Her mother had always told her what to do; how could she now know what to do by herself? Unfortunately, Diane had not achieved an autonomous identity and had no confidence in her own ability to function as a separate being.

As it occurred in Diane's situation, anorexia often begins when life changes are requiring new or unfamiliar skills about which the person feels inadequate; such changes include going off to college, getting married, or even reaching puberty. The characteristic conflict activated by such events seems to be, on the one hand, a desire to achieve autonomy and, on the other, a pronounced fear of obtaining the status of an independent adult. Food then becomes the phobic and obsessional context in which this drama is played out.

Not infrequently, the disorder begins as an extension of the ritual of normal dieting, which is very common in young women. What distinguishes the normal dieter from the one who converts dieting into a dangerous flirtation with disaster still remains a mystery. In any event, there seems to be increasing acknowledgment that the syndrome of anorexia may be the extreme end of a continuum. Thus it is somewhat reasonable to speak of a preanorectic state, in which individuals have extreme, but not yet self-injurious, aversions to food.

Anorexia in young women is thought by some psychoanalytic theorists to represent sexual conflicts, possibly involving fear of impregnation, and to function as a stratagem for avoiding the adult sexual role. Whether or not this theory holds true, anorexia does indeed severely modify the female sexual characteristics: Breasts and hips shrink dramatically, and amennorrhea is common. In Diane's case, her feelings about losing her breasts and menstrual cycle were negligible, possibly indicating that other factors were operating. It was the therapist's sense that Diane's overriding wish was to unconsciously "get even" with her mother, and that defiance of her mother's wishes was a most important factor.

HOW DOES A PERSON WHO HAS AN EATING DISORDER FEEL?

Typical of the anorectic syndrome is, in the face of dwindling energy resources, an unfailing denial of the growing seriousness of the condition. The anorectic individual feels out of control. As was stated earlier, when the backgrounds of anorectic adolescents have been examined by researchers, the initial impression is usually one, not of pathological disturbance, but rather of an unusual freedom from developmental difficulties. As children, these patients generally appeared to have been outstandingly good and quiet. If one were to superficially examine Diane's scholastic record and interactions with her peers, the picture would have been one of normalcy.

Upon closer investigation, however, these presumably positive personality characteristics, and the parental reactions to them, turn out to have a distinctly negative aspect. Foremost is a history of a lack of individual initiative and autonomy, a lack of a sense of oneself as a distinct individual, capable of determining and accomplishing one's goals. Instead, consciously and unconsciously, anorectics are likely to have feelings of being enslaved, exploited, not being permitted to lead lives of their own. Diane felt enslaved to her brother. She was not allowed to have a life of her own beyond that of a babysitter. She lacked a clear sense of her emerging self, despite prolonged struggles to be perfect in the eyes of others. She eventually had an obsessional need to be in control of every aspect of life, with particular concern about losing control over her body. Diane was preoccupied with thoughts of food and engaged excessively in food- and weight-related behavior.

Diane's mother had exerted such firm control and regulation during childhood that Diane found it difficult to establish a sense of identity and confidence in her decision-making ability. Her parents manifested intrusive concern and overprotection, not encouraging Diane's separation and autonomy. Parental discomfort with the child's autonomy leads the parent (usually the mother) to reinforce reliance on her, which stifles the child's development of self. These parents are likely to have encouraged their children to become perfectionistic overachievers. Furthermore, such a regulated child may become so focused on external cues and controls as determinants of behavior that, like the obese child, she has not learned to respond appropriately to differential cues originating within herself, both physiological and psychological.

Many bulimics have extremely low self-esteem, particularly regarding their bodies; self-loathing is not uncommon when they fail to meet their own expectations. Self-denial and need for approval are also features of their struggles with themselves. The act of purging seems to be an attempt to regain the power and control that they lost as a result of their binge eating. They seem to harbor an all-consuming rage, which is often expressed through eating. Boskland-Lodahl (1976) seem to feel that the rage stems from the guilt bulimics feel at not living up to parental standards of "adorableness." They also report that the women observed in their study both feared and hated men, who they saw as defaming their self-worth and as being capable of destroying their self-respect.

Anorexia and bulimia appear to revolve around certain family dynamics. The mothers of bulimics tend to doubt their own ability to be tender and are unresponsive to their daughters' needs, which results in the daughters' doubting their own self-worth. Self-sufficiency is seen as a desired trait because dependency is believed to be "bad." Although bulimics appear to be dependent, their needs are actually meshed in a pseudoindependence because they feel that others do not want to respond to their dependency. Fathers are seen as maintaining distant relationships but having high expectations, especially concerning their daughters' personal appearance and performance. It appears that the integration of associated ideals of independence and ambition with the traditional concepts of femininity may be particularly difficult for these women.

In Elaine's case, as soon as she was able to achieve some separation from her family and was succeeding in her first year at a small college, she abruptly left. She then went on to a larger university, where she felt like just one of a number of competing students. Her first year of tranquility and stability was still disrupted, however, this time by intense striving for achievement with the other students. This rivalry and competition for the position of her parents' best child was first noted in her rivalry with her older sister. It repeated itself many times, even in treatment, when she attended a support group for compulsive eaters and began to insist that the other members were more attractive and successful than she. At this point, her tenuous control over her eating was quickly broken, and she again returned to binging and purging, which always resulted in self-loathing. She would also often project onto the therapist a feeling of not getting anywhere, not accomplishing anything in treatment or in her life. This seemed to underlie an accusation that the therapist-mother would never be able to give her anything worthwhile.

THE CLIENT'S DILEMMA

The anorectic woman is viewed by some theorists as fearing an unconsciously hated, domineering mother. The intrusion of this mother into the anorectic's psyche and body image then forces her to reject eating, which would ultimately render her similar to her mother. The anorectic therefore rejects the feminine qualities of receptivity and passivity, which both oral and sexual needs would only accentuate.

On the other hand, some theorists believe that bulimic women seem to fear sexual contact, not because of fear of pregnancy or sexuality, but because of fear of rejection. Performance anxiety and resultant rejection were critical childhood issues for them. The conflict with mother and the resultant hatred was more of a conscious phenomenon. Moreover, rather than rejecting the female role and its socially accepted aspects, the bulimic appears to identify *too* intensely with what she perceives as the "proper female role." In contrast to the anorectic's defense against anxiety and depression by ritualism and perfectionism, the bulimic tries to become a caricature of a perfect little woman. This notion is partly supported by Boskland-Lodahl (1976), who found that bulimic women were particularly sensitive to rejection by men. This fear of rejection often resulted in avoidance of men to the extent that it prevented the possibility of their gaining any nurturance and pleasure at all from male companions.

Conflicted and assailed by self-doubts, the "preanorectic" girl becomes distressed as she experiences all the physical changes of adolescence — undeniable proof that she is turning into an adult. She is dismayed as her menstrual cycle begins and her body starts to assume a more womanly shape. The menses is a sudden and mysterious change over which the preanorectic feels no control. Consciously, she may be obsessed with the thought that she is "too fat," but at a deeper level she is very depressed. The prospect of having to leave the safety and security of childhood, with all its comforting rules and regulations, is more than she can bear.

What is far more traumatic to the preanorectic adolescent, however, is that she experiences sexuality in a passive and receptive way. This realization of the passive-receptive aspect of feminine life makes puberty an unbearable transition which the potential anorectic dreads and is determined to fight with her divided ego. Thus, she experiences the body as an object outside the self on which to spy, destroying its needs, fighting its demands, and creating a sense of false euphoria from which she foresees a final state of emancipation.

The hunger strike thus serves a multitude of purposes. As the anorectic diets, her feminine curves disappear, and she becomes as flat-chested and angular as any prepubertal girl. Once she drops below a certain weight, her pituitary gland shuts down, and she stops menstruating—almost as if she has managed to turn back the biological clock. Her unwillingness to eat understandably arouses all sorts of parental concern; here, too, because she is seen as sick, she has reverted to a more childish role. Her half-starved condition requires her family to take care of her. At the same time, her refusal of food and her emaciated appearance seem to constitute an unconscious accusation. It is as if she is saying to her parents—in particular to her overprotective mother—"See what you've done to me? I'm afraid to grow up." There may also be an element of defiance: "I've had to be such a good child all these years, and now I'm not going to listen to you. I won't even eat. This is a part of my life that I, and only I, can control, no matter what you want me to do."

Anorexia nervosa, then, is a very puzzling and paradoxical disorder. Its victims, seemingly without intention, engage in a protracted program of self-destruction, refusing others' desperate efforts to rescue them. The young girl, often in response to maternal encouragement to lose weight, embarks on a physical program which reaches obsessional levels, in an all-out defiant stance against an intrusive, domineering mother.

Elaine, the bulimic destroyer, never perceived herself as a competent, worthwhile person who had a unique place in her family. She felt shunted off, rejected, and unfavorably compared with others by her family. Underneath her constant need to strive, to compete with her sister and later on her peers and colleagues, was an unconscious fear that she would amount to nothing. She was at times convinced that others did not notice her and that her sister could obtain and easily consume all the praise, loving care, and nurturance to which she did not feel entitled. She hated her sister and envied her attractiveness, success, and the respect she could so easily obtain from others. If she, Elaine, could not obtain it, then perhaps she could destroy everyone else's happiness and gratification. These were, after all, only momentary and transitory kinds of feelings.

The client's compulsive need to feed herself was meant to satisfy ambivalently held needs. It reassured her that she could love and feed herself, without having to depend on the attention of others, with whom she could not establish trust. It humiliated and disgusted her that she needed to "stuff down" the mounting tension and anger that threatened to overwhelm her control and her life. Her increasing use of "junk food" for quick gratification and a feeling of self-control, comfort, and pleasure could never really satiate her. In fact, she doubted whether anybody could satisfy her and whether life itself could ever be a rewarding or satisfying experience. The tireless efforts of others to reassure and rescue her provided only momentary reassurance that she was not an unattractive, unlovable, unworthy person who could quickly negate their efforts into nothingness. If her rage could destroy both their efforts and herself, then her life had no meaning or feelings, except through the magic of food and the people it enabled her to control.

THEORIES AND EXPLANATIONS OF EATING DISORDERS

Psychodynamic

Psychodynamic theorists conceptualize the etiology and treatment of the various psychophysiological disorders in essentially the same way that they conceptualize the neuroses. Thus, in explaining the causes of anorexia, psychodynamic theorists are still concerned with anxiety, defense mechanisms, and trauma at various psychosexual stages. Diane had remained at an early stage of development; she had failed to individuate from her mother. The supportive, nurturing environment and the encouragement she needed in order to develop a separate identity were missing.

These theorists have proposed that anorectic individuals, when faced with the anxiety-arousing prospect of genital sexuality at adolescence, regress to already-existing oral fixations. Denial of eating is thought to reflect denial of sexuality over the unconscious, defended-against wish to be impregnated through the mouth. Some of Crisp's et al. (1980) findings place particular emphasis on the biological regression of the anorectic client to a subpubertal weight, which he views as avoidance or as a defensive posture of the anorectic character. He also suggests that both the anorectic and her family emphasize oral, dependent aspects of development rather than aggressive, sexual, and independent strivings. The result is a narrow range of coping mechanisms and restricted ego growth.

Ego Psychology and Object Relations

Bruch (1978) focuses on the early feeding relationship between mother and child as the prototype learning experiences for later relationships. If the maternal response is dysjunctive, and if she superimposes her own needs on the child so that she cannot distinguish fatigue, helplessness, and frustration from nutritional needs, then the ego centers of the child's cognitive structure become fixated in Piaget's preconceptual stage. Due to this confused conceptualization of body stimuli and the parent's rigid attitude toward verbalizations, the child's language usage is determined not by conceptual notions, but by a literal mindedness.

The child's present subjective experience is not distinguished from the concept of the object and object reality. The anorectic equates her own maturing body with her experience of the maternal object. She attributes unacceptable experiences of her self to a concrete expression of her bodily processes. The liberal incorporation of the bad object (mother) becomes equated with her own body. The anorectic ego's aggressive, hateful feelings need to be defended against in order for her not to become depressed. Thus, the anorectic retains just enough loving feelings of symbiotic oneness with mother to prevent a schizophrenic catastrophe. She also defends herself against a hateful, frustrating mother in order to forestall a permanent state of depression.

Palazzoli (1978) believes that anorexia nervosa is a special defense structure between schizo-paranoia and depression. The incorporated bad object can never be split, but remains whole, just like the body with which it is identified. The anorectic hovers between schizophrenia and depression, and her body experience is equally ambiguous, lying half-way between the non-I and the bad-I, both alien and her own, a destructive non-self invading the self. Using the defense mechanism of projection, the client protects herself from experiencing personal delusions and preserves the ability to socialize and relate. Anorexia is also a safeguard from suicide.

Family Systems

Minuchin (1978) asserts that operant conditioning is necessary to initiate weight gain. Subsequent family therapy plays a central role. It is his view that although lifesaving is the most important goal in the initial stage of treatment, long-term success without relapse depends on reorganization of maladaptive patterns of family interaction. Those who emphasize family factors tend to rely on data that suggest that families of anorectics engage in disturbed patterns of interaction.

Family systems theorists have emphasized conflicts around issues of independence and the transition from childhood to adulthood. They feel that anorectic children are likely to appear in families that are excessively enmeshed. They assert that anorectics tend to have overprotective parents and lack effective ways of directly resolving conflicts. Thus the anorectic girl may be seen as asserting her independence in the only way she can—by refusing to eat. Although Diane's parents may not have been overprotective, they certainly were overcontrolling and intrusive, refusing to allow her the freedom of expression she needed in order to grow psychologically. This intrusive concern with the child's psychobiological needs results in a hyper-vigilance on the part of the child, who becomes a "parent watcher."

Crisp and colleagues (1974), in a study of 15 females, provide some evidence that is consistent with a family systems point of view. They found that parents of daughters who showed the least improvement with therapy had significantly higher levels of psychopathology, as measured by a questionnaire. Even more relevant is their finding that successful treatment of the daughters was associated with an *increase* in parental disturbance. This increase in parental disturbance was especially marked when the marital relationship was poor; mothers tended to show an increase in anxiety and fathers an increase in depression. The authors concluded that the daughter's illness sometimes served as a protective function for one or both parents when they were threatened by the prospect of the daughter's independence.

Minuchin and coworkers (1978) report a success rate for family therapy of 86 percent after follow-up periods ranging from three months to four years. This impressive result is probably reflective of the substantial degree of effectiveness of Minuchin's family therapy approach to the disorder.

Social Learning

Some psychologists view family factors and social learning as causes of anorexia nervosa. From this viewpoint, the adolescent is likely to get considerable attention and reinforcement for early attempts at weight loss. Later, when the condition becomes serious, the child gains even more attention and may in fact become the center of family concern as the parents seek various treatments. Modeling of parents who are very slender or are highly concerned with weight and diets is also suggested as an additional cause (Bemis 1978) by these theorists.

Diane's family seemed to be overconcerned with weight. Her mother tended to be weight-conscious, as were the other women in the family. Thus, thin women were set up as positive role models. Certainly, once Diane became anorectic, she received additional attention from relatives, who expressed concern over her failing health. In this sense, Diane received a great deal of secondary gain by remaining "sick."

Biological

It seems likely that anorexia nervosa involves a substantial psychological component, although its features and modes of operation remain largely a matter of speculation. There is some suggestion of a biological cause, since there are some known physical conditions, such as pituitary gland disorders, that can result in massive weight loss. It is speculated that at some point in the process of withdrawal from eating, biological factors seem to develop their own demands, taking the behavior beyond conscious control and making it exceedingly difficult to reverse.

The best guess is that the biological component responsible is located in the region of the hypothalamus, a richly interconnected structure in the brain involved in the regulation of motives and emotions. Although biological factors may play a part in the etiology of primary anorexia, perhaps an impairment of the release of gonadotropin from the anterior pituitary gland or a defect in the feedback control mechanisms for certain neurotransmitters, for example, dopamine, psychological influences appear to be dominant. Most individuals who are diagnosed with primary anorexia have had all known physical etiologies ruled out. The belief that all these individuals are suffering from a biological disorder, then, is highly speculative. The motivating effects of the associated psychological factors and the use of the body as a receptive vehicle for the management and discharge of distraught emotional feelings are, without doubt, significant factors in the illness.

PRACTICE TECHNIQUES

The approach used by the therapist in the treatment of anorectics needs to be one of careful timing in order to avoid prematurely interpreting their unconscious motives. Such premature interpretations will only add to the anorectic's denial and reinforce her sense of alienation from the world. An approach of first gathering the facts of their lives, and a focus on understanding what they have to say and how they feel, reinforces their sense of self and reality. These clients, as previously stated, do not have a firmly established use of language and concepts appropriate to their age and background. They sometimes use language oddly or differently. Therefore, premature cognitive clarification of reality or premature use of interpretation of their mysterious behavior is discouraged, for it would be dangerous to their fragile egos and might overwhelm them. In any case, a close scrutiny of the client's ego capacity for facing her primitive emotions and an assessment of the state of her ego defenses are necessary prior to beginning work toward helping the client to realize her underlying self-destructive motivation.

Bruch's (1978) position that clients need to feel, act, and learn about themselves and their lives, sharpened by their coming to grips with reality expectations, makes sense in that it helps eliminate the deep-seated cognitive and perceptual blocks that have dissociated from consciousness and from the anorectic's early primitive body cues. With these precautions in mind, the following multidimensional approach is suggested when treating these eating disorders.

1. Induce the client to begin eating again.

The most effective therapy for anorexia nervosa is probably one
that involves a combination of techniques. First, the patient must
be induced to begin eating again, and here some form of behavior
modification seems useful. This involves shaping the client's eating
behavior with a behavior modification approach. The behavioral
method is based on operant reinforcement procedures. The client is
given social rewards, such as time spent with peers, for the appropriate consumption of food. Since the primary initial concern is
with weight gain, clients can be reinforced with special privileges
whenever they show improvements in their eating or when they gain
weight. If the client is not hospitalized, the client and therapist can
contract to increase rewards as the client begins to gain weight. In
Diane's case, since she was not hospitalized, she and the therapist
agreed upon a food regimen, which involved Diane's monitoring
her own behavior and presenting the therapist with a summary during each session. Maintaining a weight sufficient for survival is the
goal. This reduces the client's suspiciousness of the therapist's motivation. Diane's intake was steadily increased until it reached a normal level. Before progressing to a higher increment, however, the
client should evidence clear judgment and initiate rather than responding just to please the therapist.

The fact that most patients are initially treated in a hospital
makes it somewhat easier to arrange for reinforcement. The patient
can eat meals with the therapist and improvement can be reinforced. In a hospital setting, other reinforcers, such as access to television, could also be provided when the client eats a certain
amount of food. Some hospitals use modified bed rest, high calorie
intake, and supportive nursing care. The use of bed rest, the gradually increasing levels of activity, and the increased privileges all are
dependent on weight gain, thus producing a positive schedule of increased reinforcement. It may be more than that, however: Putting
the client to bed helps to break through the denial and restricts her
activity under medical supervision, thus providing needed external
structure which does not easily enable loss of control.

2. Help the client deal with feelings of hopelessness and despair.

Try to help the client overcome her underlying sense of conflict and despair. Younger clients often dread growing up. Both their attempts to starve themselves and their bodily preoccupations represent a desperate attempt to exert control over events that are threatening to overwhelm them—namely, adult responsibilities.

Underneath Diane's good, conscientious, cooperative facade was a paper-thin kind of person, pathetically unsure of herself. She had never experienced pleasure in most of her accomplishments and had never felt a sense of control over her life and relationships with others. She was never allowed to think for herself, so whenever self-determination was called for, she became terribly insecure. Therapy helped Diane to understand that she could be less than perfect and still succeed in life. Her primary psychotherapeutic goal was personal and self reorientation to enable her to see herself as having a separate identity from her parents, and therefore as deserving of some self-respect. It was crucial to build her self-confidence and to assist her in acquiring a greater sense of autonomy so that she could direct her own life and choose self-satisfying goals.

3. Help the client deal with cognitive deficits and distortions.

Another treatment goal is to enable the client to avoid the retreat in the solace of the perfect body as a solution to her existential problems in living. One client had a magical, concrete goal of 95 pounds, to which she felt she must return if she was ever to feel in control and happy again. She almost completely avoided and denied having to come to grips with her problems of not having an adequate job (despite college graduation with honors), not having dated in college, and feeling trapped in her home, where she felt forced to live with a deprecating, blaming mother. Her episodic hysterical crying, yelling, and sobbing while living with her parents can be viewed as a need to be dead psychologically in order to be immune from the pain and disgrace she felt living in her mother's home.

Anorectics' need for concretization of their interpersonal shortcomings and of daily problems, all of which are focused on their bodies, is like a macabre drama in the theatre of the absurd of which they seem quite unaware. A therapeutic dialogue must be directed at helping the client realize (later on in the treatment) the secrets locked into their needing to express their deprecatory attitude toward their body and living through body language and primitive regressive symbolism.

4. Enlist the support of the client's family.

Once the anorectic is out of immediate danger, she and her family can benefit from a more dynamic form of treatment. After Diane had started eating again and was out of immediate danger, it was important to work with her family in an effort to alter the family dynamics that might have encouraged Diane's anorectic behavior. How had the family sustained and inadvertently nurtured the anorectic behavior? How had the family transmitted the mental attitudes of anorexia as the only solution to the complex issues of individuation and separation?

In family therapy, one must proceed cautiously with the mothers of anorectics, who feel that their sacrifices for the families have already been overwhelming. The therapeutic goal does not stop with the immediate need to gain weight. In fact, focusing solely on the weight within the family sessions serves merely to reinforce the client's fear that her family wants only to "stuff" her with food while ignoring her anxiety. It also serves to reinforce the notion that the problem lies within the anorectic individual (the identified patient) and that her problem is separate and apart from the family situation.

The family's role in the ongoing maintenance of the anorexia must be examined. What gains did Diane's mother receive in keeping Diane dependent upon her? If it served the purpose of helping her to feel needed and adequate as a mother, then what other roles could she develop in the family that would serve to nurture her child's psychological growth? The families of these clients are often rigidly defensive about maintaining the status quo, present loyalties, and secret coalitions, so that family stability is preserved at the cost of individual growth. How did the family benefit from Diane's "sickness" and her accompanying constricted emotional role within the family? If Diane were not "sick," would the family focus then shift—perhaps to marital dysfunction? If that were to happen, would the parents be prepared to confront their marital issues so that their needs would not intrude on Diane's fragile autonomy?

It was crucial to examine these questions in order to alter any dysfunctional patterns so that long-term symptom-free behavior would be maintained. Thus, opening up some poorly resolved issues on which harmony was tenuously achieved shakes the basis of family stability. Perhaps that is necessary for a while, but with therapeutic support and empathy, a new harmony can be achieved. The family need not fear disintegration, for powerful forces kept it together in the past, and so it will remain together in the future—but for different reasons.

4. Utilize long-term group treatment.

Once Diane had gained a sufficient amount of weight and had worked through separation and individuation issues with her parents, and once the family's dysfunctional patterns had been explored, it was the therapist's opinion that Diane could benefit from participating in supportive group psychotherapy. These sessions allowed her to express her concerns, thoughts, and fears, and enabled her developing psychological autonomy and growth.

WHEN DO YOU REFER THE CLIENT?

If the client is not adhering to the behavioral routine suggested by the therapist (e.g., not eating to gain weight in a consistent, scheduled way), then hospitalization and medical supervision is required. Although this may interfere with the transference and may induce feelings of being controlled or exploited by the therapist, the issue of failing health or of life and death is the more important issue that must take priority in the treatment. The need for medical supervision is explained to the client, and when her health is restored, treatment can resume. The therapeutic problem becomes one in which neither the therapist nor the client is any longer in control.

Medical emergencies do exist for anorectics, and the services of an internist may also be necessary to monitor the client's disturbed electrolytic balance and general health. In the bulemic, the excessive use of laxatives or purgatives may have caused a chemical imbalance in the body, so that the psychological issues cannot be addressed at this time.

Severe undereating and the consequential malnutrition and serious weight loss may accompany a variety of psychological disorders ranging from schizophrenia to depression. However, the clinical picture in primary anorexia nervosa is remarkably similar from one client to another.

The eating disorders generally respond best to long-term psychotherapy. It is believed that a multimodal treatment approach is most appropriate. As stated earlier, referral for medical evaluation is always necessary, and a team approach is usually the most effective.

Chapter 6

Substance Abuse: The Self-Indulgent and Avoidant Client

WHAT IS ALCOHOL ABUSE AND HOW DO YOU RECOGNIZE IT?

Drug abuse problems span the globe and have been with us for centuries (Austin 1978). In the early 1600s, the use of tobacco became very controversial in England. Similar historical reactions to opium were observed in China from 1700 through the mid-1980s. History provides evidence that various cultures have found it difficult to control drugs. If a sufficient proportion of the population provides a demand for a drug, it appears that the laws are never completely effective in stopping its use or abuse. In the United States, the failure of a national prohibition against alcohol, which was instituted in 1920 and repealed in 1933, provides one of the clearest examples of this failure. It is apparent that something other than legal sanctions and controls is necessary to stop the use of many of the substances that have been abused over the past 400 years. One of contemporary society's major concerns is preventing the use of any drug from developing into a maladaptive pattern of abuse.

The use of drugs, including alcohol, provides one of the clearest examples of how a behavior pattern can range from a totally acceptable and adaptive behavior to a serious, maladaptive pattern. Using alcohol is an acceptable social custom in many cultures, and it is kept under control by most individuals who do drink. However, there are approximately 9 to 10 million alcoholics in the United States. Of the estimated 90 million people in the United States who drink, 81 million are social drinkers. The other 9 million are alcoholics, and of these, at least 3 million are female.

Although the incidence of alcoholism is thought to be increasing in women, estimates still indicate that there are about four times as many male as female alcoholics. In some respects, however, alcoholism in women differs from alcoholism in men. Although many of the basic symptoms are the same, women alcoholics are more likely than men to drink alone, to hide their drinking, and to feel guilty and ashamed. Because the alcoholic woman is strongly stigmatized in our society, she may make unusual efforts to conceal her drinking. Her best friends may never have seen her drunk. The alcoholic woman bears a double burden — she not only suffers from the stigma of drinking, but she is also looked upon as more of a moral transgressor than the alcoholic man. Alcoholic women more often suffer from associated depression and seek medical help for nervousness and insomnia. Because their drinking is not often recognized as the cause of these complaints, many of the women — more often than alcoholic men — also develop a secondary dependence on prescribed sedatives and tranquilizers. There is also a notable difference in the age of onset and the progression. In general, alcoholism starts considerably later in women than it does in men and progresses much more rapidly once it starts.

There do appear to be some clear ethnic differences in the incidence of alcoholism (McCord et al. 1960). Rates of alcoholism in ethnic groups that emphasize the use of alcohol for religious or dining purposes, such as the Jews and the Italians, are generally lower than in ethnic groups that use alcohol for recreational use, such as the Irish. Alcoholism is also more common in urban areas. The vast majority of alcoholics (70 percent) live at home with their families.

The skid row alcoholic who lives from one bottle to the next on the streets or in the woods accounts for less than 5 percent of the alcoholics in America. Although alcoholism is generally a middle-age disorder, there has been an alarming increase in alcoholism among young people, including adolescents and college students. Recent government estimates suggest that 20 percent of 14- to 19-year-olds drink alcohol on a regular basis. Estimates for college students indicate that as many as 70 to 95 percent drink, and that up to 25 percent will at some point in their lives have problems with their drinking (Ingalls 1978).

Recent analyses of survey data by Cahalan (1978) indicate that a great percentage of alcohol-related problems tend to occur in younger persons. When a number of specific problems, such as excessive drinking; problems at work due to drinking; and problems with spouse, friends, or neighbors, were included, the youngest group studied (21- to 24-year-olds) had by far the highest prevalence of problems. Thus, although we often think of the typical alcoholic as the 40- to 55-year-old, this may be a very misleading impression.

In contrast to approaches that examine only the incidence of alcoholism, Calahan (1978) took a more comprehensive approach by looking at various personal, family, social, health, and behavioral problems associated with drinking. His data suggested that alcohol-related problems are more common than would be expected. Based on summary scores of alcohol-related problems, 15 percent of the men and 4 percent of the women had relatively severe problems associated with alcohol, while another 28 percent of the men and 17 percent of the women had moderate difficulty. These findings suggest that the impact of alcohol abuse and dependency may be more pervasive than might have been anticipated, since 43 percent of the men and 21 percent of the women had at least moderate problems linked to alcohol.

The cost of alcoholism is enormous, to individuals, their families, and society at large. The male alcoholic who has maintained a chronic drinking habit for several years usually creates and experiences the highest cost to himself and to society. He often has lost his family, his health, his employment opportunities, his financial resources, and his self-respect.

A substantial proportion of homicides and suicides are related to alcohol abuse. The majority of highway deaths and accidents involve drivers who were drinking and who would have been considered to have serious problems with alcohol. Problem drinkers usually have poor work performance and high rates of absenteeism. Furthermore, there are the high costs to the local, state, and federal health agencies who provide medical and other treatment services to alcoholics. The total expenditure for dealing with alcoholism is many billions of dollars. Estimates indicate annual costs to industry of more than $9 billion, cost for automobile accidents of more than $6 billion, and a health care bill of over $8 billion (National Institute of Alcohol Abuse and Alcoholism 1974). These personal and economic costs are likely to increase dramatically in the next decade. This is primarily due to increasing rates of drinking problems among adolescents and women. It also appears that a growing number of individuals who formerly abused other drugs are now turning to alcohol.

Although alcohol is America's most abused drug, and although much time and money has been invested in studying it, its action on the brain remains unclear. Many things *are* known, however: (1) It is primarily a depressant drug; (2) tolerance develops to the effects of alcohol; (3) after prolonged use of moderate to high levels of alcohol, addiction occurs; (4) a sudden decrease in alcohol intake in an alcoholic will result in a dangerous withdrawal syndrome called delirium tremens (DTs).

To some degree, the definition of addiction and the identification of addicts are arbitrary. Addiction does not simply imply negative personality traits or criminal behavior. Rather, it is a description of how the body adapts to foreign substances. To be addicted, a person must use drugs to the extent that four conditions are present:

Cellular tolerance. After a period of time, it becomes clear that more and more of the drug is required to produce the same effects or the level of intoxication experienced initially. Tolerance may develop slowly, over a number of years, as it does in alcoholism, or it may develop rapidly, within a month, as it does with heroin.

Loss of control. The addicted person eventually cannot control the timing and/or the dosage of the drug he uses. Often the individual will crave the drug if he has not used it recently, and taking even one dose will produce the urge to take another and another, until physical or financial disability prevent further use. Another form of loss of control is seen in alcohol users who can control the amount of alcohol they use at any one time, but cannot stop using the drug, even for brief periods of time.

Withdrawal. Once an individual's body has adapted to the presence of the drug, its absence will initially upset the equilibrium of the cellular environment. Severe discomfort may occur, including pain, tremors, profuse sweating, nausea, and irritability when the drug cannot be obtained. Withdrawal symptoms usually appear within a few hours of the last dose of the drug and may persist for several days.

Disruption of life-style. Often added to the list is a fourth criterion of addiction, which reflects psychological or social changes, rather than physiological ones, attributed to use of the drug. Persons addicted to drugs often find themselves unable to meet others' expectations with regard to family maintenance, job performance, and social responsibility. At times even the smallest demand exceeds the addict's capacity. Their coping mechanisms and social responsibility are hindered.

Although alcohol in moderate quantities generally produces pleasurable changes in mood, its effects are often unpredictable. In some cases alcohol will produce a "glow" or a "high"; at other times it will have no effect at all; sometimes it will intensify a depressed mood. Much depends on the individual's physical and emotional state.

Prior to the 1950s, alcoholism was viewed as a moral problem, and since it was seen as a moral issue, the subject was not discussed in scientific circles. The alcoholic was simply a weak individual who suffered from lack of moral fiber. Just as Kinsey and Masters and Johnson made sex an acceptable topic for discussion, E. Jellinek developed a disease concept of alcoholism, thereby freeing the alcoholic from moral guilt. Jellinek (1952) provided the classic description of alcohol addiction as a four-stage process.

Stages of Alcohol Dependence

Although the distinction between alcohol dependence and alcohol abuse may prove to be an important diagnostic consideration in the future, most research at this time has not attempted to make this differentiation. Thus, most of what is described in this section applies to those who have been classified simply as "alcoholics" in the past.

Although every alcoholic will not show the same pattern, Jellinek (1971) described the typical developmental course in alcoholic dependence. In spite of Jellinek's heavy reliance on a disease model, his discussion of the development of alcoholism is important to nondisease approaches because his view emphasizes the gradual development of alcoholic behavior patterns. In other words, a person does not become an alcoholic overnight. Instead the complex behavior patterns associated with excessive reliance on alcohol develop gradually, over a period of years.

In the earliest stage, the *prealcoholic phase,* normal social drinking provides the individual with considerable relief of tension and anxiety. As drinking increases to achieve tension relief, tolerance to the effects of alcohol develop. The individual, who had previously been drinking only socially, often finds herself tense and unable to handle problems. After experiencing relief from these tensions while drinking, the person discovers that it is not the situations or the people that relax her, but the drug. After heavy social drinking for a period of six months to two years, the future addict may enter the second, or prodromal, phase.

In the *prodromal phase*, the complications of excessive drinking begin to accumulate. The individual may begin to experience some subjective discomfort associated with the use of the drug. The individual may notice a "need" for the drug and feel tense and apprehensive when not using it. *Blackouts* — losses of memory for certain periods of time — may occur. For example, the person may not remember where he was the previous night or how he returned home. The person may think about drinking throughout the day and engage in it while alone. The actual drinking behavior may change; the individual often begins to drink very rapidly, gulping drinks rather than sipping them. Unpleasant emotional reactions to drinking, such as depression, guilt, or extreme anxiety, may also develop during this phase. The person becomes reluctant to discuss his drinking behavior.

During the *crucial phase,* alcoholics lose control over their drinking, and further deterioration in psychological, social, and physical functioning occurs. The transition from the second to the third stage occurs quietly, almost imperceptibly. The alcoholic feels that he cannot abstain from drinking; or, if he can, the first drink leads to continuous use, until unconsciousness or depletion of funds stops the spree or binge. Because the body is now adapted to the presence of alcohol, cessation of drinking may lead to withdrawal symptoms.

Severe psychological and physical disturbances may also occur. Self-esteem and self-confidence decline, and social obligations which were previously met are now ignored. With continued excessive drinking, appetite is lost, and eating is avoided for long periods of time. As nutritional status declines, various physical complications, including brain damage, can occur if this pattern is maintained.

If the person is unable to obtain alcohol for any length of time and blood alcohol levels drop too rapidly, delirium tremens (DTs) may occur. The person's heart may race, his body may shake uncontrollably, and perspiration may be profuse. Visual or tactile hallucinations may occur. The person may be restless, unable to sleep, apprehensive, and fearful. Increased defensiveness, in the form of denial and projection, eventually leads to a life-style of social isolation and sudden hostility and aggression toward others.

Physical and psychological deterioration set in during the *chronic phase*, when the more extreme consequences of alcoholism are experienced as the person "hits bottom." During this stage, the alcoholic usually suffers from malnutrition, loss of feeling in the hands and legs, tremors, chronic nausea and gastritis, and, eventually, irreversible brain damage. Unable to work or to stay with the family, and possessing little money, the alcoholic typically gravitates to the poorest of neighborhoods, often drinking with those in a lower socioeconomic class. Personal grooming and hygiene may be neglected in favor of obsession with obtaining the drug.

Jellinek believes that it is only at this stage that the person will give up the struggle with alcohol and seek treatment for the addiction. Drinking is almost continuous during this stage, and the person may drink *any* alcoholic substance—including hair tonic, mouth wash, shoe polish, toxic wood alcohol, and even sterno—when regular alcoholic beverages are not available. Social contacts

center around interactions with other alcoholics, as contacts with
former friends, family, and employers are usually lost. The alcoholic may now be living on the streets.

As stated earlier, other psychological symptoms, such as hallucinations and paranoid fear, develop in some individuals. The alcoholic who stops drinking at this time may experience DTs. When
these individuals reach the final phase, it becomes increasingly difficult for them to accept their behavior. Some will admit to their addiction and seek help; others will live out this destructive pattern
until an earlier-than-necessary death. Again, it must be remembered that these are only general phases of alcoholism. Many alcoholics seek treatment prior to progressing to the advanced stages of
alcoholism.

The following list summarizes the four stages of alcohol dependence:

1. Prealcoholic Phase
   a. Alcohol produces marked release from anxiety or other
      discomfort
   b. Frequency of drinking increases
   c. Tolerance for alcohol increases
2. Prodromal Phase
   a. First memory blackouts
   b. Preoccupation with alcohol
   c. Hidden drinking, drinking alone, avoidance of discussion
      of drinking
   d. Gulping of drinks
   e. Guilt about drinking and behavior.
3. Crucial Phase
   a. Loss of control over drinking (starting to drink usually
      leads to full drunkeness, but can still sometimes avoid tak-
      ing the first drink; frequent morning drinking)
   b. Rationalizes drinking as acceptable
   c. Lowering of self-esteem
   d. Loss of friends and family, and impairment of job func-
      tioning
   e. Begins to neglect nutrition
4. Chronic Stage

a. Frequent, often constant, drinking, with no control
b. Impairments in thinking
c. Lack of concern with social standards, shift of friendships to other heavy drinkers
d. Will drink any source of alcohol
e. Fears, hallucinations, and tremors often develop
f. Often admits defeat

Jellinek's four-stage descent into alcoholism used to be cited almost routinely in textbooks, but as vivid as it appears to be, it is no longer considered entirely accurate. Critics (Marlatt et al. 1973, Pihl and Spiers 1978, Polich et al. 1980) claim that although it appears to capture some features of alcoholism, it is too rigid to apply to every case. Knupfer (1972), in fact, claims that alcoholics do not conform to any single pattern, perhaps because alcohol abuse is so widespread. She interviewed a sample of adult males drawn at random from the San Francisco area. She discovered that a rather high percentage of the group — about 30 percent — admitted to having a serious drinking problem. Approximately half of these men described their consumption as "excessive." Yet relatively few fit Jellinek's four-stage model, and, even more intriguing, a third of the very heavy drinkers had already "reformed." Most had quit on their own, and practically none of them could articulate a clear reason for breaking their dependence.

Knupfer's assessment has been bolstered by another very intensive research project. Polich and colleagues (Polich et al. 1980) conducted a four-year study of alcoholics, all men who had contacted one of the Alcoholism Treatment Centers funded by the National Institute on Alcohol Abuse and Alcoholism. These subjects underwent extensive interviews and a variety of tests, both psychological and medical. In order to ensure that the information they were furnishing was accurate, their friends and relatives were also interviewed. Most important of all, the researchers made a strenuous attempt to keep track of their subjects over the four-year period and succeeded in determining what had happened to 85 percent of them (an exceedingly high proportion for any follow-up effort thus far). Some alcoholics, the researchers note, were still drinking heavily. Others had quit and then resumed. Still others had stopped and were remaining abstinent. A small percentage (8 percent) had been able to return to controlled drinking. And finally, quite a few (almost 15 percent) had died—at a rate "two and one half times the rate that would be expected in a population of a comparable age and racial distribution" (p. 175). Thus, while it appears that Jellinek's model may be useful in some cases, it is not relevant in all cases. Recent research also indicates that there is no one alcoholic pattern; rather, people appear to respond to alcohol, at least initially, according to their own unique personality constitutions.

Another significant point to be made is that most of the studies on alcoholism have been limited to males. Experts traditionally believed that alcoholism was far more common among men than among women. They now believe, however, that female alcoholics are quite numerous and that their ranks may be increasing (Gomberg 1974). Some theorists have suggested, in fact, that alcohol abuse has been fairly common among women all along; it has simply been less visible, they claim, because women are generally quieter about their drinking behavior. They are more likely to drink in secret and less likely to become violent when intoxicated (Pihl and Spiers 1978, Wilsnack 1973).

In addition to intoxication, alcohol abuse can lead to other alcohol-induced states that often bring clients to emergency rooms. Alcohol-induced hallucinations and DTs are examples. Alcohol-induced hallucinations are not diagnosed easily. In acute *alcoholic hallucinosis,* the individual generally will experience hallucinations of some type, usually auditory, will usually have appropriate reactions to the hallucinations (for example, fear if the hallucinations are fear provoking), will have no delirium or confusion, and will have no easily identifiable signs of heavy alcohol use. An example of this process is as follows: First the individual may hear a voice speaking simple statements. With time, however, the hallucinations usually extend to the voices of several people, all of them critical and reproachful. The individual's innermost weaknesses, particularly sexual ones, may be itemized, and various horrible punishments then proposed. The person may hear the clanking of chains, the sharpening of knives, the sound of pistol shots, or footsteps approaching in a threatening manner. Terror stricken, the individual may scream for help or attempt suicide.

In some cases, the individual may be misdiagnosed as schizophrenic — especially if alcohol abuse is denied, and there is no friend or family member to give accurate information. Alcoholic hallucinosis may occur in some long-term, heavily-drinking alcoholics who have stopped drinking or have reduced considerably their alcohol intake in the previous 48 hours. There are no significant differences in the type of hallucinations or other symptoms experienced by the schizophrenic and those experienced by the alcoholic with hallucinosis. The only clear distinguishing characteristic is the individual's history. This condition may continue for several days or even weeks, during which time the person is depressed but fairly well oriented and coherent, apart from the hallucinations. After recovery, the client usually shows considerable remorse and guilt, as well as some insight into what has happened.

Investigators are now less inclined than they had previously been to attribute this type of psychotic reaction solely to the effects of alcohol. Rather, it seems to be related to a broader pattern of maladaptive behavior. In other words, while the psychotic symptoms can be triggered by the alcohol, it is probable that they could have been similarly brought about by other drugs, illness, exhaustion, or other types of stress.

The other alcohol-induced state, *delirium tremens,* is relatively easy to identify. Delirium tremens is probably the best known of the various alcoholic psychotic reactions. A fairly common occurrence among those who drink excessively for a long time, this reaction may occur during a prolonged drinking spree or upon the withdrawal of alcohol after prolonged drinking. The DTs are a sequence of symptoms resulting from a continuing decrease in alcohol levels in an alcoholic. There are usually four stages of symptoms. The first stage begins with the psychomotor agitation and hyperactivity of the autonomic nervous system that continues throughout all four stages. The shakes and anxiety may begin within two to three hours of no alcohol intake. The shakes (most noticeably, the hand tremors) become progressively more intense and disruptive, until the individual might not even be able to feed himself. This initial stage is also characterized by a very rapid heart rate, profuse perspiration, hypertension, insomnia, and loss of appetite. In the absence of treatment or further alcohol intake, these symptoms progress.

It may be four, six, or eight hours after the last drink, but the appearance of hallucinations will mark the beginning of the second stage. These hallucinations may affect any sensory system — visual, auditory, or tactile — and are similar to those that occur in alcoholic hallucinosis. The differential diagnosis is easily rendered, however; none of the first-stage symptoms are present in alcoholic hallucinosis.

In the third stage, delirium develops and delusions begin — intermittently at first and then for increasing durations — followed by amnesia for the entire episode. Disorientation to time and place is common. All of the earlier stages may develop in the first 24 hours after the last drink, or it may take 96 hours for the stage to appear. The time course of DTs depends on the rate at which alcohol levels decrease.

Finally, the fourth stage is marked by severe grand mal seizures that may occur frequently, and sometimes cause death. The four stages overlap, merge, and are sometimes missed as discrete stages. The clinical situation is never quite like the typification described here. Thus, the delirium is usually preceded by a period of restlessness and insomnia, often accompanied by general uneasiness and apprehensiveness. Slight noises or suddenly moving objects may produce considerable excitement and agitation.

Once the symptoms fully appear, they may include the following: (1) disorientation to time and place (the client may, for example, mistake the hospital for a church or a jail, or no longer recognize friends, or identify hospital attendants as old acquaintances); (2) vivid hallucinations (particularly of small, fast-moving animals like snakes, rats, and roaches) which are clearly localized in space; (3) acute fear, often provoked by the hallucinated animals' changing form, size, or color in terrifying ways; (4) extreme suggestibility, in which a person can be made to see almost any form of animal if its presence is merely suggested; (5) marked tremor of the hands, tongue, and lips; and (6) other symptoms, including perspiration, fever, rapid and weak heartbeat, coated tongue, and foul breath.

The delirium typically lasts from three to six days and is generally followed by a deep sleep. When the person awakens, few symptoms remain, aside from possible remorse, but most clients will have been badly scared and may not resume drinking for several weeks or months. Without therapy, however, drinking eventually begins again, only to be followed by a return to the hospital with another attack. The death rate from delirium tremens as a result of seizures, heart failure, and other complications used to be approximated at 10 percent (Tavel 1962). With drugs such as chlordiazepoxide (Librium), however, the death rate during delirium tremens and acute alcohol withdrawal has been markedly reduced.

In actual practice, a client clearly "going into" DTs would be hospitalized — usually on a medical unit since the medical problems are more critical at that point than the psychiatric problems — and treated with a long-lasting benzodiazepine, usually chlordiaz-epoxide (Librium). The benzodiazepine has cross tolerance with alcohol and will substitute for the alcohol, thus inhibiting withdrawal (DTs). The amount of benzodiazepine is gradually reduced until discontinuation in four to seven days, at which point the individual has been detoxified to alcohol.

Korsakoff's psychosis, another of the psychoses associated with alcoholism, was first described by the Russian psychiatrist Korsakoff in 1887. The outstanding symptom is a memory defect (particularly with regard to recent events) which is concealed by falsification. Individuals may not recognize pictures, faces, rooms, and other objects that they have just seen, although they may sense that these people or objects are familiar. Such persons increasingly tend to fill in gaps with reminiscences and fanciful tales that lead to unconnected and distorted associations. These individuals may appear to be delirious, hallucinating, and disoriented to time and place, but ordinarily their confusion and disordered conduct are closely related to their attempts to fill in the memory gaps. The memory disturbance itself seems related to an inability to form new associations in a manner that renders them readily retrievable. Such a reaction usually occurs in older alcoholics, and only after many years of excessive drinking.

The symptoms of this disorder are now thought to be due to Vitamin B deficiency and other dietary inadequacies. A diet rich in vitamins and minerals generally restores the patient to more normal physical and mental health. However, some personality deterioration usually remains, in the form of memory impairment, blunted intellectual capacity, and diminished moral and ethical standards.

Another alcohol related disorder is *pathological intoxication.* This is an acute reaction that occurs in persons whose tolerance to alcohol is chronically low (such as epileptics or those of an unstable personality makeup) or in normal persons whose tolerance to alcohol is temporarily lessened by exhaustion, emotional stress, or other conditions. Following the intake of even moderate amounts of alcohol, these individuals may suddenly become disoriented and may even commit violent crimes. This confused, disoriented state is usually followed by a period of deep sleep, with complete amnesia afterward.

While 80 percent of alcoholics can be expected to experience some withdrawal symptomatology (Mello and Mendelson 1979), only 5 to 15 percent develop the more serious withdrawal symptoms—convulsions, confusion, disorientation, and hallucinations (Schuckit-Rorpes 1979, Sellers and Kalant 1976). Although most alcoholics experience at least some of the less severe symptoms of withdrawal, DTs occur in only 5 percent of alcoholics hospitalized for major withdrawal (Victor and Adams 1953), with an estimated incidence among alcoholics of between 1 and 15 percent (Gross et al. 1973).

DSM-III SYMPTOMS

In the first edition of the DSM, published in 1952, alcoholism was included among personality disorders, subsumed under the sociopathic personality disturbances. Although it was still a part of the personality-disorder grouping in DSM-II (1968), alcoholism was no longer considered an antisocial behavior. Rather, it remained part of an overall grouping that also included the sexual deviations and drug dependence. However, the latest edition, DSM-III (1980), separates the newly named substance-use disorders, which include both alcoholism and the drug dependencies, from any other conditions, thereby removing the official stigma placed on the addictions by virtue of their contiguity to the worst transgressions of society's moral code.

Although a specific blood alcohol level, at least 0.1 percent, is used in most states to determine legal intoxication, DSM-III specifies different criteria for a diagnosis of alcohol intoxication. For this diagnosis, *all* the following criteria must be present:

1. recent ingestion of alcohol
2. maladaptive behavioral effects, such as fighting, poor judgment, and so on
3. at least one of the following: slurred speech, uncoordination, unsteady gait, nystagmus (rapid involuntary movements of the eye), flushed face
4. at least one of the following: mood changes, irritability, excessive talking, impaired attention
5. none of these effects may be due to any other disorder

The defining characteristic of this form of maladaptive behavior is that the excessive use or dependence on the substance is interfering with the person's general functioning. In addition to certain physical complications, including death from overdoses that can occur with some drugs, the individual suffers in other ways. The substance abuse may result in poor interpersonal relationships, loss of employment, deterioration of family life, and legal complications.

There are two general categories of substance use disorders. The first category is *substance abuse*, in which the pattern of maladaptive behavior impairs social or occupational performance. Individuals in this category may fail to meet obligations to family, friends, or employers, as their behavior becomes increasingly erratic and impulsive. Furthermore, the substance abuser will often develop a psychological dependency on the drug. Psychological dependence on a drug usually refers to an overwhelming desire to use the substance on a very regular basis. The person may attempt to stop using the drug but be successful for only short periods of time. A maladaptive pattern of drug abuse may develop in which the abuser remains under the influence of the drug throughout the day on a regular basis or experiences certain complications, such as overdoses.

The second general category of substance use disorders is *substance dependence* which is considered a more severe and advanced disorder. In addition to patterns which are characteristic of abuse, the person shows signs of tolerance or withdrawal or both. These signs have often been considered indications of a physical addiction to a drug. Tolerance occurs after prolonged use of certain drugs; that is, the same dose or amount of the drug has less of an effect. With tolerance, larger doses are needed in order to achieve the effects that were originally experienced when the person first began using the drug. Withdrawal symptoms, which can be fatal, occur when drug use stops or when the amount of drug is diminished.

In sum, approximately 9 to 10 million Americans either abuse or are addicted to alcohol, which functions as a central nervous system depressant. DSM-III has differentiated between alcohol dependence, or true alcoholism, and alcohol abuse. In advanced alcohol dependence, there are clear signs of a physical addiction to alcohol in that withdrawal symptoms begin 8 to 72 hours after drinking has been stopped. These symptoms range from extreme tremulousness ("the shakes") to severe forms of withdrawal such as delirium tremens, in which the person may have vivid and frightening hallucinations of small animals, snakes, or insects. Withdrawal can be severe enough to cause death unless medical attention is provided.

Because tolerance to alcohol develops — that is, larger amounts are required to have an effect — an alcoholic might consume enormous quantities of alcohol and have a high blood alcohol level, yet not show any gross signs of intoxication. However, although the person may not appear intoxicated or drunk, there are usually behavioral indications of dependency, such as the chronic urge to drink, repeated failures at trying to stop drinking, inability or disturbances in meeting responsibilities, hiding liquor for later use, or early morning drinking to forestall withdrawal symptoms. The alcoholic is also likely to show certain physical complications due to the excessive and chronic use of alcohol. Cirrhosis of the liver, hepatitis, severe gastrointestinal problems, and brain dysfunction are some of the more serious physical problems encountered in advanced alcoholics. As a result of the physical complications, it is not uncommon for such persons to look much older than their age. Furthermore, the alcoholic's life expectancy is about 10 to 12 years shorter than that of the nonalcoholic. The criteria for alcoholism (physical alcohol dependence) according to DSM III, therefore centers on four criteria: signs of physical addiction, tolerance, psychological dependence, and medical complications.

Individuals who have problems associated with alcohol but have not developed a physical dependence are considered to have the less severe pattern of alcohol abuse. These individuals often have a multitude of problems: with the law — arrests for drunken driving or public drunkeness; on the job — work missed due to hangovers; with family or friends — fighting, child abuse, or wife abuse while drinking; or with extreme drinking rates — a fifth or more of liquor a day. Others experience difficulties as a result of drinking only in certain situations, such as becoming drunk before all social engagements.

CASE DESCRIPTION

Richard L. presented himself in a counseling session as a shy, awkward 29-year-old man. He complained of anxiety attacks which he could not control. He blamed these attacks on his probation officer, who he felt had intruded excessively into his life. He thereby displaced his problem and disowned his drinking behavior, and he seemed somewhat frightened of certain aspects of his life. He also appeared to have poor interpersonal skills. He gave a life history that indicated enmeshment with his family, who expected him to fail (despite their stated belief that he could accomplish great things). His family had often come to his rescue, but they resented his acting-out behavior and drinking. They felt that he had chosen a life of failure and deviance, primarily as a way of punishing them and rebelling against the family mandates.

It was apparent early in the therapy that he was a young man who had poor judgment and little conflict-free individuality and who lived impulsively. He acted out in order to avoid recognizing his own painful, negative feelings. He seemed to have needed more protection and understanding as a child than his parents were capable of giving him. Instead, he was burdened with impossible expectations and was physically abused by his mother.

He had been a breech delivery and had rheumatic fever at age 8. In school he often fought and was teased by the other children. He stated that if someone tried to pick on him, "I would punch him out." As a child he had suffered from hyperactivity and inability to concentrate on tasks, and was thus an academic underachiever. He was continually in trouble, and his mother would often slap him around. She reminded him often that he was a disappointment to the family. She continually compared him to his brother, who was "the good one." His father, an engineer and inventor, was a successful businessman. Richard believed that his parents' marriage was an unhappy one. Richard recalled that his parents "were always fighting about something." His father was demanding and critical. Richard was labeled the "family black sheep" and everyone's "cross to bear." Richard also remembered that his father would drink alcohol every time he had to speak in front of an audience. His only happy memory was of having been accepted by his classmates when he was 16 years old; he had his driver's license and was considered to be a lot of fun. Four months short of graduation, however, Richard impulsively quit high school.

Soon after, Richard enlisted in the navy, where he served as a corpsman stationed in North Carolina for one year. His duties consisted of handing out medication for the men on sick call. Richard stated that he never felt as though he "fit in" in the navy. He did not feel comfortable with any of the other men. He was introduced to the use of drugs while in the service. Shortly thereafter, he offered Valium to a man sitting next to him at a bar. The man turned out to be a narcotics agent. Richard was charged with selling drugs, but the charge was eventually dismissed. With his parents' help, and the services of an attorney, Richard obtained a general discharge from the navy.

Richard left the navy and returned to live with his parents. He met and married a young woman, and they moved to Florida. He began to feel that his work as a respiratory therapist was depressing, and he found himself dwelling on existential issues of life and death. He began distancing himself from his wife; she felt rejected, and the relationship ended. Richard continued his cycles of drinking, depression, withdrawal, and drinking.

Approximately five years before he entered treatment, he threatened a man in an automobile with a gun (which, according to him, was unloaded). He was intoxicated at the time and wanted the man to give him money for more alcohol. Following this incident, he once again moved back in with his parents. He became increasingly depressed and began drinking more heavily—over a quart of vodka a day. He was also taking prescription drugs — analgesics and codeine. He resorted to self-medication whenever he felt unable to cope with his problems or fears. He also reported having seizures, which were directly related to his alcohol and drug intake.

Richard was eventually hospitalized in a Veterans Administration hospital for two months. His presenting complaints were that he suffered from racing thoughts and confused thinking. At that time, he was being medicated with 2 milligrams of chlorpromazine (Thorazine) daily.

After discharge from the hospital, Richard returned to the New York area. His parents arranged for him to live in an adult home for four months because they felt that he might benefit from a structured, supervised way of life. Richard resented this, however, feeling that they were intruding into his privacy and trying to control his life.

WHAT DOES ALCOHOL ABUSE LOOK LIKE?

Alcohol abuse affects many dimensions of behavior, including motivation, cognition, affect, motor skills, and self-care capacity. Often, the alcoholic's sole motivation is alcohol; his life is dominated by overwhelming interest in and desire for alchol, to the exclusion of other activities and interests. Disrupted families and unemployment are often the result.

Cognitive changes are also common. Alcoholics often lack self-confidence and maintain a generally negative view of themselves. It is not clear whether negative self-esteem develops after the alcoholics begin to fail in their endeavors, or whether these views were present prior to the development of the alcoholic behavior. As previously noted, the advanced alcoholic may experience other cognitive problems, such as memory blackouts, hallucinations, and eventual intellectual deterioration.

Alcoholics undergo a number of affective changes. The most common affective reactions are depression, anxiety, guilt, anger, and hostility. These affective reactions are common in many patterns of maladaptive behavior, however, and therefore cannot be used as precise criteria for identifying alcoholics.

Motor difficulty is also common. Loss of coordination and slurred speech during intoxication, and tremors and seizures during withdrawal are examples of alcohol-induced motor impairment. The alcoholic may lose the motor skills necessary for, as well as interest in, self-care. Deterioration in appearance, poor hygiene, malnutrition, and neglected health are common in the late stages of "true" dependence.

HOW DOES THE ALCOHOL ABUSER FEEL?

The Roman poet, Horace, in the first century BC, wrote about the effects of wine: "It discloses secrets; ratifies and confirms our hopes; thrusts the coward forth to battle; eases the anxious mind of its burthen; instructs in arts. Whom has not a cheerful glass made eloquent! Whom not quite free and easy from pinching poverty!"

Alcohol tends to depress activity in all living cells, and in that sense it is a true depressant. The casual observer of a cocktail party or a college beer party might wonder about just how depressing alcohol is as she notices the drinkers' loquaciousness, laughter, and general expansiveness. The explanation is that alcohol, initially at least, selectively depresses those more recently evolved parts of the cerebral cortex that are concerned with self-evaluation and control, thus serving to release the emotional motivational centers from these control centers. There is evidence, however, that some metabolic products of alcohol may more directly produce stimulating effects, possibly by increasing levels of certain neurotransmitters, such as norepinephrine (Lahti and Majchrowicz 1974). In addition, it is probably true that some of the uninhibited behavior associated with alcohol probably results from learned expectations about how to behave when intoxicated. After a certain level of alcohol accumulates in the blood, the well-known syndrome of drunkenness occurs, with increasing impairment of cognitive functioning and physical coordination. If consumption continues, the result is a state of total incoordination and incapacitation, leading to loss of consciousness.

Continued use of alcohol in large quantities has a variety of physical consequences, the least serious of which is the chronic irritation of the stomach lining, resulting in indigestion or ulceration. Extensive use also results in the accumulation of fat in the liver, reducing its functioning and eventuating, if continued, in a marked impairment of this organ called *hepatic cirrhosis*. X-ray scanning procedures have shown that cerebral atrophy is associated with extensive and chronic alcohol abuse (Fox et al. 1976). A number of other debillitating and potentially lethal consequences can also follow chronic and extensive use, including damage to the cardiovascular system and the development of a life-style that renders the chronic abuser vulnerable to a variety of serious diseases. How much these effects are due to the direct pharmacologic effects of alcohol and how much to the life-style that accompanies chronic and protracted use is not always clear, nor may the question be entirely relevant to the need to stop the destructive processes.

THE CLIENT'S DILEMMA

The disease concept of alcoholism can be explained as follows. Some persons — the persons who eventually become alcoholics — are born with a specific vulnerability to the physiological effects of alcohol. Because of this vulnerability, they react to alcohol more intensely than do others, and they develop a much greater need for alcohol — a need that becomes an obsession and ultimately leads to addiction.

The disease lies dormant until the susceptible individual begins to drink, at which time a predetermined, predictable process is initiated. It is not a sudden, all-at-once process; it is a gradual, progressive one. Its full development may take years, sometimes as many as 15. At first drinking is moderate and for pleasure. Later it becomes heavier as alcohol is used for relief from anxiety and escape from emotional and daily-life problems. The drinker next finds that he needs alcohol not only for relief and escape, but also just to be able to perform the ordinary tasks of life and work. At this stage the drinker has become psychologically dependent on alcohol, but it is not yet an addiction; the drinker can still control his intake.

Along with this behavioral progression, however, a crucial physical change has been taking place. As a result of prolonged exposure to high concentrations of alcohol, an alteration takes place in the body's tissues. Somehow the metabolic process of the cells are altered to incorporate alcohol as an ingredient. Now the cells must have alcohol in order to carry on their normal functioning. If they are deprived — if the individual does not drink — the body reacts with severe disturbances, known as withdrawal. In its mildest state, this syndrome — or group of symptoms — takes the form of severe shakes. In its most extreme form, it is manifested in DTs.

According to the disease concept of alcoholism, the drinker has progressed from psychological dependency to physical dependency, or true addiction. Now not only does the psyche demand alcohol, but the body demands it as well. Since this craving is outside voluntary control, the drinker may be unable to resist it.

From a psychological point of view, people who become alcoholics are alcoholism prone, not because of a physical disability, but because of psychological disabilities. These are people who, in childhood, went through disturbing emotional experiences, such as parental rejection, parental cruelty, inability to make friends, lack of success in school, lack of fulfillment and gratification, constant parental conflict, alcoholism in the family, a broken home, or other such difficulties. As a result of these distressing experiences, these children developed feelings of anxiety, depression, insecurity, loneliness, repressed anger, and low self-esteem — feelings they carry into their adolescence and adulthood.

In addition to this handicapping burden from childhood, these individuals are also hindered by a cluster of personality traits that limit their capacity to deal realistically with emotional problems and the daily problems of living. These traits include low tolerance for frustration and suffering, the need for immediate gratification, poor impulse control, and limited ego strength (the ability to cope with and overcome problems).

Persons so disposed have an urgent need for (1) relief from emotional distress; (2) an easy, instant source of pleasure, gratification, and self-esteem; and (3) a way to deal with a reality they cannot handle. Alcohol provides all of these. It anesthetizes emotional pain, produces euphoria, inflates the deflated ego, beautifies the ugly self-image, and modifies reality so that the drinker does not have to deal with it.

The condition becomes progressively worse, not because of some preexisting physical disease, but because of a step-by-step destruction of the person's psychological control over his own behavior and a step-by-step submission to an unreal, fantasy experience in which right and wrong, responsibility, goals, achievement, and societal acceptance no longer have any meaning. By then, escape and oblivion are all that matter from hour to hour, from day to day.

THEORIES AND EXPLANATIONS OF ALCOHOL ABUSE

Alcoholism appears to be related to a variety of factors that can operate in different ways in different individuals. It appears that there is no single etiological agent that can be traced in all, or even most, cases. As with other types of abnormal behaviors, there are probably multiple factors underlying each case of alcoholism. It is also likely that the relative importance of factors will vary from individual to individual. In general, though, as is the case for schizophrenia, biological factors, such as a genetic predisposition to alcoholism, and psychological factors, such as social learning and high stress, appear to be major causes of alcoholism.

Psychoanalytic

Psychoanalytic theorists believe that alcoholism is the overt symptom of unconscious emotional problems. Some psychoanalytic theorists feel that alcoholism is a symptom of unsatisfied dependency needs. This dependence, in turn, is thought to stem from an oral fixation. It is proposed that the future alcoholic remains developmentally immature, fixated at the infantile oral stage. This fixation is thought to explain the dependency, low frustration tolerance, excessive ingestion of alcohol, and antisocial tendencies of adult alcoholics. Alcohol, these theorists feel, provides a substitute milk that nourishes and reduces fear (Menninger 1938). The substitute nourishment, while sustaining the individual, does not contribute to ego maturation and the development of good object relationships.

Another similar psychoanalytic view holds that as an infant, the male alcoholic was overly close to a mother who did not satisfy his oral needs. Turning to the father, however, stirred homosexual impulses, which were then repressed. Unable to accept these impulses, the male alcoholic drinks to reduce both homosexual fears and hostility toward women. As alcohol fails to meet these needs, the person drinks more and more as a passive means of suicide (Fenichel 1945).

There is some evidence that alcoholics may in fact have more intense oral needs than other people. For example, alcoholics are much more likely than nonalcoholics to be heavy cigarette smokers (Maletzky and Klotter 1974). Other research has shown that boys with strong oral needs are more likely than others to become alcoholics.

As for the dependency of the alcoholic, this theory is supported by a wealth of research data (McCord et al. 1960) and is likely to receive the hearty assent of anyone who has lived with an alcoholic. It is no secret that alcoholics are not self-sufficient people, willing to take responsibility for their actions. On the contrary, they tend to seek out anyone or anything — including the alcohol — on which to pin the blame for their troubles. It was not they who caused the accident or the divorce; it was the alcohol. It is important to note, however, that most of the evidence for the dependency theory is retrospective evidence, and it is therefore possible that the dependency of alcoholics develops out of their drinking problem rather than vice versa, or at least that the two problems feed each other in a vicious cycle.

Somewhat the opposite of the dependency theory is the second major theory to develop out of current research — that alcoholics are power seekers who begin drinking in order to foster within themselves the comforting illusion that they are in control. McClelland and co-workers (1972) have built an entire treatment program around this theory. Despite the credible aspects of this theory, however, there is an absence of empirical data to support these psychoanalytic notions (Frank 1970).

Thus, early psychodynamic views theorized that the alcoholic was fixated at the oral stage of psychosexual development and had extreme dependency needs. Out of this traditional view came the search for the so-called alcoholic personality that was prone to the disorder. Although some studies have suggested that, relative to their nondrinking peers, young drinkers are more aggressive, impulsive, anxious, and depressed and have lower self-esteem (Braucht et al. 1973), there has been no solid evidence to support the basic notion of the alcoholic personality.

Social Learning

Since the 1960s, more attention has been given to a social-learning interpretation of alcoholism. According to this view, individuals learn to be alcoholics, even though biological predispositions may also play a role in the development of alcoholism and other addictive behaviors. The social-learning view focuses on four factors in the development and maintenance of excessive drinking: positive and negative reinforcement, tension reduction, modeling, and cognitive factors such as beliefs and expectations (Davidson 1974; Miller 1976).

The generally pleasant consequences of drinking tend to be reinforcing in themselves. These pleasant consequences include the immediate, relaxing physiological effects of the alcohol; the attention and approval of friends; and positive changes in behavior, like increased gregariousness and friendliness, which may lead to other reinforcers. Considerable research has, in fact, shown that alcohol is a powerful *positive reinforcer* which alcoholics will work very hard to obtain (Davidson 1974; Nathan and O'Brien 1971). Research has also shown that animals will consume sufficient quantities of alcohol to become intoxicated, but usually only if the alcohol has been mixed with more pleasant-tasting substances, such as fruit juices, or if it has been substantially diluted with water. Interestingly, most human drinkers, including those who later develop drinking problems, have a history of initially drinking mixed drinks before they develop a taste for straight liquor (Davidson 1974).

According to the learning-theory position, the development of alcoholism is also an operant-conditioning procedure based on negative reinforcement. Specifically, the dynamics are as follows. We all have our share of troubles—anxiety, self-doubt, depression, guilt, anger, and so forth. In the process of emitting different behaviors in an attempt to reduce our psychological discomfort, some of us will take a drink. And alcohol can definitely do the job. Acting as a depressant, it dulls or deadens entirely whatever psychological distress we are experiencing. Alcohol thus becomes associated with the alleviation of psychological pain. And because of this negative reinforcement, the drinkking behavior is likely to be repeated.

Actually, learning theory views the development of alcoholism as a two-stage process. At first, persons may drink excessively only at times of psychological stress. In our society, however, regular heavy drinking is frowned upon. Individuals may therefore begin to feel guilty about their episodes of heavy drinking and about behaviors that accompany it. In short, the solution to stress (alcohol) becomes itself a source of stress. And what do these persons do in order to relieve this increasing stress? They resort to the behavior which they have learned is effective in reducing psychological stress: drinking. Hence, they drink to reduce the feelings of guilt and anxiety that have developed because they drink too much — a vicious cycle.

Negative reinforcement can also play a powerful role in alcoholism since drinking is also reinforced by the reduction or elimination of some unpleasant condition. If drinking helps to reduce anxiety, guilt, depression, pain, or other forms of discomfort, the individual is likely to increase or at least continue drinking. This basic principle emphasizes the following sequence: a stressful situation leads to an unpleasant feeling, which leads to excessive drinking, which results in relatively immediate tension reduction. As Miller (1976) has indicated, the more frequently this sequence occurs, the more likely it is that the person will drink excessively to cope with stress; the more stress, the more important the reinforcing properties of alcohol become. In the advanced stages of alcoholism, when the person is clearly addicted to the alcohol, reducing the discomfort of withdrawal symptoms is likely to be another important factor in maintaining the alcoholic pattern.

Although the *tension reduction* properties are readily apparent, it is not entirely clear how important this factor is in maintaining drinking behavior. In the early 1960s, it was believed that tension reduction was the primary explanation for the development of alcoholism. In recent years, however, it has been found that alcohol does not always reduce anxiety, depression, and other unpleasant conditions (Cappell and Herman 1972). In some cases, alcohol may actually increase anxiety or depression, especially in chronic alcoholics (Nathan and O'Brien 1971). There may be, for example, a "kickback" effect. An individual feels tense. She has a drink to reduce the tension. It appears to work. As the alcohol wears off, the tension may reappear, only it's more uncomfortable than it was before. Now an even greater volume of alcohol is needed in order to reduce the tension.

This cycle is somewhat supported by a study by Williams (1966), which also suggests that the amount of alcohol consumed is an important variable in determining its effect on anxiety and depression. Moderate levels of alcohol reduce unpleasant emotions, but continued drinking will eventually begin to increase the anxiety and depression to near the levels that the person had prior to drinking. In summarizing the issue, Miller (1976) suggests that the role of discomfort reduction for the alcoholic is quite complex. For example, certain stressors do appear to lead to increased drinking in alcoholics, whereas other stressors do not. Social stressors increase drinking rates (Miller et al. 1974), while threat of pain does not appear to have the same effect (Higgins and Marlatt 1974).

Modeling is the third learning factor that helps to explain alcoholism (Bandura 1969). Modeling theorists suggest that persons will imitate what others do, if the person being observed has a high reward value (is respected or has power) and is reinforced for his behavior. A number of studies (MacKay 1961; Wood and Duffy 1966) have shown that alcoholics are much more likely than nonalcoholics to have had an alcoholic parent. It is therefore possible that young persons, when confronted with problems — and since they have been raised in a home with an alcoholic parent, their problems are likely to be substantial — resort to the same coping mechanism they saw their parent resort to: drinking.

We have already noted that alcoholism tends to run in families. In addition to the genetic interpretation of this finding, it is possible that the child observes the parent's behavior and learns through modeling to engage in the same or similar drug-taking behavior. Later in life, the person is more likely to drink excessively around other drinking models — friends, relatives, or spouse. Marlatt

(1974) showed in an experimental situation that heavy drinkers do consume significantly more alcohol when they are with someone who drinks at high rates than when they are with light drinkers.

Finally, the importance of *cognitive factors* is drinking behavior has recently received considerable attention (Marlatt 1978, Wilson 1978). These authors summarized several studies that show the powerful influence of cognitive factors on drinking behavior. One of the major factors studied was the influence of cognitive expectations about alcohol and its effects. Marlatt and colleagues (1973) found that alcohol consumption was influenced more by cognitive factors than by the actual presence of alcohol in drinks. In a study designed to test expectancy factors, they found that expectancy had a significant effect on how much beverage the subjects drank. Both the alcoholic and social drinkers drank more if they *believed* the beverages contained alcohol, regardless of whether the drinks actually contained alcohol. When subjects, including alcoholics, expected nonalcoholic beverages, they drank relatively little, even when an alcoholic drink was provided.

Other studies have shown that expectancy factors have a significant effect on the influence of alcohol on sexual and aggressive behavior (Marlatt et al. 1973, Wilson and Lawson 1976). Other studies have found similar effects of expectation on increasing aggression (Lang et al. 1975) and on increasing sexual arousal to deviant stimuli depicted in a tape of a simulated forcible rape (Briddell et al. 1978). These results clearly show that certain expectations about alcohol can powerfully influence behavior.

Humanistic-Existential

The predominant humanistic theory is based on the work of psychiatrist Eric Berne, who developed an approach called *transactional analysis* (TA). This theory proposes that persons play circular games that produce no change or growth in their lives. A *game* is a program or set of principles that guides persons' lives, the manner in which they live, and the decisions they make. Games are often based on early experiences, and decisions may thus be ill conceived, forced, and immature. Once persons decide to play a game, they develop a script in order to get others to cooperate with them.

Steiner (1969), using the TA model, talks about three games alcoholics frequently play, called, "Drunk and Proud," "Wino," and "Lush." The details of the games differ, but they share the same general existential position, which can be phrased as, "I'm no good and you're OK (Ha! Ha!)." In each of these games, in order to obtain some attention and social reinforcement, alcoholics put themselves in a position in which others will disapprove of them. On the surface, those who disapprove of the alcoholic's behavior appear to be virtuous and blameless; however, they are soon put in a position in which they are made to feel foolish and guilty. This twist represents the "Ha! Ha!" part of the script. Each game has its own dynamics, aims, rules, and roles to be taken by family members and friends; also included are roles in the helping professions. Some of these roles include Patsy, Dummy, Rescuer, Persecutor, and Connection.

In "Drunk and Proud," the alcoholic says, "You're good; I'm bad (and try and stop me)." The alcoholic misbehaves while under the influence of alcohol and then apologizes. If you accept the behavior, you appear foolish and helpless (a patsy)! If you reject the behavior, you appear to be the persecutor of a "sick person." No matter how noble your intentions are, sooner or later the alcoholic's behaviors provoke an angry outburst, which proves that you really do not care. In "Lush," the alcoholic says "I'm crazy or depressed and only you can make me feel better." Because of a lack of reinforcement, the alcoholic hurts himself and receives sympathy, attention, and reinforcement (*strokes*, in TA terminology) from various rescuers. Therapists and social workers are quite often induced into playing this game.

In the game of "Wino," in which the alcoholic is saying, "I'm sick; you're OK (Ha! Ha!)," he drinks until physical deterioration has set in. In this case, the alcoholic believes that services and goods are given out by people in power only to those who are helpless and crippled. This attitude probably results from severe deprivation in early childhood. A judge often becomes the patsy in this game by sentencing an alcoholic to jail or a hospital in the winter, where he gets exactly what he wants (food, clothing, shelter, sympathy, and care). Unfortunately, the life plan or goal of these games is eventual self-destruction.

Richard, our previously described case, certainly liked to play victim. He was the poor, unfortunate one who was under the control of others, an object of their abuse. While there were times when he was also the recipient of help from others, he always defeated their efforts by starting to drink again, placing himself once again in the victim position; their efforts failed him.

He remembered a dream he had had as a child, in which he was forbidden by his mother to go to the store to buy candy. He rebelled, however, and went anyway. On his way to the store, he was hit by a car and his bicycle was mangled. He then witnessed his own funeral as a detached spirit, watching everybody cry over his death. If we see the death of the child as his true self, then the spirit is the detached and disowned part of himself who is only vaguely interested in what is happening. His mother is the inhibiting force, and the bicycle is the lost autonomy; he will never again do as he truly wishes.

The humanistic-existential perspective views the alcoholic as someone who has rejected, or indeed someone who has never located, a real identity. Instead of giving expression to their true selves and accepting the risks involved in such a choice, alcoholics attempt to cope with life's problems by playing roles that are unacceptable to themselves and that are not favored by, but are understandable to, society. In so doing, they give up their freedom to choose self-actualizing behaviors, behaviors that would be more congruent with their true selves. The longer they continue this self-defeating behavior, the more isolated they become from their true selves and from other human beings.

Family Environment

The disease model of drug abuse has led investigators to emphasize individual factors in the search for explanations of this phenomenon. Recently, however, there has been a move to explore the role of small social groups, such as families and gangs, as well as the part played by the larger social system in the maintenance of drug use and abuse. One group that exerts a good deal of influence on behavior is the family. However, attempts to pinpoint a particular family constellation that produces drug abuse in its members have been as fruitless as the search for the "addict personality."

Initial family research on alcoholism focused on the wife of the male alcoholic. She was thought to be dependent and neurotic, and it was alleged that to prevent exposure of her own inability to be independent, she started her husband drinking and encouraged him to continue even when he seemed about to stop. Research has demonstrated, however, that many personality problems exhibited by the wives of alcoholics were consequences of their attempts to cope with the situation, rather than causes of their husbands' drinking (Kogan and Jackson 1965). In addition, the personalities of wives of alcoholics could not be distinguished from those of wives of nonalcoholics (Kogan and Jackson 1965).

Jackson (1968) has identified the stages through which a family proceeds in its attempts to cope with an alcoholic husband. These stages parallel Jellinek's in some respects. At first *excessive drinking* puts a strain only on the marital relationship. Drinking episodes eventually become more public, however, and the family suffers *social isolation.* The third stage begins when the *family gives up* efforts to control the excessive drinking and no longer supports the alcoholic member. Now the *wife takes control* of the family, reassigning to herself and to capable children what used to be the husband's tasks. By *isolating the drinking member,* the family is then able to regain its equilibrium and reduce stress.

This stage may continue toward a physical separation between the husband and wife, and lead to eventual divorce. At this point, however, the husband usually begins to seek treatment. If he maintains sobriety and attempts to reenter the family, he may find that he no longer has a "slot." The family may be unwilling to go through the stress of another reorganization. The husband's rejection and isolation may be a factor in his later resumption of excessive drinking.

More recent work on the possible role of the family in alcohol abuse views the family as a system in which the behavior of each member is interrelated and coordinated with the behavior of others. In this approach, developed by Steinglass and associates (1971), drinking is either a signal of stress within the family system or an integral, adaptive part of family maintenance. In one of the families studied, the wife used alcohol to increase assertiveness in coping with threats to the family from the outside world when her husband refused to assert himself.

Research support comes from Gorad (1971), who found that in families with an alcoholic, both the husband and wife were competitive, escalated conflicts, did not handle outside stress well, and did not work toward achieving joint goals. Alcohol was used by the partner who was unable to compete directly to help maintain his or her position and the family equilibrium. Although the role of the family in maintenance of drug abuse is just beginning to be explored, it is clear that the family is a major factor in passing along drug-related behaviors and attitudes from one generation to the next.

Biological

Some evidence suggests that a biological predisposition, possibly controlled through genetic transmission, may be important in alcoholism. There is considerable evidence, for example, that alcoholism tends to run in families (Winokur et al. 1970). It is quite common to find that alcoholics had a parent, usually the father, who was also an alcoholic. This does not necessarily mean, however, that genetic factors are involved in alcoholism. It may simply mean that the person learned the behavior while growing up with a parent modeling drinking behavior as a means of handling problems.

Early studies on adoption, in fact, suggested that adopted children of alcoholics were not more likely to become alcoholics themselves (Roe et al. 1945). However, more recent studies conducted in Denmark suggest that there is a genetic predisposition to alcoholism; Goodwin and colleagues (1973) compared a group of 55 male children who were adopted from alcoholic biological parents to a matched group of 78 control subjects who were also adopted but did not have an alcoholic biological parent. The children were adopted within 6 weeks of their birth and had no knowledge of or contact with their biological parents. They were interviewed when they were adults (average age 30) by a psychiatrist who did not know that the subject's biological parent was alcoholic. Ratings and information gathered by the psychiatrist pointed to several differences in the two groups of adoptees. Some 18 percent of those with alcoholic parents were themselves alcoholic, in contrast to a 5 percent alcoholism rate among the controls. In addition to being almost four times more likely to become alcoholic, the children of alcoholics had significantly more divorces, psychiatric hospitalizations, and treatment specifically for drinking problems. In general, the conclusions were that a biological predisposition might be relevant in alcoholism because of the comparatively high rates found in the adopted offspring of alcoholic parents.

Goodwin and co-workers (1974) conducted a further investigation using some of these same experimental subjects who happened to have siblings who were raised by their alcoholic parents. This study found high rates of alcoholism in both the adoptees and those who were raised by their alcoholic parents. The groups did not differ significantly from each other. In other words, those who were raised by their alcoholic parents were no more likely to become alcoholic than those who were adopted and raised by nonalcoholic foster parents. Again, the evidence suggests the importance of a biological predisposition.

Miller (1976) and others have suggested that some individuals may inherit certain characteristics that will make them more or less likely to become alcoholic. For example, nonalcoholics may have a more immediate adverse reaction to alcohol because of gastrointestinal sensitivity or other physiological differences. There is some suggestion that Orientals, who have generally low rates of alcoholism, may have this type of sensitivity to alcohol (Ewing et al. 1974).

PRACTICE TECHNIQUES

Regardless of which theory or combination of theories prevails, alcoholics can be helped. The basic goal of treatment is to break the dependency on alcohol, to rid them of the compulsive need to drink. Various methods are used to achieve this goal—physical, psychological, and a combination of both.

The potential for recovery from alcoholism is greatly enhanced when treatment begins in the early stages—before the dependence has become firmly entrenched and before the drinker's entire life is alcohol centered. Alcoholics in the late stages, especially those in whom physical and physiological deterioration is far advanced, have very poor prospects for recovery. Also, it is generally agreed that individuals whose alcoholism starts early and develops rapidly have a poor prognosis, a poor chance of being treated successfully. Patients whose alcoholism starts later in life and develops slowly are regarded as having a better prognosis, provided, of course, that they seek treatment. The prognosis is also good, in general, for those who have remained socially involved; have had good achievement in work, business, or raising a family; and have a capacity for warm, deep personal relationships.

Statistics on the long-range outcomes of treatment for alcoholism vary considerably, depending on the population studied and on the treatment facilities and procedures employed. They range from low rates of success for long-term alcoholics to recoveries of 70 to 90 percent when up-to-date treatment and aftercare procedures are used. Although individual psychotherapy is sometimes effective, the focus of psychosocial measures in the treatment of alcoholism more often involves group therapy, behavior therapy, and the Alcoholics Anonymous (AA) approach.

Detoxification

Any treatment of alcoholism generally begins with a medical treatment called *detoxification* — that is, removing the alcohol from the alcoholic's system and seeing the alcoholic through the withdrawal symptoms. The patient is hospitalized, and a tranquilizer such as diazepam (Valium) or chlordiazepoxide (Librium) is substituted for the alcohol. Withdrawal to the substitute drug is usually completed in five to seven days. High levels of vitamins, especially the B complex, are administered daily to counter the nutritional deficiencies. Since dehydration is also common in withdrawal, a high liquid intake is maintained. Finally, depending on the severity of the alcoholism, an anticonvulsant such as phenytoin (Dilantin) may be administered to eliminate the possibility of seizures.

Once detoxification is completed, the difficult part of treatment begins — the effort to change the alcoholic from a drinking social dropout with disrupted interpersonal, family, and job relationships, to an integrated, self-sustaining, coping member of society. This is not an easy task, however. Since rehabilitation affects so many aspects of the alcoholic's life, the most effective alcohol rehabilitation programs are *multimodal* in nature. Within a supportive and nonthreatening environment, alcoholics are provided with occupational therapy to help them learn or relearn occupational skills; relaxation therapy to teach them how to reduce tension without alcohol; and group and individual therapy to help them learn something about themselves and to teach them how to relate to others without a drink in their hands. Family or marital therapy is then useful, to resolve some of the problems that may have contributed to or resulted from the drinking; vocational counseling then helps get clients back to work, thus keeping them busy, boosting their self-esteem, and relieving their financial worries. Often included are lectures and films dealing with alcoholism, physiology, psychology, and human relations. These are designed to help the patient understand the disease, why they succumbed to it, how it affects them physically and psychologically, and how it affects their relationships with family members and others. These forms of treatment proceed concurrently, and most, if not all, clients participate in them daily.

Psychodynamic Treatment

Psychodynamic treatment of the alcoholic aims not so much at the symptom — that is, the drinking — as at the underlying psychic cause, since according to psychodynamic theory there will be no symptom relief until there is relief of the unconscious conflict. However, psychodynamic therapy has a relatively low success rate with alcoholism and is generally not a common form of treatment for this disorder.

Behavioral Treatment

Traditional psychodynamic psychotherapy attempts to deal with unconscious conflicts presumed to be at the bottom of a psychiatric illness. In the case of alcohol dependence, the assumption is that when the conflict is resolved, the alcoholism will be easier to overcome. Behavior therapy, on the other hand, which ignores the psychological dynamics of the illness, concentrates on the excessive drinking itself. The drinking is regarded as inappropriate learned behavior that can be unlearned — eliminated — through a variety of behavioral techniques.

One of the most rapidly developing forms of treatment for alcohol abuse disorders is behavior therapy, of which several types exist. One is *aversive conditioning*, involving a wide range of noxious stimuli. A noxious (offensive) stimulus — such as an emetic drug or an electric shock — is administered along with the taste, smell, and sight of an alcoholic drink. The procedure is repeated daily for several weeks. Ultimately, the pain, revulsion, and discomfort produced by the shock or by vomiting become associated with alcohol in the drinker's mind. This negative association works to extinguish the drinker's desire for alcohol.

Today a variety of pharmacological and other deterrent measures can be employed after detoxification. In order for the alcoholic to unlearn the drinking response, this response must be either extinguished — that is, no longer reinforced by anxiety reduction — or made aversive through some kind of punishment. Since it is difficult to arrange things so that alcohol intake is not followed by a reduction in anxiety, most behavioral treatments of alcoholism rely on the use of aversive techniques.

One such aversive method involves the use of drug called disulfiram (Antabuse), a chemical that interferes with the normal processing of alcohol for about two days after it is taken. When Antabuse and alcohol are combined, a toxic agent accumulates in the bloodstream, causing an extremely unpleasant reaction. The individual flushes, his heart rate increases, he experiences extreme nausea, and he generally feels as though he is about to die. The pairing of this reaction with alcohol is, of course, a classic case of aversive conditioning. Furthermore, Antabuse treatment is also based on the assumption that it will help the alcoholic avoid impulsive drinking (Baekeland et al. 1971), since if he wants to take a drink without becoming violently ill, he has to stop taking Antabuse at least two days in advance. A drawback to Antabuse is that many patients, after taking the drug in the hospital, simply discontinue it once they are discharged. Consequently, treatment rarely relies on Antabuse alone. Instead, the drug is used as part of a more general rehabilitation program.

Another approach involves the intramuscular injection of emetine hydrochloride, an emetic. The client is given alcohol before experiencing the nausea that results from the injection, so that the sight, smell, and taste of the beverage become associated with severe retching and vomiting. With repetition, this classic conditioning procedure acts as a strong deterrent to further drinking — perhaps in part because it adds an immediate and unpleasant physiological consequence to the more general socially aversive consequences of excessive drinking.

Other aversive methods include the use of mild electrical stimulation, which presumably enables the therapist to maintain more exact control of the aversive stimulus, reduces possible negative side effects and medical complications, and can even be administered by means of a portable apparatus that can be used by the patient for self-reinforcement. Using a procedure which pairs electrical stimulation with drinking-associated stimuli, Claeson and Malm (1973) reported successful results — no relapses after 12 months — in 24 percent of a study group consisting mostly of advanced-stage alcoholics.

Aversive conditioning with emetic drugs has been in use for decades, but on a small scale. Electric shock has come into use only during the past 15 years. Both methods are very complex, requiring hospitalization in special hospitals and the attention of specially trained professionals. Generally, psychotherapy is given along with aversive conditioning, so that the underlying conflict and the drinking habit itself are attacked simultaneously.

Another approach, called *covert sensitization,* involves extinguishing the drinking behavior by associating it with noxious mental images rather than chemical or electrical stimuli (Cautela 1967). Positive results have been reported, with the reduction of drinking for a time. However, the long-term effects of covert sensitization generally have not been impressive. To expect such stimuli as images to change a deeply ingrained life pattern is perhaps unrealistic. Covert sensitization procedures might be effectively used as an early step of alcohol rehabilitation, but other treatment procedures should later be used while the person remains abstinent. The most important effect of any type of aversion therapy with alcoholics, though, seems to be the temporary extinction of drinking behavior, making it possible for other psychosocial methods to be used effectively (Davidson 1974). Other behavioral techniques have also received a great deal of attention in recent years (see also Gottheil et al. 1982, Miller 1978, Nathan 1977, Sobell and Sobell 1973). However, Pendery, Maltzman, and West (1982) followed up on the subjects of the original Sobell study and found that only 1 out of 20 subjects was still successful in controlling drinking. Clearly, additional research will be needed to determine the success or failure of controlled drinking as a treatment approach.

Humanistic Treatment

Humanistic treatment for alcoholism, as for other disorders, emphasizes the need for individuals to look inside themselves and work hard to identify the real self, the self that they would truly choose to be. Equally important is the confrontation with the nonchosen self, the role that they have been playing. Through these therapeutic dialogues, individuals are helped to realize that they alone must make the choice between two different behavior patterns. This philosophy is actually quite close to the basic tenet of Alcoholics Anonymous. AA's position is simply that every day, alcoholics must decide anew whether they will escape from the self into alcohol or whether they will deal directly with the difficulties and anxieties they all must confront sooner or later.

Alcoholics Anonymous

The most successful of these regular nonprofessional meeting programs for alcoholics is AA. The AA program started in 1935, soon after the end of Prohibition, and has since spread throughout the world. The organization was started by two individuals, Dr. Bob and Bill W., in Akron, Ohio. Bill W. recovered from alcoholism through a "fundamental spiritual change" and immediately sought out Dr. Bob, another alcoholic, who, with Bill's assistance, achieved recovery. Both began to help other alcoholics. As a result, there are now over 10,000 groups in the United States alone. In addition, AA groups have been established all over the world. AA is not a panacea. Not all alcoholics benefit from, or can even tolerate, the group's approach. But it is an option to which every alcoholic should be exposed.

AA operates primarily as a nonprofessional counseling program in which both person-to-person and group relationships are emphasized. AA accepts both teenagers and adults with drinking problems. There are no dues or fees. The organization does not keep records or case histories, nor does it participate in political causes. It is not affiliated with any religious sect; however, spiritual development is a key aspect of its treatment approach. To ensure the anonymity of the alcoholic, only first names are used. Meetings are devoted partly to social activities, but consist primarily of discussions of individual problems with alcohol, often with testimonials from recovering alcohlics.

An important aspect of AA's rehabilitation program is that it lifts the burden of personal responsibility by helping alcoholics accept that alcoholism, like many other problems, is bigger than they are. Henceforth, they can see themselves not as weak-willed or lacking in moral strength, but rather as having a disease. They cannot drink. Just as other people may not be able to tolerate certain types of medication, the alcoholic cannot tolerate alcohol. With mutual help and reassurance through participation in a group composed of others who have shared similar experiences, alcoholics eventually acquire insight into their problems, a new sense of purpose, greater ego strength, and more effective coping techniques. And, of course, continued participation in the group helps prevent the crisis of a relapse.

The encouragement and guidance received at meetings and through informal personal associations help alcoholics to strengthen their determination and to resist the urge to drink. On admission to AA, the new member is introduced to the AA guidelines, known as the "twelve steps." Each person is encouraged to follow them at his own pace. The twelve steps consist of a series of acknowledgments and resolutions by the alcoholic: that he is in the grip of a force over which he has no power; that he has turned over his will and life to God as we understand Him; that he has inventoried all his weaknesses and shortcomings and asks God to remove them; that he will make amends to those he has harmed; that he has had a spiritual awakening and will at all times practice the twelve-step principles and carry the message to other alcoholics.

The success of AA seems to be based on two tenets: (1) once an alcoholic, always an alcoholic, and (2) no one can stop drinking without help. AA believes that alcoholics are powerless in the face of forces greater than themselves and, unaided, will always remain alcoholics. The organization sees alcoholism as a lifelong problem from which individuals never recover. This model, by focusing on internal causes of alcohol addiction, leads alcoholics to believe that their excessive drinking is a matter of lack of internal control over their own drinking behavior. Consequently, they must completely abstain from alcohol and must rely on AA for comradeship and support in doing so.

Such support is provided not only through the meetings, but also through AA's famous buddy system. When members feel that they cannot keep themselves from taking a drink, they are supposed to call AA. One or two members will then come as soon as possible to help the individual fight the urge. In the process, it is believed, they will also be helping themselves. As alcoholics become more and more involved in AA groups and activities, they become like members of a secret society, carefully observing the organization's code of words and rituals, becoming very suspicious of all outsiders. Often the AA subgroup occupies so much of the members' time that they may neglect their families, thereby creating new problems.

The effectiveness of AA has been debated. Members claim a 50 percent cure rate, but they neglect to mention the high initial dropout rate. The results of independent studies show the actual cure rate to be about 30 to 35 percent (Ditman 1967), which is about equal to the cure rate produced by other treatments.

Group Therapy

Group therapy attempts to force alcoholics to face their problem and recognize the possible disastrous consequences, but it also encourages them to begin to see new possibilities for coping with it. Often, but by no means always, this double recognition paves the way for developing more effective coping skills and taking other positive steps toward dealing with drinking.

In some instances, the spouses of alcoholics and even their children may be invited to join group therapy meetings. In other situations, family treatment is itself the central focus of the therapeutic effort. In the latter case, the alcoholic is seen as a member of a disturbed family in which all the members have a responsibility for cooperating in treatment. Since family members are frequently the persons most victimized by the alcoholic's addiction, they often tend to be judgmental and punitive, and the alcoholic, who has already passed harsh judgment on himself, tolerates this further devaluation very poorly. In other instances, members of a family may unwittingly encourage an alcoholic to remain addicted, as, for example, when a wife with a need to dominate her husband finds that a continually drunken and remorseful spouse best meets that need.

Family Therapy

Family therapy is based on the theory that stress and conflict in the family are capable of provoking emotional disorders in one or more vulnerable members of the family. Treating the patient individually might help to eliminate some of the symptoms, but this gain would be undone by the persistence of the strains within the family. The aim of family therapy is to treat the family members together in order to undo the mutually destructive patterns operating within the family and to relieve pressures that are playing on the vulnerable individual's weakness. When there is alcoholism in the family, therapy is directed, in part, toward changing the family interactions that tend to reinforce the alcoholic's vulnerability. Efforts are made to enhance the alcoholic's psychological growth so that he will accept more constructive roles in the family and refrain from using alcohol as a coping device.

Follow-up

One part of the most successful rehabilitation programs is a follow-up treatment component. The ex-patients usually meet one or more times a week for three to six months, or perhaps for the rest of their lives. This continued contact provides support for the individuals, reminding them once again that they are not the only alcoholics in the world and that people are there to help them. Furthermore, the follow-up meetings give alcoholics the opportunity to continue working on their problems and to learn additional interpersonal coping skills.

In their extensive four-year follow-up of a large group of treated alcoholics, Polich and colleagues (1980) found that the course of alcoholism after treatment was variable. In some respects the findings of this study were not encouraging and seemed to emphasize the treatment failures among alcoholics. Only 7 percent of the total sample (922 males) abstained from alcohol use throughout the four-year period; 54 percent continued to have alcohol-related problems. Some 36 percent of the sample demonstrated alcohol-dependency symptoms, and another 18 percent suffered adverse consequences (e.g. arrests while drinking).

On the positive side, the study can be viewed as demonstrating a clear beneficial effect of treatment for at least some individuals. Although 54 percent had drinking problems at follow-up, over 90 percent of the subjects had had serious drinking problems at the beginning of treatment — a significant reduction.

The outcome of treatment is most likely to be favorable when the drinking problem is discovered early, when the individual realizes the need for help, when adequate treatment facilities are available, and when alcohol-use reduction is an acceptable treatment goal (as opposed to strict abstinence). In their study of various treatments of chronic severe alcohol problems, Brandsma and colleagues (1980) found that direct treatment, whether professional or paraprofessional, insight-oriented or rational-behavior based, was more effective than an untreated control situation. One important finding was that professional treatment was more effective than nonprofessional treatment, although either of the two major therapeutic orientations (insight-oriented versus rational-behavior therapy) was equally effective. AA was the least effective, partly due to a high dropout rate.

As with other serious maladaptive behaviors, the total alcoholic treatment program usually requires measures to alleviate the patient's often destructive life situation. As a result of their drinking, alcoholics often become estranged from family and friends, and their jobs are lost or jeopardized. Typically, the reaction of those around them is not as understanding or supportive as it would be if they had a physical illness of comparable magnitude. Simply helping them learn more effective coping techniques may not be enough if the social environment remains hostile and threatening. For alcoholics who have been hospitalized, halfway houses, designed to assist them in their return to family and community, are often an important adjunct to the total treatment program. The concept of a *community reinforcement approach* has been developed to focus on helping problem drinkers achieve more satisfactory adjustments in key areas of their lives, such as marriage, work, and social relationships. This approach seems to offer a promising conceptual basis for future treatment programs.

WHEN DO YOU REFER THE CLIENT?

As has been already noted, the biological components of the disease of alcoholism (whether causative or a consequence of the illness) can be conducive to creating the need for sustained drinking behavior. Thorough medical assessment is therefore necessary for helping the alcoholic back to recovery.

Referral to AA meetings or to Alanon is also a necessary initial step in helping alcoholic clients back to feeling that others understand their plight. These meetings also allow alcoholics to realize that there are some constructive options for dealing with dysfunctional aspects of their lives. The alcohol-free climate of these groups, together with positive steps toward accepting those dysfunctional aspects of their behavior (which had previously induced only more guilt, anxiety, depression, and hopelessness), now make it possible to confront and eventually put to rest old patterns on the road to recovery. These groups provide the environment for acceptance, caring, and revitalization of aggressive or frustrated feelings which have been so typical of the alcoholic's way of life.

If, during the treatment process, the problem drinking has given way to alcoholic alibis and rationalizations of drinking behavior so that the physical demands for drinking occur together with loss of control, then referral to an alcohol counselor is necessary. These clients need to be educated about the fact that internal needs have substituted for the previous reactive drinking despite the periods of abstinence. Acceptance of help from a source outside the self is necessary.

During periods of prolonged drinking, the alcoholic client may need an alcohol-free environment and a source of an external structure, such as hospitalization, for detoxification. This may prevent physical problems and accidents while also providing time to convince the client to make a commitment to a new way of dealing with old problems.

Information about alcoholism and treatment resources can be obtained from the National Clearing House for Alcohol Information, P.O. Box 2345, Rockville, Maryland, 20852, or from the National Council on Alcoholism, 733 Third Avenue, New York, New York, 10017. The council can direct therapists to many helping resources in the United States.

Chapter 7

Post-Traumatic Stress Syndrome: Situational Traumas Leading to Personality Disruptions

WHAT IS POST-TRAUMATIC STRESS SYNDROME AND HOW DO YOU RECOGNIZE IT?

In 1942, the disastrous Coconut Grove nightclub fire in Boston took the lives of 492 people. More than 50 percent of the survivors required treatment for severe psychological shock (Adler 1943). In 1972, two commuter trains collided in Chicago. The collision left 44 persons dead and over 300 injured. The tragedy also left scores of persons with feelings of fear, anxiety, and guilt. Psychological evaluation of 8 of the 64 survivors after the collision of two jet planes on Santa Cruz de Tenerife Island in 1977, in which 580 people died, indicated that all the survivors studied suffered from serious emotional problems which stemmed directly from the accident (Perlberg 1979).

With few exceptions, people who are exposed to plane crashes, automobile accidents, explosions, fires, earthquakes, tornadoes, sexual assault, or other terrifying experiences experience severe psychological shock. The symptoms may vary widely, depending on the nature and severity of the terrifying experience, the degree of surprise, and the personality of the individual.

Stressful events may be loosely characterized as *acute* or *chronic*. Acute stress results from sudden, intense events, such as natural disasters, rape and other violent crimes, and loss of a spouse. Chronic stresses, on the other hand, are the relatively constant demands of living in social systems, attending school, working, and maintaining personal relationships. These events may impart meaning and purpose to life, but they are also inevitable sources of stress. This chapter focuses on acute stress.

A "disaster syndrome" has been delineated which appears to characterize the reactions of many victims of such catastrophes. This syndrome may be described in terms of the reactions during the traumatic experience, the reactions initially following it — the acute post-traumatic stress — and the complications that may arise later or be long lasting — the chronic or delayed post-traumatic stress.

Initial Disaster Syndrome and Acute Post-Traumatic Stress

The initial responses to a disaster typically involve the shock stage, the suggestible stage, and the recovery stage. It is in the third stage that acute post-traumatic stress disorder may develop.

During the *shock stage*, the victim is stunned, dazed, and apathetic. Frequently unaware of the extent of personal injuries, the victim tends to wander about aimlessly until guided or directed. The victim is generally unable to make more than minimal efforts to help either herself or others. In extreme cases, the victim may be stuporous, disoriented, and amnesic about the traumatic event.

During the *suggestible stage,* the victim tends to be passive, suggestible, and willing to take direction from rescue workers or others less affected by the disaster. The individual often expresses extreme concern over the welfare of other victims and attempts to be of assistance; however, performance of even routine tasks tends to be inefficient.

In the *recovery stage*, individuals may be tense, apprehensive, and generally anxious, but they gradually begin to regain psychological equilibrium. The person may feel a need to repeatedly describe the catastrophic event. The clinical picture may be complicated in some cases by intense feelings of grief and depression. If victims feel that their own personal inadequacy or incompetency contributed to the loss of loved ones in the disaster, they may experience strong feelings of guilt. In this case, the post-traumatic stress may continue for months. Many victims experience *survivor guilt* which seems to center around the feeling that they did not deserve to survive.

Chronic or Delayed Post-Traumatic Stress

Some individuals who undergo terrifying experiences exhibit a reaction pattern that may endure for weeks, months, or even years. As has been noted, the post-traumatic stress reaction would be clinically diagnosed as *chronic* if it continued for longer than six months. If it did not begin until six months after the catastrophe, it would be diagnosed as *delayed*.

In either case, post-traumatic stress includes the following symptoms:

1. *Anxiety,* varying from mild apprehensiveness to episodes of acute anxiety, commonly associated with situations that recall the traumatic experience
2. *Chronic tension and irritability,* often accompanied by feelings of fatigue, insomnia, inability to tolerate noise, and the complaint of "I just can't seem to relax"
3. *Repetitive nightmares,* reproducing the traumatic incident either directly or symbolically
4. *Impaired concentration and memory*
5. *Depression*

Some individuals withdraw from social contact and avoid experiences that may cause excitation. This is commonly manifested in the avoidance of interpersonal involvement, loss of sexual interest, and a need for peace and quiet at any price.

The post-traumatic syndrome may be complicated by a physical mutilation that necessitates changes in the victim's way of life; it may also be complicated by the psychological effects of receiving disability or legal compensation or damage suits, which all tend to prolong post-traumatic symptoms (Okura 1975).

DSM-III SYMPTOMS

Many factors influence an individual's response to stress. The impact of stress depends not only on its severity but also on the individual's preexisting vulnerabilities. Psychosocial stressors are numerous and varied, and individuals will respond to them in different ways. In attempting to deal with stressful events, for instance, individuals may react with task-oriented or defense-oriented mechanisms. Extreme or prolonged stress can bring about psychological decompensation.

The diagnostic criteria for post-traumatic stress disorder as listed in DSM-III are as follows:

1. Existence of a recognizable stressor that would evoke significant symptoms of distress in almost everyone.
2. Reexperiencing of the trauma as evidenced by at least one of the following:
   a. recurrent and intrusive recollections of the event
   b. recurrent dreams of the event
   c. sudden acting or feeling as if the traumatic event were recurring, because of an association with an environmental or ideational stimulus
3. Numbing of responsiveness to, or reduced involvement with, the external world, beginning some time after the trauma, as evidenced by at least one of the following:
   a. markedly diminished interest in one or more significant activities
   b. feeling of detachment or estrangement from others
   c. constricted effort
4. At least two of the following symptoms that were not present before the trauma:
   a. hyperalertness or exaggerated startle response
   b. sleep disturbance

    c. guilt about surviving when others have not, or about behavior required for survival

    d. memory impairment or trouble concentrating

    e. avoidance of activities that arouse recollection of the traumatic event

    f. intensification of symptoms by exposure to events that symbolize or resemble the traumatic event.

Psychological research and clinical observations of the relationship between stress and psychopathology are so substantial that the role of stress in symptom development is now emphasized in diagnosis and assessment. In DSM-III, for example, the diagnostician can specify the condition on Axis IV.

The DSM-III diagnostic categories for classifying individual problems in response to stressful situations can be found in two different sections of the manual—in a section devoted to adjustment disorders and in a separate section included with the anxiety disorders. In the section on adjustment disorders, several categories are available for classifying psychological adjustment problems of mild severity. More severe psychological disorders in response to trauma or excessive stress—such as imprisonment, military combat, rape, and natural disasters—may be classified as post-traumatic stress disorders (under the anxiety disorders section in DSM-III). These disorders may involve a variety of symptoms, including intense anxiety, denial, repression, apathy, depression, and the lowering of ethical standards. In most cases, the symptoms recede as the stress diminishes, especially if the individual receives brief supportive psychotherapy.

In adjustment disorders, the stressor is usually a common one such as divorce, but the individual's response, which occurs within three months of the stressor, is beyond what one would normally expect in terms of impaired social or occupational functioning. Furthermore, the individual's response is not merely one instance of overreaction to stress, but rather a continuing pattern that typically lessens or disappears after (1) the stressor has subsided or (2) the individual learns to adapt to the stressor. Individual predisposition is not involved.

In post-traumatic stress disorder, the stressor is an uncommon one (an extremely traumatic experience, such as rape), and the symptoms, which begin immediately or soon after the trauma, are typically dramatic, including (1) a recurring sense that one is reexperiencing the actual traumatic event, (2) a general lack of responsiveness to the present environment, and (3) a variety of psychological disturbances. The time frame is important here: An acute post-traumatic disorder begins within six months of the stressor; a chronic post-traumatic disorder is long lasting—that is, it typically lasts six months or more. Finally, there is a category for a delayed post-traumatic disorder, which is defined as beginning at least six months after the stressful event.

Of the post-traumatic stress disorders, the delayed post-traumatic stress disorder is less well defined and more difficult to diagnose than disorders that emerge immediately or shortly after the precipitating incident. In fact, some have questioned whether these disorders should be diagnosed as post-traumatic stress disorders at all. Instead, they would prefer to use other anxiety-disorder diagnoses.

CASE DESCRIPTION

Nancy R. is an unmarried 52-year-old woman. While on vacation in the Poconos, she was abruptly awakened in the night by an unidentified male, beaten, and raped. She entered the center for Service to Rape Victims Program in crisis three months later.

Nancy's presenting problem included extreme feelings of anger and periods of panic during the night. She was experiencing eating and sleeping disturbances and periodic flashbacks of the attack, all common to rape trauma syndrome. The symptom that led Nancy to seek treatment was an uncontrollable flashback during which she reported she could actually feel the weight of the rapist's body on top of her and still smell him.

Nancy was masculine in appearance. She wore no makeup, her hair was cropped short, and her fingernails were cut straight across, causing even her hands to appear mannish. Nancy sat with her legs apart, leaned forward, rested her hands on her knees, and spat anger with every word during the first sessions. Her anger was directed at everyone. Her venom had alienated many of her friends, and her job was now in jeopardy because of displacement of her angry feelings onto her coworkers.

Nancy had never seen her assailant. He woke her as he clubbed her on the head, causing bleeding, while he was threatening to kill her. Nancy believed him and her eyes avoided his face at all times in order to survive. It was as if as a survivor, she was unable to fix the feelings of anger and hate on a particular face. To complicate matters, the police had arrested a black male several months later for a similar crime and were trying to tie the two cases together. Nancy was unsure of even the man's race.

The initial focus of the crisis intervention was to enable Nancy to focus her anger on an appropriate object or person. For Nancy this became the motel in which the assault occurred. The lack of appropriate locks and the absence of a telephone became the basis for a lawsuit.

Several sessions later, Nancy began to feel that she was making progress. Her anger with the world had subsided considerably, and she appeared to be functioning at a level comparable to that prior to her assault. It was at this point in treatment that someone knocked at her door at 1:00 A.M., and her world fell apart. She reported that she grabbed an 8-inch knife and, in a panic, waited near the door. It was not until her landlord called at the door that she was able to move. She screamed at him for frightening her. She then reported that she sat on her bed, knife in hand, clutching her knees, for over an hour before the taste of fear in her mouth left and she was able to put the knife down.

Nancy feared her world would never be safe again. She discussed her deceased mother frequently and expressed a longing for the comfort and safety of the past. The focus of sessions in this short-term type of counseling revolved around exploring how safe her world was before the attack and the manner in which she negotiated her surroundings at that time as opposed to after the attack. Achieving insight into the fact that the world is not less safe now, nor was it entirely safe before, Nancy was able to call on her inner strength. She drove to New York to meet a friend and gradually became more confident in both familiar and unfamiliar situations.

WHAT DOES THE CLIENT WITH POST-TRAUMATIC STRESS SYNDROME LOOK LIKE?

Individual reactions to stress vary considerably, but when stress is prolonged or intense, it often brings about some pattern of reaction that includes one or more of the following characteristics (Davidson 1978, Dubos 1965, Horowitz 1976, Selye 1976).

Affective reactions. The most common reaction to severe, sudden stress is *anxiety.* This may occur during the period of stress or some time afterward. In addition to anxiety, specific fears of things or events related to the stress, such as fear of driving automobiles after an accident, may also result. After a stressful event, the individual may become and remain depressed for a considerable period of time. Depending on the individual and the situation, this depression may be intense or mild and may be accompanied by disturbing thoughts, physical complaints, and guilt. Stress may also leave the person more vulnerable to other minor stresses and irritations. Perhaps the most serious damage done by stress-induced irritability is that people often think that minor irritations are the cause of their anger rather than recognizing them as the precipitating factor. The minor irritants are so much the focus of attention that the real cause — stress — often goes unnoticed.

Cognitive reactions. Under intense stress, individuals sometimes find it difficult to concentrate or think clearly. This effect of stress on concentration often leads to accident proneness. After the stress has receded, unpleasant recollections of the event may intrude in thoughts, sometimes repeatedly (Becker et al. 1973).

Biological reactions. Stress sets off an automatic physiological reaction through the sympathetic nervous system that prepares the body for a "fight or flight" response. Blood is diverted from the skin and digestive system to the crucial skeletal muscles; heart rate, blood pressure, and respiratory rates increase in order to better supply the body with oxygen; adrenaline is released; muscles are tensed; and so on. These reactions, while perhaps adaptive hundreds of years ago, are not adaptive in today's society. People are generally not able to fight or run from the stressors facing them today. As a result, physiological arousal is often useless and may even be harmful.

When stress is intense, and especially when it is prolonged, overarousal can result in a variety of problems, including migraine headaches, urinary and bowel dysfunction, muscle aches, sleeplessness, trembling, and increased menstrual discomfort. Excessive arousal also commonly produces high blood pressure and releases blood fats that may contribute to heart disease (Ursin et al. 1978). Whether these physiological reactions will occur, and their seriousness if they do occur, depends on the severity and duration of the stress and on the individual psychological constitution of the person involved.

In addition, people often react to stress through changes in what they eat and drink. They may eat more or less than usual. Often they will consume more alcohol, caffeine, tranquilizers, tobacco, or other drugs. It is clear that the drugs counteract the effects of stress to some extent. Overeating may accomplish the same thing by distracting the eater or even by lowering arousal by diverting blood from the brain (Selye 1976). At other times, stress can produce a loss of appetite.

Other reactions. Stress reactions may affect other behavioral dimensions. Severely stressful events can bring about a brief period of "irrational" or "bizarre" behavior. Such reactions are infrequent, however, and are usually transient.

Not all reactions to stress are maladaptive, however. Stress can call forth bravery, cooperation, and our best coping strategies. In floods and fires, some men and women risk their lives to save others rather than flee in panic. Disasters, enemies, and other stressors often bring people together in a common cause that allows them to forget minor animosities.

Many factors influence reactions to stress.

Intensity and duration of stress. In general, the more intense or prolonged the stressful event, the more serious the stress reaction will be. The intensity of the traumatic reaction also seems to be dependent on the suddenness of the event and the degree to which the situation is life threatening. Events such as the death of a spouse or loss of a job are more likely to produce serious stress reactions than a cancelled vacation (Rabkin and Struening 1976).

Presence of other stress. Each source of stress is assumed not only to produce its own reactions in the individual but also to make the individual more vulnerable to other stresses. The studies of Holmes and Rahe (1967), showing a link between serious illness and the number of stress events in an individual's life, provide some evidence for this belief.

Prior experience and forewarning of stress. Stress reactions are generally more severe and intense when the individual has had no prior experience with the particular stress or with similar events, and when the individual has had no warning of the stress (Cassel 1970).

Characteristics of the individual. Some individual characteristics and circumstances have been identified that appear to typify the people most likely to react strongly to stress. A survey conducted at the University of Chicago and the National Institute for Mental Health (Uhlenhuth et al. 1974) suggests that individuals who are young, female, white, Protestant, of lower socioeconomic status, and living alone tend to experience more severe reactions to stress than do others. There appear, however, to be individual differences with regard to how people react to stress. Psychologists also often speak of the differences among individuals in their abilities to cope with stress and in their tolerance for stress (Dohrenwend and Dohrenwend 1969). Because these terms are often not operationally defined there is little research to help specify what the components of coping and tolerance are and to determine if they differ in some meaningful way. Research has demonstrated, however, that some individuals chronically react more intensely to stress than others (Glass and Singer 1972, Golin 1974, Horowitz et al. 1973). However, it is difficult to determine whether this reaction stems from genetic or other causes, or some unknown combination.

Social support. A clear relationship is apparent, however, between the magnitude of the stress reaction and the presence of social support, which is defined as satisfying relationships with friends and/or family (Habif and Lahey 1979). Individuals who live alone are much more likely than those who live with families to react to intense stress with serious illness or behavior disorders (Webb and Collette 1975).

Personal control. An additional factor influencing the severity of stress reactions is the degree to which the individual can predict or control the stress events. Symptoms of stress may persist because the person's customary sense of self-confidence and mastery has been badly undermined. The world, which previously seemed at least reasonably safe and predictable, has now become an untrustworthy place. Now that the stressful event has occurred, the victim is continually on the alert for new threats (Krupnick and Horowitz 1981). At the same time, however, the person feels somewhat "shaky," no longer sure of being able to cope with any situation that might arise.

Stress takes its toll on the body. It causes the pituitary and adrenal glands to oversecrete their hormones and throws the nervous system out of kilter. It disrupts the individual's efforts to preserve a sense of homeostasis (Cannon 1929, 1932). When the mind is stressed, so too is the body, and the effects are presumably all the more powerful when the stress is unusually intense.

Once all these vital functions have become altered, the body may not return to its former, comparatively tranquil, well-balanced state. The nervous system may continue to overreact for a considerable period after the traumatic event.

HOW DOES THE CLIENT WITH POST-TRAUMATIC STRESS SYNDROME FEEL?

Like phobias, post-traumatic stress disorder is precipitated by a specific event. The objects or events that set off the phobia are quite commonplace — for example, crowds, embarrassment, cats, illness, and so on. The precipitant of post-traumatic stress disorder, in contrast, is a catastrophic event *beyond* the normal range of human suffering — for example, an earthquake, a rape, combat, or imprisonment in a concentration camp. Three symptoms that result from the catastrophe define the disorder: (1) numbness in experiencing the world, (2) reliving the trauma in memory and in dreams, and (3) symptoms of anxiety. The anxiety symptoms include excessive arousal, hyperalertness, poor concentration, memory impairment, and phobic avoidance of situations that are reminders of the trauma. In addition, the individual may be wracked with guilt about surviving the catastrophe when others did not.

THE CLIENT'S DILEMMA

The catastrophe that brings about a post-traumatic stress disorder need not be experienced en masse, as is the case in flood, war, and concentration camp confinement; it can be solitary. Rape is perhaps the most common such catastrophe in modern American society. The rape situation itself involves severe psychological and physiological reactions on the part of the victim — reactions that reveal the shock and trauma of the event. Psychologically, the victim experiences feelings of anger, terror, exhaustion, racing thoughts, worry, shame, humiliation, helplessness, and fear. Physiologically, victims experience common fear reactions: racing heartbeat, rapid breathing, shaking and trembling, as well as pain (Veronen et al. 1979). A person's reaction to rape looks very much like post-traumatic stress syndrome and has been called *rape trauma syndrome* (Burgess and Holmstrom 1979).

Most power-oriented and anger rapes result in extreme trauma for the victim. The reactions can be divided into two phases: the *acute* (disorganization) and the *long term* (reorganization). The acute phase begins immediately following the rape and may continue for hours, days, and often several weeks. The acute phase is characterized by severe disorganization of one's life, accompanied by strong psychological and physiological reactions. In the hours immediately after the attack, the victim experiences a variety of emotions, including shock, disbelief, fear, anger, and extreme anxiety. Although these reactions tend to be the same for almost all victims, the outward behavior may be *expressive* (releasing feelings through crying, smiling, restlessness, or tenseness). In the *controlled* reaction, the victim will generally appear subdued and matter of fact. Her feelings are constricted and inhibited.

Physiological reactions in the acute phase include the physical trauma of being beaten, general soreness from the attack, and muscle tension including headaches, fatigue, and severe sleep disturbances. Gastrointestinal problems are common, in the form of stomach pains, loss of appetite, and nausea from antipregnancy medication and from the attack itself. Genitourinary problems are also frequent, including vaginal discharge, itching, burning upon urination, and general vaginal pain. Some physical symptoms may be due to the assault itself and not to the emotional trauma. Injuries such as bruises, abrasions, and vaginal or rectal tears require a period of healing.

After the initial shock or disbelief has begun to fade, rape victims typically experience deep feelings of fear, anger, and anxiety. Some victims appear hysterical; others try to mask their horror with a calm facade. Many are in terror lest the rapist return. Some extend their fear to all strangers or situations. At this time, the victims need to talk about the experience, to try to make sense of their horror, to be reassured that they are not alone and still prey to the assailant, to feel that they are still valued and cared for by their friends and loved ones.

The acute phase continues for several weeks after the attack, and feelings of humiliation, fear, embarrassment, anger, revenge, self-blame, and concern about future physical violence are common. The fear experienced by victims is a central part of the rape trauma. Even though these reactions diminish greatly after about three months, there still remains a core of fear and anxiety concerning many previously routine aspects of social life. Some victims never lose their fear in any situation in which there is the potential that they might be treated aggressively or in which they might lose control.

Next, the victim experiences symptoms that strongly resemble reactions to floods, combat, and concentration camp confinement, particularly anxiety and reliving the rape. Physical symptoms also appear—inability to fall asleep or sudden awakening, stomach pains, genitourinary disturbances, and tension headaches. Persons/victims who had been suddenly awakened by the rapist found that they would awaken each night, at about the same time the attack had occurred, screaming from rape nightmares. Dreams and nightmares of the rape continued for a long time, with one third of the victims reporting terrifying rape dreams.

Like flood victims, rape victims startled easily in response to even minor episodes, such as being alone. In addition, fear, depression, humiliation, embarrassment, anger, and self-blame became dominant emotions, particularly fear of violence and death. Like the victims of flood and concentration camp confinement, these victims sometimes developed phobias. Persons who had been attacked indoors developed phobias of the indoors, and those who had been attacked outdoors developed phobias of the outdoors.

Even though the extreme fear and anxiety reactions of the acute phase diminish three to six months after the attack, they are still very much present. Nightmares are common and fear of places and situations suggestive of the rape are frequent (Kilpatrick et al. 1979, Veronen et al. 1979). The reason for these fears is that a very crucial learning process takes place during the rape. Through classical conditioning, characteristics of the rape situation (activities, body parts, the person, the place) become associated with the fear and violence experienced. After the rape, similar places, situations, noises, people, and other reminders evoke the same fear and anxiety responses the victim experienced during the rape. One of the very real problems in dealing with rape in the counseling situation is that these situations must be unlearned and removed from the victim's life.

During the *reorganization phase* of rape trauma, severe reactions seem to diminish, but the problems of restoring one's life to normal remain. How quickly and completely the victims reorganize their lives depends on several factors, including psychological characteristics, their social support networks (including friends, relatives, spouses, and rape counselors), and the manner in which they were treated as a victim (Burgess and Holmstrom 1978, Atkeson et al. 1982).

In the long-term process of reorganization, most victims take action to ensure safety. Feelings of fear and nervousness often continue during the second, long-term reorganization phase. Victims may fear retaliation by the rapist. Women often change their place of residence during this time. Many persons who are raped change their telephone numbers, and approximately half of them make trips home to seek support from family members. Half of the victims move. Many of the victims begin to read about rape and write about their experiences. Some become active in rape crisis centers and assist other victims; of these, 70 percent recovered in a few months. When contacted four to six years after the rape, three quarters of the victims in this study felt that they had recovered, half of these within a few months and the other half within several years. One quarter of the victims felt that they still had not recovered (Burgess and Holmstrom 1979).

Clinicians have reported some of the long term consequences as occurring more frequently than others; difficulty trusting members of the opposite sex and avoidance of interpersonal involvement are among the more common. Metzger (1976) suggests that in the case of women victims that they see men as protectors and providers and are therefore profoundly affected by the sense of betrayal the rape produces. Survivors of acquaintance rape are especially fearful of men and distrust their ability to judge who is safe. Young women and recently divorced women have the highest incidence of acquaintance rape. In addition to their relationship problems, these women, whose egos may be fragile or immature either developmentally or as a result of their circumstances, are often left with severe self-concept and self-esteem problems.

Most women are terrified when they are raped, for they are afraid they are going to be killed. Even the minority who do not consider the possibility of death, experience rape as extremely frightening, degrading, and stressful.

Burgess and Holmstrom (1976) found that rape victims tried a variety of coping mechanisms. Before the attack, many got the vague sense that something was wrong—noticed that a man was hanging around and wondered uneasily what he was up to. Reactions to this awareness of impending danger included trying to escape; memorizing what the man looked like in order to identify him afterward; talking to calm the man down, disuade him, or at least stall for time; bargaining; asserting their rights; threatening; joking; screaming; trying to fight the attacker off; and blowing a rape whistle to attract attention. However, one third of the victims were too frightened to do anything. They were paralyzed by fear, totally overpowered physically, or too shocked by an acquaintance's unexpected behavior to do anything to prevent it.

Women who have been raped report that they are depressed and afraid, plagued by nightmares and mood swings. The immediate impact of rape brings about a wide variety of reactions. After the extreme fear of a life-threatening situation, the woman may be glad simply to be alive. But they may also feel humiliated, angry, vengeful, embarrassed, or guilty. Their moods may change unpredictably. Thoughts of the attack may haunt them night and day. Many find it hard to eat and sleep, and their bodies may be sore all over. According to Resnick et al. and Ellis (1981), depressive symptoms seem to disappear in most rape victims within about four months.

Rape continues to disrupt victims' lives for weeks and months afterward. Many women find it difficult to work but feel vulnerable at home. They may change their door locks, telephone numbers, and apartments, but the fear of being attacked again persists. Disturbing dreams, terror at being alone, and paranoid reactions to strangers and even acquaintances make it difficult for victims to feel free and safe anywhere.

Sexual fears are fairly common after rape, and some women are unable to resume normal sexual activity. Rape can precipitate sexual difficulties for the woman; she may have fearful or negative feelings about sexual relations in general, particularly about intercourse. Becker (1984) theorizes that sexual problems are a result of a "two factor" social-learning theory. They explain that the fear and anxiety or negative reaction experienced by the assault survivor at the time of the incident is generalized to other sexual situations, resulting in a conditioned response to avoid or withdraw from sexual activity or inhibit sexual feelings entirely.

Given the sexual focus of the personal violence and fear in rape, most victims find themselves conditioned by the rape to have certain responses to sexual activity. This figure included 38 percent who refrained from sex entirely for at least three months following the rape. Only a minority of rape victims studied by Burgess and Holmstrom — 19 percent — reported no change in sexual activity. Among these women, however, 50 percent reported changes in their responses to sex, including flashbacks, worrying about their partner's reaction, aversion to certain sexual activities, discomfort and pain, difficulty with sexual feelings in general, and lack of orgasmic response. A minority (9 percent) of the victims in this study increased their sexual activity following the rape. Sometimes this increase was an attempt to counter the negative rape experience with positive sexual interaction. In other cases, however, the increase reflected a change in sexual self-concept along the lines of abandoning previous sexual values. Burgess and Holmstrom (1979) reported that some women engaged in sexual intercourse with almost any available male, and some began prostitution. The incidence of these reactions is not clear, but they can be assumed to be relatively rare.

Sexual relationships are thus no comfort for these women, for they are usually marred by associations with the rape. Sensitive partners may wait patiently until the woman's fear is gradually replaced by willing interest in sex. But some insist on asserting their own "sexual rights" immediately, much to the rape victim's distress. Some double-standard husbands have subtly blamed their wives for what happened and have even divorced them, saying, "I don't know how I could forgive her, although I know it's not her fault" (Renshaw 1978, p. 717).

The rape experience affects not only sexual activity, but sexual satisfaction as well. Feldman-Summers and Linder (1979) measured the self-reported sexual satisfaction of rape victims one week before the attack (retrospectively), one week after the rape, and two months after the rape. They found that for several dimensions of sexuality, sexual satisfaction dropped significantly one week after the attack and then increased slightly in the following two-month period. The level of sexual satisfaction two months after the rape was still significantly less than it had been before the rape.

These findings have important implications for helping rape victims recover and regain their previous sexuality. Reentry into sexual interaction is best accomplished gradually, by means of those activities that are not fear-conditioned by rape. This approach allows for positive feelings to be associated with sexual interaction and opens the way for communication with one's partner about fears and anxieties about life in general and sex in particular.

Reentry into sexuality can be a complex and difficult process. In addition to making the decision to resume sexual activity and dealing with her own emotional and physiological responses to sex, the victim is often concerned about her partner's reactions (Burgess and Holmstrom 1979). Common concerns include how her partner feels about the rape itself: Does he think it was her fault? Does he believe her? Does he think she enjoyed it? Does he think she wanted to be raped? She is also anxious about how her partner feels about her. Does he see her as spoiled and undesirable? Does he see her as different? How does he feel about her being sexual with another man?

These are all concerns which are frequently difficult for the victim to discuss with her partner, but which may be confronted in the counseling situation in the context of understanding and communication.

The time it takes rape victims to learn to cope with their experience depends on their ego strength, how close and supportive their friends and relatives are able to be, and how health and law-enforcement officials treat them as victims. The support, or lack of it, from people around her makes a significant difference in a woman's ability to cope with rape trauma. If she decides to report the rape and suffer the additional stress of police, hospital, and courtroom procedures, she should be accompanied by an advocate to help her handle the difficulties she most assuredly will encounter.

Short-term rape counseling usually has two major goals. One is to help the victim gain control over the stressful memories of the rape. Confronting the victim directly by talking about what happened tends to dilute the pain and fear they experience. The second goal is to help the victim feel accepting of and reassured about herself again. Some rape victims may feel that others will reject them. They need supportive persons around who will reassure them that they are worthwhile, loved, and appreciated. Other women need help with feelings that they have lost control over their emotions. They may feel that it is wrong to express anger and want very much to be emotionally stable again. Others need help with feelings of weakness, helplessness, and insecurity. Women who believe that they were not powerful enough to fight off their assailants may need to feel that they are strong in all situations. Courses in self-defense may restore their sense of physical competence. Also, opportunities to counsel other rape victims may give them a sense of usefulness and accomplishment (Burgess and Holmstrom 1974).

In a later study, Burgess and Holmstrom (1979) found that rape victims differed as to their recovery rates and the types of strategies they used. These researchers found that the victims who recovered most rapidly used more adaptive strategies, including positive self-assessment, defense mechanisms of explanation, minimization, suppression, and dramatization; and increased action. Victims who had not yet recovered used less-adaptive mechanisms, such as negative self-assessments, inaction, substance abuse, and acting on suicidal thoughts.

"Teenage rape trauma syndrome" refers to a pattern of behavior common to some victims after being raped. The syndrome typically has three phases: a phobic phase, followed by a denial phase, followed by a psychosomatic phase. In the phobic phase, the young women demonstrate many fears: fears of leaving the house, fears of strangers, resistance to relationships with the opposite sex, and frequent nightmares that reenact the rape scene. The girls may request tranquilizers or sleeping pills. It is more important, though, for the young woman to be encouraged to talk about her fears and nightmares to her counselor.

In the denial phase, about two months after the rape, these girls begin to socialize again and generally deny that the rape continues to trouble them, in spite of evidence to the contrary, including persistent nightmares, insomnia, sleeping with a nightlight, and complete avoidance of the location of the rape. They may begin to dress sloppily, wearing loosely fitting garments. At this point in the therapeutic relationship, these victims may discontinue follow-up care, claiming that they have no need for it.

Later, six to eight months after the rape, these girls enter the psychosomatic phase, complaining of headaches, abdominal pain, or dizzy spells. The time of onset is often vague, and the victim may not inform a new physician that she has been raped.

A rape victim should immediately call a crisis center and a sympathetic friend. Her first priority is to get medical care for injuries and instructions on dealing with possible disease or pregnancy. The presence of a close friend and a knowledgeable rape crisis counselor will help ensure that the victim receives proper and comforting treatment. A rape victim also needs sound advice, without pressure, to make a decision about whether to report the crime to the police and whether to pursue prosecution if the rapist is apprehended. The crime should be reported promptly, and the victim should save all physical evidence, make note of her assailant's characteristics, and obtain a written report of her injuries and laboratory results. A number of counseling modalities have been described that seem to be effective with rape trauma survivors during the first three months following the incident.

The following are general suggestions for counseling teenage rape victims. (1) Offer all adolescent rape victims the opportunity for counseling immediately after the rape or in the near future; (2)

Avoid unnecessary repeated descriptions of the details surrounding the rape; (3) Look for signs of suicidal ideation; (4) Be alert to signs of the "teenage rape trauma syndrome"; and (5) Offer support in dealing with family, community, and police.

For an example of a step-by-step early-intervention program for counseling rape survivors, refer to Kilpatrick and colleagues (1979). For further information, write to the National Center for Prevention and Control of Rape, U.S. Department of Health and Human Services, 5600 Fishers Lane, Rockville, Maryland, 20857.

THEORIES AND EXPLANATIONS OF POST-TRAUMATIC STRESS SYNDROME

Ego Psychological

The ego-psychological view is that coping ability and adaptability require a degree of order and predictability (Erikson 1950, 1968, Hartmann 1939, Kardiner and Spiegel 1947). The challenges that one faces must remain within reasonable limits and not overtax existing resources — which, as Erikson describes it, is one's ability to make sense of experience. If these challenges prove too overwhelming or become more than one can bear, then, almost inevitably, one will cease to function normally and begin to become disorganized.

Cognitive Behavioral

Seligman (1975), a cognitive behaviorist, offers a similar explanation. Excessive stress causes individuals to become disturbed because it is uncontrollable and unpredictable. Previous learning is suddenly upset. The connection between what people do and what happens to them has been disrupted.

A great deal of attention has recently been devoted to the topic of preventing maladaptive reactions to stress through *stress inoculations*. The idea involves using cognitive techniques to inoculate persons to stress so that they are better able to deal with difficult life situations. Meichenbaum (1974) has proposed a more elaborate program of cognitive stress inoculation for use with adults under stress. His procedure involves (1) explaining the relationship between stress and anxiety and stress reactions, (2) teaching clients that they can consciously control reactions to stress, (3) teaching progressive muscle relaxation, and (4) giving clients controlled laboratory practice in reacting calmly to stressful films, imagined stressful events, and unpredictable electric shocks.

Social Learning

More recently, social-learning therapy has been adapted for the treatment of serious acute stress reactions (Sank 1979). In the case of chronic stress, perhaps changing occupations, for example, or seeking marital counseling can help to reduce stress (Bourne 1969, Fraser 1973). Learning theorists believe that stress is a reaction to situations in which reinforcement has abruptly become noncontingent. Thus stripped of their usual ability to anticipate and control life events, people give way to feelings of helplessness and fail to cope with normal, everyday stressors.

PRACTICE TECHNIQUES

Until recently, there was a lack of awareness of all the therapeutic alternatives available for those suffering from post-traumatic syndrome. Due mainly to the mental health movement, however, clinicians are now more familiar with the problem. Although many victims may not be aware that therapy is available (Katz and Mazur 1979), they can seek assistance from such providers as walk-in clinics that practice crisis intervention, "rap groups" for Vietnam veterans and rape counseling centers.

Post-traumatic stress disorders develop in persons whose sense of control and mastery has been powerfully undermined. The world that once seemed orderly and benign now appears unpredictable and menancing. An extraordinarily threatening experience—or series of incidents—has completely shaken their very identity and sense of self, and their trust in themselves and their ability to cope has been shattered. Whether or not they are explicit about it, therefore, most therapists seem to assume that they are helping their traumatized clients regain what they have lost—their self-confidence and ability to cope.

1. Help clients to express their feelings about the terrifying event.

It is most important to bring clients face to face with the traumatizing experience. It is necessary that they express their emotions or achieve some sort of catharsis. Even therapists who are not psychodynamically oriented may unwittingly be providing their clients with some type of emotional release. Discharging tension and anxiety to a comforting and reassuring expert reduces the feelings of terror associated with the traumatizing events.

2. Help clients establish social support systems.

If social support can help prevent post-traumatic disorders, it can also help victims recover (Butcher and Maudal 1976). In some situations, the best person to offer such support may be another victim. Clients often report that they originally thought that their symptoms were unusual, that no one else had felt as distressed as they did after the ordeal. They are often relieved to discover that others have felt the same way.

3. Help clients to control their symptoms.

After victims have brought their experiences and feelings into the open, their symptoms can be worked through and brought under control. The client's feelings should be explored to a point at which both therapist and client feel comfortable with them. Using triggering situations to enable the client to experience some of the symptoms without losing control and feeling humiliated is helpful. The ability to control both internal and external events at their own discretion can rebuild the client's sense of environmental mastery. Progressive muscle relaxation and systematic desensitization can be employed to relieve anxiety. For a detailed description of these techniques, see Benson 1975, Goldfried and Trier 1974, Jacobson 1938, Mathews and Gelder 1969. A number of studies have also demonstrated that meditation, modified to remove its metaphysical-religious aspects, may be as effective as more formal relaxation techniques (Clopton and Risbrough 1973).

4. Help clients to increase their assertiveness and sense of environmental mastery.

Clients can be trained in assertiveness and other skills that will help them feel less vulnerable. In Nancy's case, resuming her friendships, exploring her social encounters, and moving progressively back into the world all helped her to feel like an active, competent person again. By the end of the twelve sessions offered by the rape counseling program, Nancy had begun to wear makeup and nail polish. Her hairdo was less severe and she wore the color pink to a session for the first time. Although Nancy believed that she was over the worst and that her crisis had passed, one of the coping mechanisms upon which she relied heavily was blocking the memory of her assault.

The knowledge that she would have to relive the entire event in detail for her lawsuit was sometimes anxiety provoking. She planned to rely on her feelings of hate, anger, and revenge to carry her through the ordeal. Nancy perceived the lawsuit as necessary to her mental health, and she believed that she would be able to utilize the support of her friends to sustain her.

WHEN DO YOU REFER THE CLIENT?

Rape counseling typically does not involve long-term psychotherapy. Most victims need to feel as though they have gained control over the effects of the memories of the rape. They also need to learn to feel comfortable with themselves again. They may fear that others will reject them. Helping them to mobilize a support group is an effective way of enabling them to cope with these feelings.

For other women, however, the impact of the rape is long lasting.

These women carry the emotional scars of the rape for years and seem unable to come to terms with the emotional aftermath of the traumatic event. Years later, they may be afraid to venture out of the house or may feel extremely vulnerable when left alone. Others may be very reluctant to enter into an intimate relationship with a member of the opposite sex. For these women, long-term psychotherapy would be more appropriate.

Post-traumatic stress syndrome in general often involves short term therapy. Adjustment times typically do not exceed 24 months. Prior levels of functioning should be taken into consideration. Clients who, prior to the traumatic event, were high functioning and who had adequate coping skills to begin with, tend to return to their normal level of functioning more readily than those who were not. If, after 6 months of psychotherapy, the client has made little progress, psychiatric evaluation is warranted.

Chapter 8

Sexual Dysfunctions: The Otherwise Functioning Client

WHAT ARE THE SEXUAL DYSFUNCTIONS AND HOW DO YOU RECOGNIZE THEM?

Maintaining a sexual relationship involves all levels of human behavior. On the biological level, a delicate series of hormonal, physiological, and muscular functions work together to produce an integrated response during the act of sexual intercourse. Things are more complicated, however, on the psychological level, where the pleasure associated with sexual activity is frequently accompanied by anxieties, inhibitions, questions, and doubts about social definitions and expectations, emotional reactions to one's partner, and the interpersonal patterns of sexual and social relationships. On the sociocultural level, one's sexuality is affected by cultural prescriptions and proscriptions, social patterns, expectations, and norms that help to determine where, how, with whom, and under what circumstances sexual behavior will take place.

It is only in recent times, thanks in large part to the pioneering work of Kinsey and associates (1948, 1953) that we have come to understand how widespread and severe are individual problems with sexuality in our own culture. Because of the very nature of the sexual dysfunctions, the format of this chapter differs slightly from previous formats. In this chapter, instead of one case history presentation, several shorter case histories will be described. One reason for this is that there are many sexual dysfunctions. The second, more complicated, reason is that the practice of counseling and sexual therapy requires specialized training. To present counseling techniques for sexual problems in the space of one chapter would be oversimplifying the issues and perhaps misleading readers. Most training programs for counselors and therapists provide one or, at best, two courses in sexuality, which does not prepare the student to practice sexual counseling or sexual therapy. We will focus here, therefore, on providing the reader with a description of the various disorders, and we will take the professional stance that individuals with sexual dysfunctions should be referred to professionals trained in the field of sex therapy.

The term *psychosexual dysfunction* refers to impairment either in the desire for or in the ability to achieve sexual pleasure or gratification or both. With few exceptions, such impairments generally occur, not as a result of anatomical or physiological pathology, but rather because of faulty psychosexual adjustment and learning. The dysfunctions vary markedly in degree and, regardless of which partner is alleged to be dysfunctional, the enjoyment of sex by both parties in the relationship will probably be adversely affected. Whatever the dysfunction may be, it is reasonable to assume that it can create much misery and unhappiness in the lives of both the individuals affected by the disorder, and their partners.

Several dimensions of maladaptive behavior can occur in sexual dysfunctions. As stated before, the *biological reaction* is clearly influenced since sexual arousal and behavior can be easily disrupted by a malfunction in this area. Major problems are also likely to occur in the other dimensions of behavior. For example, common *psychological reactions* to sexual behavior are intense anxiety prior to or during sexual activities, guilt over certain sexual behaviors, or depression because of the difficulties caused by the sexual dysfunction. Another dimension involved is the *cognitive reaction*. In cases of sexual dysfunction, there is typically some negative evaluation of sexual behavior in general. These negative beliefs are often based on cultural or religious proscriptions against sexual activity. These proscriptions against sexual behavior often also affect individuals at a psychological level. Both men and women with sexual dysfunctions tend to develop diminished self-esteem and self-confidence. Like people with any type of problem, those with sexual dysfunctions often tend to worry excessively about the disorder. These affective and cognitive effects usually lead to decreased interest in sex, which usually then interferes with current or potential sociosexual relationships.

The individual with a sexual dysfunction generally does not have any other major forms of maladaptive behavior and may be well adjusted to other aspects of life, such as work settings or nonsexual social relationships. Munjack and Staples (1976) found that, based on psychological tests, women with sexual dysfunction were virtually identical to "normal" controls. The only difference was that the controls were slightly less depressed.

Thus, difficulty in achieving satisfactory sexual relations has significant physiological, emotional, interpersonal, and cultural effects. Psychotherapists tend to emphasize the psychological factors, however, and most professionals agree that psychological factors seem to account for nearly three fourths of all sexual difficulties.

Psychosexual dysfunction is probably one of the most common of all human problems. Practically every man has had trouble at one point or another achieving or maintaining an erection, and almost every woman has difficulty reaching orgasm from time to time. For some people, however, such sexual dysfunctions become chronic. Some men are impotent; that is, they can rarely, if ever, sustain an erection long enough to enjoy sexual intercourse. There are also women who are completely anorgasmic; some experts prefer the term *preorgasmic* (Ersner-Hershfield and Kopel 1979). Such women are unable ever to have an orgasm. The variety of sexual behaviors is vast, and in our increasingly permissive contemporary culture, it is basically up to couples to decide for themselves what kind of sexual relationship they wish to have. Thus, the definition of sexual dysfunction is largely subjective and experiential.

Male Sexual Dysfunctions

Impotence, or Erectile Insufficiency

The two most widely recognized experts in the field of sexual dysfunction are Masters and Johnson (1970). According to them, the most common male sexual dysfunction, *impotence*, refers to the inability to obtain and maintain an erection that is sufficient to complete sexual intercourse. This disorder is now known as *erectile insufficiency*. In many cases, a male, for some reason or other, begins to worry about whether or not he will be able to achieve erection. This fear can become so anxiety-eliciting that it can eventually lead to actual impotence. Other psychological factors involved in impotence are performance anxiety, spectatoring (mentally observing and evaluating one's sexual performance while it is occurring), and guilt.

Masters and Johnson (1970) differentiate between primary and secondary impotence or erectile insufficiency. In *primary* impotence or erectile insufficiency, the most difficult to cure of all the forms of inadequacy, the male has never been able to sustain an erection sufficient for the successful completion of intercourse, usually defined as including intravaginal ejaculation. This is a chronic type of disorder. The individual with *secondary* impotence or erectile insufficiency usually has a history of having been able to have sexual intercourse at least once but currently cannot maintain an erection. This male has had at least one episode, usually many episodes, of successful intercourse. Primary erectile insufficiency is a relatively rare disorder, but it has been estimated that at least half the male population has experienced the secondary variety at least temporarily, especially in the early years of sexual exploration. It should be again noted that the man who occasionally cannot perform sexually because of extreme fatigue, excessive alcohol consumption or the like would not be classified as impotent. Under some situations, however, these "normal" failures can result in secondary impotence if the individual is overly anxious and allows the temporary condition to distress him to the extent that it interferes with subsequent functioning.

Chronic or permanent erectile insufficiency before the age of 60 is relatively rare and is usually due to psychological factors. In fact, according to the findings of Kinsey and colleagues (1948, 1953), only about one fourth of males become impotent by the age of 70, and even then many cases are a result of psychological factors. More recent studies have indicated that men and women in their 80s and 90s are quite capable of enjoying sex (Kaplan 1974a; Masters and Johnson 1976). To the degree that men do experience some difficulties in their older years, it appears that in some cases they may simply be assimilating and complying with the societal expectation and definition of declining sexual performance with age (Tollison et al. 1977).

Some cases of erectile insufficiency—estimates are approximately 15 percent (Kaplan 1974a)—are caused by a variety of organic conditions, including certain types of vascular disease, diabetes, neurological disorders, kidney failure, hormonal irregularities, and excess blood levels of certain drugs, including alcohol (Wagner and Metz 1980). Masters and Johnson (1970) have also listed some psychological and social causes of secondary impotence or erectile dysfunction: frequent premature ejaculation, intemperate alcoholic consumption, excessive maternal or paternal domination in childhood, inhibitory religious orthodoxy, homosexual conflict, and inadequate sexual counseling.

The primary therapeutic goals in treating impotence or erectile dysfunction are to remove the individual's fear of failure, to eliminate the spectator role by reorienting the client's emotions toward active participation in sexuality, and to remove his partner's fear of his impotence. Masters and Johnson's treatment program for impotence of erectile dysfunction typically progresses in the following manner: (1) pleasuring without direct attempt to produce an erection, (2) penile erection through genital pleasuring, (3) extravaginal orgasm, (4) penetration without orgasm, and (5) full coitus with orgasm. According to Masters and Johnson (1975), the woman's role in the treatment of impotence or erectile dysfunction cannot be overemphasized. They believe that unless she shows compassion over his erectile failure, his feelings of anxiety and guilt will only increase. Masters and Johnson report a success rate of 59.4 percent in treating cases of primary impotence and 73.8 percent in cases of secondary impotence.

Premature Ejaculation

Some men have no difficulty achieving erection but ejaculate so quickly during intercourse that both partners are left feeling frustrated. This problem is called *premature ejaculation*. The erection is easily achieved, but the male is unable to postpone his ejaculation long enough to satisfy the female. Ejaculation takes place immediately before, immediately upon, or shortly after insertion, resulting in unsuccessful intercourse.

Exact definition of premature ejaculation is not possible because of pronounced variations in both the likelihood and the latency of female orgasm in sexual intercourse. Premature ejaculation is defined in many different ways by many different therapists. Masters and Johnson (1970), for example, believe that the individual involved has not learned to control his sexual response. Before Masters and Johnson (1976) the definition of premature ejaculation was based on the amount of time insertion could be maintained before ejaculation (Kinsey et al. 1948) or how many thrusts could occur after penetration but before orgasm. Ejaculations occurring less than a minute after penetration were considered to be premature. This emphasis on time, though, was avoided by Masters and Johnson (1970), who defined the problem as reaching ejaculation before the female reached orgasm on 50 percent of the sexual encounters. However, this definition is not without problems either. For example, if the female partner has difficulty achieving an orgasm even when there is sufficient stimulation over an extended period of time, should this be considered premature ejaculation by the male? LoPiccolo and Heiman (1977) suggest that an inability to tolerate as much as four minutes of stimulation without ejaculation is a reasonable indicator that a male may be in need of sex therapy. Although the exact definition is a difficult problem for the researcher and the clinician, it is usually the man or his partner who decides that it is a problem and who then seeks help.

Generally, the treatment for premature ejaculation involves teaching the individual to recognize the signs of impending and imminent orgasm. Using the *squeeze technique*, which will be discussed later, the woman stimulates the man until the point of inevitability of orgasm. At that moment he signals her, and she then stops stimulation. Once the ejaculatory urge has subsided, she resumes sexual stimulation. This start-stop procedure was first discussed by James Semans (1956), who suggests that the couple repeat this procedure several times, after which the man is allowed to ejaculate. Four trials are recommended. The couple then proceed to sexual intercourse, during which the same start-stop pattern is repeated.

Retarded Ejaculation, or Ejaculatory Incompetence

Somewhat the opposite problem is *retarded ejaculation,* also referred to as *ejaculatory incompetence.* Ejaculatory incompetence is a rare condition in which the male is able to achieve erection and insertion but is unable to ejaculate within the woman's vagina. He may be able to ejaculate by masturbating or, in the case of a married man, he may be able to ejaculate with a woman to whom he is not married; in other cases, he may be unable to ejaculate at all. Occasionally, a man with a predominantly homosexual orientation will experience ejaculatory incompetence with women (see Kaplan 1974a, p. 333). Relatively few cases of ejaculatory incompetence or retarded ejaculation are seen by sex therapists, but Kaplan (1974b) believes that the problem is widespread. It is possible that many men are too embarrassed by it even to contemplate therapy for it.

Treatment of retarded ejaculation involves the woman initially stimulating the man to orgasm extravaginally. Once he does ejaculate, even if it is outside the vagina, Masters and Johnson believe that the couple has overcome a major hurdle. This orgasm means that the man can allow himself to be pleasured by the woman, and it enables her to express to him her positive feelings about having pleasured him. After this has been accomplished on several more occasions, a technique called *bridging* is used. This involves the woman manually stimulating the man to the point of orgasm. Right before he ejaculates, he signals her and she stops. At this point, she places his penis inside her vagina and he continues to thrust, producing orgasm through this means alone. Once orgasm occurs intravaginally, Masters and Johnson believe much of the man's anxiety and conflict seem to disappear. They report a success rate of 82.4 percent using this technique.

Female Sexual Dysfunctions

Arousal Insufficiency

Arousal insufficiency, formerly known as "frigidity," is in many ways the female counterpart to erectile insufficiency (DSM-III lists both as forms of inhibited sexual excitement). Not uncommonly, it is accompanied by complaints of an absence of sexual feelings and unresponsiveness to most or all forms of erotic stimulation. Its chief physical manifestation is a failure to produce the characteristic lubrication of the vulva and vaginal tissues during sexual stimulation, a condition that may make intercourse quite uncomfortable and often painful.

Orgasmic Dysfunction

Many women are readily sexually excitable and otherwise enjoy sexual activity, yet they experience difficulty in achieving orgasm. Formerly, *any* failure to gain sexual gratification on the part of the female was listed under the all-inclusive misleading heading of "frigidity." Masters and Johnson (1970), however, have distinguished various forms of female sexual dysfunction. The major sexual impairment for women is *orgasmic dysfunction,* which refers to inability to experience orgasm. According to these researchers, there are two basic types of this problem. In *primary* orgasmic dysfunction, the woman has never achieved orgasm through coitus, masturbation, or any other means. In situational, or *secondary*, orgasmic dysfunction, the woman is orgasmic only in certain situations and not in others. For example, the woman could have experienced orgasms in the past but is no longer able to do so or can only have an orgasm under specific circumstance. For example, she may experience orgasm only by means of manual stimulation, or only when coitus takes place in the bathroom. The diagnosis of orgasmic dysfunction is complicated by the fact that the subjective quality of orgasm varies widely among females and within the same female from time to time, making precise evaluations of occurrence and quality difficult (Singer and Singer 1972). As has been stated, orgasmic dysfunction is in some ways the female counterpart of impotence. In recent years, many women have been as concerned about being nonorgasmic as men are concerned about being impotent.

Because of social pressures, personal expectations, and/or the sheer desire to be orgasmic, some women will fake orgasms, presumably to please their partners. Some women seen in therapy report that they had faked orgasms for years prior to being able to communicate honestly with their partners about their nonorgasmic condition. Recently, there has been some research indicating that faking orgasms also occurs among men. Many nonorgasmic women report some traumatic sexual experience in the past and/or parents who held extremely rigid and negative views about sex. In some cases, orgasm may have taken on some other meaning to them, such as submission to the male or loss of self-control. In other cases, the intensity of orgasm may be frightening, and the woman may be afraid to "let go."

Treatment of organsmic dysfunction involves freeing the woman from the now seemingly involuntary control of the orgasmic reflex. In therapy she is taught to focus on the sensations produced by mounting sexual tension. She is made aware through psychotherapy of her sexual functions and attitudes. She is also told what an orgasm is, what it feels like. She is encouraged to fantasize during foreplay and masturbation. She learns the progression of sexual responsiveness and the sexual events that generally terminate in orgasm.

The woman is usually first taught to experience an orgasm through masturbation. This may involve working through feelings of shame and guilt about the activity. Once she is able to have an orgasm alone, she then learns, by bridging, to have one with her partner. Next she learns to experience orgasm through clitoral stimulation by her partner and, finally, she experiences orgasm through sexual intercourse, usually, again, through the use of bridging.

Masters and Johnson report an 83.4 percent success rate for primary orgasmic dysfunction and a 77.2 percent in cases of secondary orgasmic dysfunction.

Vaginismus

Vaginismus and dyspareunia are less common sexual dysfunctions. In *vaginismus,* the outer third of the vagina spasmodically contracts when penile insertion is attempted, rendering intercourse either impossible or very painful. Some women who suffer from vaginismus also have arousal insufficiency, possibly as a consequence of conditioned fears associated with a traumatic rape experience. In other cases, however, they are afflicted with this disorder despite sexual responsiveness.

This form of sexual dysfunction is relatively rare, but when it occurs, it is likely to be extremely distressing for both the affected woman and her partner (Tollison et al. 1977). In severe cases of vaginismus, the attempt to introduce the penis into the vagina may produce agonizing pain, rendering penile penetration impossible. In less severe cases, vaginal spasms may delay intromission or make it difficult. Some married women with vaginismus report that their marriages were never consumated. Although the woman may not have been able to have intercourse because of specific anxieties about being penetrated, she may be capable of sexual arousal orgasms. Some of these couples will engage in sexual activities other than intercourse, such as mutual masturbation. Other women with vaginismus are also nonorgasmic and may engage in little or no sexual activity.

Masters and Johnson believe that the major factor involved in vaginismus is an impotent male whose repeated attempts at intercourse followed by failure have so frustrated his partner that she unconsciously protects herself by closing her vaginal doors. Other psychological factors that they feel are involved are anticipated pain of first sexual intercourse, fear or guilt about coitus, inhibitions formed by emotionally traumatic experiences such as rape, conflict growing out of homosexual tendencies, and physical abnormalities that render intercourse very painful. Mace (1971) believes that the woman is unconsciously saying, "I am afraid to let you come into my life by opening myself freely and trustfully to you."

Treatment of vaginismus involves first explaining to the couple exactly what is occurring. The woman is next encouraged to relax as much as possible. She is told to take a long, relaxing bath and then to go to bed and begin stroking her body until she feels she is ready to begin stroking her genitals. During therapy she discusses the sensations she experienced and what they meant to her. She is next told to insert one finger into her vagina and to then contract the vaginal muscles. The purpose of this exercise is to help her learn to control these muscles; once she can contract the muscles at will, she will be able to relax them at will. She inserts two fingers into the vagina and then progresses to three. Once she can accommodate three fingers, she can physically accommodate a penis. At this point her sexual partner is included in the therapy. He repeats what she has learned: First he examines her genitals. Then he inserts first one finger into her vagina, then two, and then three. At the time of first intercourse, the penis should be well lubricated; the woman guides the penis into her vagina. The couple then rest for a few minutes, during which they discuss how they each feel about the experience. They then proceed slowly to more involved forms of sexual foreplay.

Vaginal dilators are also used in the treatment of vaginismus. The woman inserts them one at a time, starting with the smallest and proceeding to the largest, which is approximately the size of a penis. When the woman can accommodate the largest dilator, her partner is involved in the therapy and, as just described, they proceed in small steps, culminating in sexual intercourse. Such treatment of vaginismus is almost always successful in a relatively short period of time.

Dyspareunia

Dyspareunia, or painful sexual intercourse, can occur in men but is far more common in women. Men generally suffer from dyspareunia only if there is severe, intense pain at orgasm. The pain is usually the result of congestion of the prostate, seminal vesicles, or ejaculatory ducts or of an inflamed verumontanum. Although dyspareunia can occur in men, it is much more common in women. The great majority of the sexual dysfunctions involve psychological factors, but dyspareunia can be caused by certain organic conditions, such as tumors, deformities, vaginal infections, or insufficient lubrication. Tension, fear, and anxiety are the psychological factors involved.

Inhibited Sexual Desire

Inhibited sexual desire, or lack of interest in sex, is another sexual dysfunction described by Masters and Johnson (1970). Inhibited sexual desire may be generalized (chronic) or situational and can affect both men and women. The man or woman shows little or no sexual drive or interest. The individual may experience little desire with one partner and not with another, or it may be a generalized response whereby the individual simply is not interested in sex. It is estimated that approximately 40 percent of all sexual problems in males and females result from inhibitions of desire.

Sexual Aversion

Masters and Johnson (1970) define *sexual aversion* as a negative reaction of phobic proportions to sexual activity. It can be situational (varying with different partners or situations); it can involve a physiological component (the individual can exhibit certain symptoms, such as heart palpitations, nausea, and sweating); or it can be psychologically based. Most often it is caused by psychological factors. Its onset may be abrupt (after a rape, for example) or gradual. It is a consistent reaction to sexual behavior, and it is three times more common in women. This disorder is very different from inhibited sexual desire: Persons with inhibited sexual desire simply are not interested in sex; those with sexual aversion are repulsed by it. It is a much stronger reaction and can reach phobic proportions, whereby individuals structure a good deal of their lives so that they avoid any activity that is even remotely related to sexuality.

Sexual Anesthesia

Kaplan (1974a) describes what she calls *sexual anesthesia* in women. Sexual anesthesia occurs when a woman suffers from a hysterical conversion neurosis and as a result reports that she "feels nothing" after sexual stimulation is started. She may enjoy the physical closeness and warmth that sexual activity typically involves, but clitoral stimulation produces nothing more than the sensation of being touched. She may even be unable to ascertain when the penis enters the vagina.

DSM-III SYMPTOMS

The sexual dysfunctions appear to be very common (Kaplan 1974b, Khatchadourian and Lunde 1972, McCary 1973). They are much more prevalent than one might think. Every sexually active person has probably experienced some dysfunction at one time or another. Masters and Johnson (1970) estimate that fully half the marriages in the United States suffer from some form of sexual inadequacy. The actual number of clients with sexual problems is undoubtedly much higher than the surveys indicate. And the vast majority of cases, particularly those involving female sexual dysfunction, often go untreated. This estimate is supported by Frank and colleagues (1978). They found that, of 100 couples, 80 percent reported having happy and satisfying sexual relationships. However, 40 percent of the men reported problems with erection and ejaculation, and 63 percent of the women reported having trouble becoming sexually aroused or reaching orgasm.

DSM-III states that "the essential feature (of the psychosexual dysfunctions) is inhibition in the appetitive or psychophysiological changes that characterize the complete sexual response cycle." The categories listed include the following: inhibited sexual desire, inhibited sexual excitement, inhibited female orgasm, inhibited male orgasm, premature ejaculation, functional dyspareunia, functional vaginismus, and atypical psychosexual dysfunction.

For a detailed description of each of these disorders, please refer to DSM-III (1980).

THEORIES AND EXPLANATIONS OF SEXUAL DYSFUNCTIONS

Psychodynamic

Freudian theory holds that sexual difficulties result from childhood sexual trauma, which led to excessive fear, guilt, or anxiety about sex. Only through a thorough psychoanalysis of these deep-seated feelings could a healthy and full sexual pleasure, which Freud believed was one of the most important aspects of life, be achieved. Freud asserted that the healthy person was one who is able to love, play, and work.

According to Freud (1905), sexual disorders represent a continuation into adulthood of the diffuse sexual preoccupations of the child. Children normally enjoy "showing off" their sexual equipment and peeking at that of others. Furthermore, according to Freudian theory, they are capable of resorting to any number of defensive maneuvers in attempting to deal with the castration anxiety and penis envy supposedly endemic to the oedipal period. In accordance with this line of thinking, psychodynamic theorists generally conceptualize sexual disorders as the result of fixation at a pregenital stage; in general, with sexual disorders as with the sexual dysfunctions, it is the oedipal stage, with its concomitant castration anxiety, that is considered the major source of mischief. Treatment then involves the therapist's interpreting symbolic remarks, behaviors, and dreams in an attempt to bring to the conscious level the unconscious sexual conflict so that it can be confronted and "worked through."

Behavioral

Behaviorists suggest that sexual difficulties may essentially be bad habits that come from the association of sexual feelings with negative outcomes. The behaviorists feel that impotence, for example, might result not from a neurotic childhood conflict, as the Freudians believe, but from a recurrent fear of sexual rejection that interferes with the ability to participate in sexual feelings. Most theorists would agree that behaviorists have had a profound impact upon the treatment of psychosexual dysfunctions, especially in recent years.

The most notable example of such treatment, unquestionably, is the Masters and Johnson (1970) program, which made headlines in the late 1960s and early 1970s. Theirs is a brief form of therapy, and ideally taking two weeks. Clinicians who favor this approach try to determine how well a given pair of sexual partners communicate. They are more interested in helping couples overcome their symptoms than in probing any deep-seated emotional conflicts. Indeed, candidates for the Masters and Johnson program are carefully screened to be sure that they are free of overwhelming psychological problems. They generally insist on treating couples who are committed to each other or are involved in a long-standing relationship.

The most common behavioral interpretation of sexual inadequacies is that they result from faulty learning, inasmuch as the child learned to associate either guilt or anxiety with sexuality or had several "bad" early sexual experiences. Behaviorists believe that many cultural patterns contribute to sexual performance difficulties. For example, the myth that women do not enjoy sex and should think solely of satisfying their male partners has probably caused many women to neglect or negate their sexual feelings and pleasure. Lack of information about sexual functioning has kept many people from learning how to stimulate themselves effectively to obtain maximum pleasure. In sum, the behaviorists believe that just as sexual dysfunctions are learned, they can be unlearned.

Masters and Johnson's treatment of married couples rests on two basic assummptions. The first is that sexual inadequacy is not an individual problem — "her" problem is "his" problem — but a problem of the marital unit, in which sexual communication has broken down. They work only with couples because they feel that there is no such thing as an uninvolved partner in a committed relationship in which there is sexual distress. This strategy shifts the therapeutic focus from the individual to the relationship. The second assumption is that in order to reactivate the individual's natural ability to respond to sexual stimuli, the couple must be relieved of all performance pressures; essentially, they must return to a goalless, nondemand petting stage in order to rediscover their ability to be "pleasured" by touching and caressing. Masters and Johnson's program uses the dual-sex therapy team because they believe that only a woman can fully understand the female sexual response and only a man can fully understand the male sexual response. This team approach increases therapeutic objectivity and balance by adequately representing male and female viewpoints and gives each partner a same-sex therapist to whom he or she can relate more easily.

Techniques used by Masters and Johnson include the following:

Hand riding. Because most sexual dysfunction occurs when the individuals involved are embarrassed to teach each other what is sexually pleasing to them, Masters and Johnson employ a technique called "hand riding." It involves the placing of one's hand upon the partner's hand and gently and slowly guiding the partner's hand over the body, indicating what is sexually pleasing. The situation is then reversed, with the opposite partner doing the guiding over his or her own body. Partners thereby learn to communicate to each other what sexually pleases them.

Squeeze technique. This technique, which is primarily used to treat premature ejaculation, involves the female's squeezing the glans of the penis between her thumb and forefinger after the male communicates to her his feeling of impending orgasm. The female places her thumb below the frenulum and two fingers above, one forward of the coronal ridge and one behind, on the shaft of the penis. Pressure is then applied for several seconds until the erection has practically subsided. By squeezing the penis in this fashion, the sensation of impending orgasm disappears and sexual intercourse is continued. In this manner, ejaculation is postponed and sexual intercourse is lengthened. This pattern should be repeated approximately four times, each trial lasting 15 to 20 minutes. The man then ejaculates during the last trial.

This technique will not work if the man himself attempts to use it. It is important also for the couple not to use the technique as a game. Eventually, through overuse of the technique, it is possible that the man will become less and less sensitive to sexual stimulation.

Kegeling. This technique is named after the physician who developed these exercises. Kegeling is designed to strengthen the pubococcygeal muscle in women. The woman is taught to stop and start her urinary flow so that she can learn which muscle is involved. She then practices this exercise regularly in order to strengthen the muscle. Since this muscle is directly involved in the physiology of orgasm in the female, Kegeling has the indirect effect of helping the female learn about her own sexual apparatus and physiological response.

Sensate focus. Sensate focus is an important technique in sexual pleasuring. Masters and Johnson (1966) define sensate focus as the use of touch to provide sensory experiences in reconstituting natural responsivity to sexual stimuli. In this manner, clients are retaught to go back in time to when they experienced the uninhibited sensual responses of early childhood. Further clients are removed from the spectator role and placed in a position in which they learn to communicate effectively with the sexual partner. Sensate focus is kept at a nonverbal level and involves the partners' touching each other for sexual pleasure. It progresses from nongenital to genital touching in three steps. In phase 1, purposeful erotic arousal, genital stimulation is carefully avoided. Tender, gentle touching is used instead. The purpose of this phase is to increase intimacy and mutual involvement. The responsibility of the man to have an erection and the pressure on the woman to create one are removed.

Phase 2 of sensate focus, which typically, but not always, follows phase 1, involves progression to touching the genital areas. The intent of this phase is to produce sexual stimulation and arousal, but not orgasm. The couples are explicitly and implicitly encouraged to engage in progressive sexual behavior not involving orgasm.

The couple progresses to phase 3 only after they consider their response to phase 2 to be positive. Phase 3 involves orgasm by noncoital or coital means. In sum, the purpose of sensate focus is to reinstitute sexual responsiveness to touching. It is a crucial component to most, if not all, of the treatments for the sexual dysfunctions, especially for vaginismus, dyspareunia, and inhibited sexual desire. Helen Singer Kaplan (1974), a psychoanalyst who combined behavioral methods with more traditional psychotherapy, believes that sexual difficulties have immediate, specific underlying causes. In her view, human sexual response is best seen as *triphasic*, or consisting of three separate but interlocking phases: desire, arousal, and orgasm. She believes that desire-phase disorders are the most difficult to treat, because they tend to be associated with deep-seated psychological difficulties. She also states that "the standard sex therapy methods seem to be effective primarily for those sexual problems which have their roots in mild and easily diminished anxieties and conflicts" (Kaplan 1974b, p. xviii). To deal with the more complex cases, she uses a longer version of sex therapy which seeks a deeper level of insight and addresses unconscious conflicts. One of her underlying theories is that a sexual disorder usually results from multiple causes, some more immediate and accessible, others more remote and hidden.

The immediate causes include physiological and medical problems, which she feels account for approximately 20 percent of the cases, and the kinds of negative learning and association that encompass bad habits and negative cultural and social conditioning. Kaplan's method of therapy, like that of Masters and Johnson, focuses first on these immediate causes. In nearly 80 percent of the cases, such therapy is successful in alleviating sexual difficulty. Only then, if couples wish it, or if therapy is not successful, are the deep personality conflicts explored.

According to Kaplan, most sexual dysfunctions involve a number of psychological components. The clinician who is trying to evaluate a given client's problem should be aware of four distinct but interrelated factors: (1) the immediate situation, (2) possible intrapsychic conflicts, (3) possible interpersonal conflicts, and (4) prior learning. With some clients, Kaplan suggests, one component may be more prominent than the rest. With others, all components may seem to play an equal part.

The details of Kaplan's treatment method differ considerably in some ways from the Masters and Johnson approach. In the treatment of premature ejaculation, for example, she advocates the use of the "stop-start" technique instead of the squeeze.

Biological

Psychogenic impotence is by far the type of erectile dysfunction most frequently encountered by therapists, accounting for more than 85 percent of the cases. There are organic reasons for this sexual dysfunction, however, some of which include such diseases as diabetes, pelvic traumas, arteriosclerosis, multiple sclerosis, cancer, spinal cord injury, and the aftermath of surgery of the prostate, colon, or bladder. Certain drugs, including alcohol, narcotics, antihypertensives, and antidepressants, can also affect sexual potency. Nevertheless, in the great majority of cases, impotence has a psychological basis. Some organic causes of orgasmic dysfunction in women are hormonal imbalance, disorders of the nervous system, genital lesions, excessive use of drugs or alcohol, and deficient sexual apparatus (lack of a clitoris or ejaculatory ducts).

Some organic reasons for dyspareunia in men are inflammation of the glans penis caused by poor hygiene habits in the uncircumsized male, or Peyronie's disease. Dyspareunia in women can be the result of disorders of the entrance to the vagina, such as an intact hymen, scar tissue, or infection; vaginal disorders, such as infections, or allergic reactions; thinning of the vaginal walls; scarring of the roof of the vagina; pelvic disorders, such as endometriosis; tumors; cysts; or tears in the ligaments which support the uterus. In general, though, dyspareunia is usually due to the psychological factors of fear and guilt. The pain can involve the vagina, cervix, uterus, or bladder. The vaginal muscles become taut, and intercourse is painful, especially if the male partner is insensitive or clumsy. Dyspareunia in postmenopausal women frequently occurs because the mucous membrane of the vagina has become fragile and thin due to the decreased estrogen production. The vagina no longer secretes sufficient lubrication for easy penile insertion.

When vaginismus is caused by organic factors, they are generally the same as those involved in dyspareunia. Again, however, vaginismus is usually psychological in origin and occurs when the woman has learned to associate fear and pain with sexual intercourse.

Organic factors involved in inhibited sexual desire include anemia, hypothyroidism, alcoholism, and Addison's disease. Certain drugs, such as antihypertensives, antihistamines (which dry up the vaginal membrane), heroin, cancer chemotherapeutic agents, and marijuana, can also diminish sexual desire. When sexual aversion reaches phobic proportions, the individual experiences physiological symptoms, such as heart palpitations, nausea, and sweating.

Social Systems

Social work clinicians, whose major concern is the person-situation constellation, would agree with Masters and Johnson (1970) that it is frequently advisable to focus therapy on the interaction of the marital pair. However, clinical experiences have led many to believe that the most chronic marital complaints are unconscious wishes. The man who complains that his wife is frigid and cold unconsciously wants his spouse to be that way. Her warmth, intimacy, and sexual impulsivity would only serve to frighten him. Similarly, the wife who complains that her husband is weak and fragile needs this kind of husband to protect her. His sexual potency would frighten her (Eisenstein 1956, Strean 1976). Moreover, the wife in the first example and the husband in the second are unconsciously conforming to each other's labels of them. If therapists do not take sides in a marital conflict, they eventually will be experienced by the client in the same way that the spouse is experienced (Strean 1976).

Mental health professionals who adhere to social systems theory, role theory, ego psychology, and psychoanalysis often support their clinical observations with a recognition of the ever-present unconscious collusion between spouses in a sexually conflicted marriage (Strean 1976). These theorists believe that Masters and Johnson (1970) and the other behavioral therapists fail to understand that a sexual conflict is always a manifestation of a psychosocial conflict that had its roots in the client's life story. People with sexual conflicts react like frightened, angry, or inhibited children, and it is their unresolved childhood conflicts that must be addressed in sex therapy. Clients need to be helped to see the parallels between the therapeutic relationship and their sexual relationship. They need to be helped to realize they are writing their own self-destructive scripts for sexual unhappiness.

PRACTICE TECHNIQUES

The treatment of sexual dysfunctions has undergone nothing less than a revolution in recent years. Once regarded as very difficult and often intractable therapeutic challenges, most instances of sexual dysfunction now yield quite readily to programs of treatment involving new techniques that are still being developed and improved (Anderson 1983, Leiblum and Rosen 1979, Nowinski and LoPiccolo 1979, Tollison et al. 1977). As a result, success rates approaching 90 percent or more for many of the dysfunctions have become quite routine.

The turning point is uniformly considered to be the publication in 1970 of Masters and Johnson's *Human Sexual Inadequacy*. The success rates claimed by this team of dedicated clinical researchers astonished the professional community and rapidly led to the widespread adoption of their general approach, which combines elements of traditional and behavioral therapy in a framework emphasizing direct intervention aimed at the dysfunction itself.

While the early confidence inspired by Masters and Johnson's reported results has waned somewhat in the interim (Leiblum and Rosen 1979, Vandereycken 1982, Zilbergeld 1980), their work has un-questionably stimulated a host of new therapeutic techniques. Despite varying emphases and methods among treatment pro-grams, there seems to be general agreement on the importance of removing crippling misconceptions, inhibitions, and fears, and fostering attitudes toward and participation in sexual behavior as a pleasurable, natural, and meaningful experience.

Malatesta (1978) has named the following five components of sex therapy: (1) education, (2) relationship enhancement, (3) struc-tured behavioral activities, (4) environmental rearrangement and skills training in sexual functioning, and (5) anxiety management and other concerns. They feel that, without exception, the effective sex therapy plan should ascertain that the presenting couple or individual has an adequate *understanding of human sexuality.* The therapist should convey to the couple that (1) sexual problems do not necessarily indicate deep-seated emotional problems but probably reflect inadequate or maladaptive learning and experi-ence, and (2) that neither partner is entirely responsible for a sexual dysfunction, and that positive change is entirely dependent on a mutually shared and mutually executed plan of therapeutic activity.

The strength of the couple's relationship is ultimately tied to the couple's motivation and the partner's involvement in the treatment process. Thus a typical therapeutic focus could be on the division of home labor, sex-role differentiation, life-style patterns, and con-flict-resolution skills.

The prescription of a systematic plan of structured sexual activi-ties remains an integral part of sex therapy. Another aspect of the behavioral prescriptions involves the extent to which couples can disengage from extraneous stimuli such as work or children, pro-mote and interesting and creative atmosphere for sexual expres-sion, and focus on self and partner sexuality. Last, when anxiety is a central feature of the sexual dysfunction, it may be important to employ more traditional methods of intervention, such as progres-sive relaxation training, systematic desensitization, or hypnosis, be-fore or during a sex therapy program (Kroger 1977, 1981, Wincze 1982, Wolpe 1958).

The following are some more concrete practice techniques:

1. Take an extensive history at the outset of therapy.

Before beginning treatment, the therapist should obtain an extensive history. This basically serves as a psychological examination and will aid the therapist in assessing the extent of the client's problem. It is crucial for the therapist to question the client about sexual fantasies, desires, and wishes. The information obtained will be invaluable to the diagnostic and assessment process. The therapist needs to determine explicit details of the couple's sexual relationship and information about the quality of their relationship in general.

2. Refer the client for a complete physical examination.

More so than in any of the other psychological disorders, it is crucial to rule out any organic cause of the sexual problem. For example, Masters and Johnson tell the story of three men who were referred to them with the presenting problem of impotence. These men had all been in therapy prior to coming to the institute; they had had a combined fifteen years of therapy with five different therapists. Still the problem persisted. Upon entering the treatment facility, a complete sexual history was taken for these men. As it turned out, none of the men had ever had an orgasm by any means, not even through nocturnal emissions as adolescents. The therapy team referred them to a urinary specialist, a physician who not only specializes in urinary problems but also thoroughly understands the sexual apparatus of men and women.

As it turned out, these men did not have ejaculatory ducts; they would never ejaculate. These men could have gone for therapy for the rest of their lives and the problem would have remained because it was not psychological. Of course, after they were told that they did not have ejaculatory ducts, they were offered psychological counseling to deal with this finding; however, no amount of psychological counseling could ever "cure" their problem. It is therefore crucial to utilize the expertise of professionals who are specifically trained in therapy, for they know which questions to ask.

3. When treating a client who has a sexual problem, work closely with a sex therapist who can be utilized for supervisory/consultation purposes.

Sexual dysfunctions often have different psychological roots than do the other, more psychologically based problems. There are times when clients simply need to be provided with accurate information about their bodies or are ignorant about sexual techniques or the sexual response. In cases such as these, a therapist who is specifically trained in this area should be consulted; these situations can usually be readily treated with sex therapy. Other problems may be more complex, arising, for example, out of either fear of failure, or a need to be in control during sexual activity, or fear of rejection if performance is inadequate. These situations can usually be ameliorated by short-term therapy. The focus here is on teaching these clients to communicate their fears and anxieties. Again, however, a clinician specifically trained in sex therapy should be consulted.

There was a case, for example, of a woman who had been in therapy for many years because of dyspareunia. She had explored in great detail with her original therapist her guilt and anxiety about sexuality in general, her feelings toward her husband, and her feelings toward her parents. Still the problem persisted. Frustrated after about five years with the other therapist, the woman decided to consult a certified sex therapist. After a detailed sex history was obtained, it became obvious that some other factor was operating. As it turned out, the woman was taking excessive doses of an over-the-counter antihistamine to relieve symptoms of sinus congestion. Most antihistamines work by drying up mucous membranes, of which the vagina is one. The antihistamine was drying up this client's vagina, thereby making intercourse painful. The therapist suggested that the woman stop taking the antihistamine for a while. The client later reported that the problem had been eliminated. A therapist untrained in the effects of certain drugs on sexual anatomy and physiology would probably have led the therapy in another direction. It is important, therefore, once it has been ascertained that the client is presenting a primarily sexual dysfunction, to consult with a colleague who is specially trained in sex therapy.

Another case example points to the need for the therapist to be aware of the effect of drugs on sexual behavior. Bob B., a 42-year-old engineer, sought therapy for impotence. Divorced, he had functioned adequately while married and initially following the break-up. The problem had first occurred about two months before he began therapy. During the initial sessions, he discussed his anger at his former wife and his fears about reentering the dating world. It was during one of these initial sessions that the therapist asked if he was taking any medication. He quickly answered, "No, nothing that would cause this problem." The therapist persisted, asking him if he was taking any medication at all. He replied that all he took was blood pressure medication, which he was certain had nothing to do with his sexual problem. In fact, however, it had everything to do with his sexual problem. He was encouraged to discuss the problem with his family physician and to request an alternate medication, one that did not carry the side effect of impotence.

Another group of clients who suffer from performance anxiety and fear of rejection are more difficult than the other two groups to treat. Others who fall into this group are those who fear romantic intimacy or sexual success (see Kaplan 1974b). The sexual problems of these individuals stem from negative attitudes toward themselves, feelings of conflict, and severe insecurity. Sex therapy in these cases is aimed at alleviating basic problems of a fragile self-esteem and guilt following the pleasures associated with sex. Here the therapist must be able to deal with unconscious motivation and conflict. It is necessary in these cases for the therapist to shift from psychotherapy to sex therapy and back again, and to recognize the crucial points at which to do so. Brief psychotherapy is generally inappropriate for these clients; their problems are associated with severe psychopathology, such as pervasive paranoia and marked hostility in relationships.

In recognition of the need for specialized training and certification in the area of sex counseling and therapy, the American Association of Sex Educators, Counselors, and Therapists (AASECT) in 1973 appointed highly qualified professionals to establish training guidelines. AASECT reviews the experience and academic training of clinicians who wish to specialize in sex counseling and therapy.

A list of qualified professionals can be obtained by contacting AASECT, 600 Maryland Avenue, S.W., Washington, D.C. 20024.

4. It is especially important when treating a client with a sexual dysfunction to be aware of one's own values and beliefs so that they are not projected onto the client.

The case of Sally and Tom L. typifies one of the cautions necessary in the practice of sex therapy. They were an upper-middle-class couple who first came for counseling because of sexual problems. Sally was not interested in sex with Tom, and they had not had sex in over three months. Tom was very upset, not understanding what the problem was. They were observant Catholics, and the therapist assumed because of Sally's strict Catholic upbringing that she felt guilty about sex. The therapist then proceeded with treatment with this assumption in mind, working to help the couple accept and alleviate this anxiety with the ultimate goal of more open sexual communication. These attempts failed, and the couple left therapy shortly thereafter, with the problem unchanged.

When Sally called the same therapist for a session a year later, she informed the therapist that she and Tom had divorced. The major reason for the divorce was that Sally was involved in an affair with her girlfriend. Although it is probably true that the divorce would have occurred anyway, it was an important lesson for the therapist inasmuch as the therapist's assumptions had caused her to lead the therapy in a particular direction. If the assumptions had been examined and perhaps explored in the therapy, it is possible that the underlying fact of Sally's homosexuality would have surfaced, in which case other, more productive, issues could have been examined.

5. Help the client to learn to communicate openly about sexuality.

Crucial to the process of sex therapy is to teach clients to communicate honestly and openly about sex. Atwood (1985) presents the following communication suggestions for clients who are having sexual problems:

1. Don't collect "trading stamps"; deal with issues immediately.
2. Attempt to reinterpret negative perceptions into more positive ones.
3. Avoid patterns of communication in which someone is a loser; aim instead for two winners.
4. Free yourself from preprogrammed responses.
5. Beware of transforming anxieties and insecurities about self into critical attacks on others.
6. Avoid patterns of denial/discounting. Responsibility shared is more rewarding than responsibility denied.
7. Listen and look. Tune into your partner.
8. Examine and evaluate feelings of guilt and anxiety.

WHEN DO YOU REFER THE CLIENT?

1. Refer the client to a medical physician or a urologist if you suspect that the problem has a biological rather than pyschological etiology.
2. The client should be rediagnosed or referred if it is suspected that the sexual problem is secondary to some more disturbing psychological problem, such as schizophrenia or depression. Depression very often leads to a lack of desire for sex. If the therapist focuses only on the sexual problem and not on the person in the context of the environment, the problem may persist.

Chapter 9

Schizophrenia: The Delusional, Fragmented Client

WHAT IS SCHIZOPHRENIC BEHAVIOR AND HOW DO YOU RECOGNIZE IT?

"The author who undertakes to write a handbook chapter on the phenomena conventionally included under the rubric schizophrenia — questions of his own sanity and proper intellectual humility aside — faces an enormously intimidating task" (Carson 1983). A tremendous amount has been written about schizophrenia, and an equally overwhelming amount of research has been conducted on the topic. This chapter will provide an overview of the problem.

The schizophrenias are a group of psychotic disorders which are characterized by gross distortions of reality. Schizophrenic behaviors are typified by withdrawal from social interaction and by disorganization and fragmentation of perception, thought, and emotion. For the most part, schizophrenia has severe consequences for the affected persons and their families. In addition, schizophrenia poses a serious problem to the mental health agencies whose main function it is to provide treatment and support. While fewer than 1 person in every 100 will at some time be diagnosed as schizophrenic, such persons do represent a signifcant proportion of the patients in inpatient and outpatient mental health facilities. The etiologies and treatment of the disorder, therefore, are matters of great concern.

Until the end of the nineteenth century, the several forms of what we now call psychosis were generally considered to be the result of a single disease. Historically, schizophrenic disorders were attributed to a type of mental deterioration beginning early in life. In 1860, Morel, a Belgian psychiatrist, described the case of a 13-year-old boy who had formerly been the most brilliant pupil in his school but who, over a period of time, lost interest in his studies, became increasingly withdrawn, seclusive, and taciturn, and appeared to have forgotten everything he had learned. Morel believed the boy's functions had deteriorated as a result of a genetic anomaly and that they were therefore irrecoverable. He used the term *dementia precoce* (mental deterioration at an early age) to describe the condition and to distinguish it from disorders of old age.

One of the first persons to classify schizophrenia as a distinct disorder was Emil Kraeplin (1856–1926), the influential German psychiatrist. In the nineteenth century, he adopted the Latin form of the term. He called the disease *dementia praecox*. It was Kraeplin who first proposed the idea that there were three separate psychoses, representing three separate disease entities: hebephrenia, catatonia, and paranoia. He used the term *dementia praecox* because he believed that the onset of the disorder was early in life, typically in adolescence. Kraepelin believed that this apparent mental deterioration of the young was an organic disorder and that recovery from it was impossible. Actually, however, as Bleuler was later to point out, the term was rather misleading, since the problems usually became apparent, not during childhood, but during adulthood, and there was no conclusive evidence of permanent mental deterioration in most cases.

In 1911, the term *schizophrenia* was suggested by the Swiss psychiatrist Eugene Bleuler, and it eventually replaced the earlier term. The word *schizophrenia* is derived from the Greek words meaning "split mind." Bleuler used the term *schizophrenia* because he thought the disorder was characterized primarily by disorganization of thought processes, lack of coherence between thought and emotion, and inward orientation, away from reality. For Bleuler, then, the "splitting" thus implied, not multiple personalities, but a splitting within the intellect and between intellect and emotion. Bleuler chose it to refer to the fragmentation of emotion, thought, and perception that characterized the disorder.

Bleuler also introduced a fourth classification of the disorder, the simple type. He believed that schizophrenia was characterized by a splintering of the psychic functions rather than by gradual deterioration, and he noted that while some schizophrenics did deteriorate, others remained unchanged, and some even improved. Thus, he was also the first to distinguish between chronic and acute schizophrenia. Like Kraepelin, Bleuler believed in an underlying organic trend toward schizophrenic deterioration. Yet he went considerably beyond Kraepelin by taking into account psychological explanations of schizophrenic behavior. Bleuler explained disordered thought in terms of attention deficits, association disturbances, and ego disintegration.

A completely different approach to the origins and cure of schizophrenia was then propounded by a contemporary of Kraepelin's and Bleuler's, Adolf Meyer (1866–1950). Meyer, an American neuropathologist, who was recognized as the dean of American psychiatry, believed that there were no fundamental differences between schizophrenics and normals and, further, that there were no differences in their respective psychological processes. Rather, he believed that the cognitive and behavioral disorganization that was associated with schizophrenia arose from inadequate early learning, and reflected "adjustive insufficiency" and habit deterioration. He felt that individual maladjustment, rather than biological malfunction, lay at the root of the disorder. Meyer's approach mandated research in an area wholly different from those of Bleuler or Kraepelin. While they strengthened the biological tradition of research in schizophrenia, Meyer gave impetus to a tradition that focused on learning and biopsychosocial processes.

Most theorists today agree that it is not clear that schizophrenia is a singular process. The existence of a single diagnostic label, in this case schizophrenia, does not in and of itself establish similarity of underlying organization in each case of schizophrenia any more than does a medical diagnosis of hypertension, which can be due to many different underlying conditions. Thus, many clinicians today believe that there may be several schizophrenias, each with a different etiological pattern and set of psychodynamics (Bellak 1980).

Since Bleuler's (1911) description of schizophrenic persons who recovered after relatively short periods of disordered behavior, a great deal of research has been focused on identifying factors that are associated with a favorable prognosis. This line of research has led to the description of two patterns of schizophrenic disorders — one associated with chronic, long-term disability and the other with shorter periods of disordered functioning. These are not considered subtypes of schizophrenia; rather, this distinction applies to all four types listed. The distinction basically refers to two different courses of the disorder. Sometimes schizophrenic disorders develop slowly and insidiously. Here the early clinical picture may be dominated by seclusiveness, gradual lack of interest in the surrounding world, excessive daydreaming, blunting of affect, and mildly inappropriate responses. This pattern is referred to as *process schizophrenia*; that is, it develops gradually over a period of time and tends to be long-lasting. It is characterized by a gradual onset of maladaptive behavior early in life, considerable social withdrawal, and poor personal adjustment. The outcome for process schizophrenia is generally unfavorable, partly because the need for treatment is usually not recognized until the behavior pattern has become firmly entrenched. *Poor premorbid personality features* or *chronic schizophrenia* are alternative terms referring to this pattern and are approximately equivalent in meaning to *process*.

In other instances, however, the onset of the schizophrenic symptoms is quite sudden and dramatic and is marked by intense emotional turmoil and a nightmarish sense of confusion. This pattern, which is usually associated with identifiable precipitating stressors, is referred to as *reactive schizophrenia* (alternatively, *good premorbid conditions* or *acute schizophrenia*). In contrast to process schizophrenia, reactive schizophrenia has a relatively sudden onset and is clearly associated with some precipitating event in the life of an individual who showed a relatively satisfactory adjustment earlier in life. The symptoms of reactive schizophrenia usually clear in a matter of weeks, although in some cases an acute episode is the prelude to a more chronic pattern.

Keep in mind that this process–reactive distinction should be viewed, not as a dichotomy, but rather as a continuum. The distribution of schizophrenic individuals can be envisioned in the familiar bell-shaped curve, with relatively few falling at either the process or reactive extremes and most falling somewhere in the middle.

Another distinction which has gained increased prominence in recent years is that between paranoid and nonparanoid symptom patterns among persons diagnosed as schizophrenic. In the *paranoid* pattern, delusions, particularly persecutory or grandiose ones, are a dominant feature. In the *nonparanoid* forms, such delusions, if present at all, tend to be rare and fleeting. Evidence is building that important differences exist between those who exhibit a predominantly paranoid symptom pattern and those who exhibit few, none, or inconsistent paranoid symptoms. In general, paranoid schizophrenic individuals tend to be more "reactive" than "process" in type and to have a more benign course and outcome (Ritzler 1981). They may also be genetically less vulnerable to schizophrenia than nonparanoid types (Kendler and Davis 1981). Adding to the confusion, though, is the finding that a substantial number of persons originally diagnosed as having paranoid schizophrenic symptoms are later diagnosed as having nonparanoid ones (Kendler and Tsuang 1981).

Whether process, reactive, paranoid, or nonparanoid in the general sense of these terms, schizophrenia encompasses many symptoms that vary greatly over a period of time in an individual's life and from one individual to another. The basic experience in schizophrenia, however, seems to be one of disorganization in perception, thought, and emotion.

Clinicians have made the following general observations of schizophrenia. Sullivan (1962) believed that when persons experiencing a dramatic first-time psychotic break have a history of good social adjustment, they may be able to treat the psychotic break as useful, leading to reorganization of the personality. Mosher (1974), Laing (1960), Bowers (1961), and others suggest a possible positive outcome of a first psychotic break if an individual receives proper treatment.

A few characteristics of schizophrenics are quite useful in predicting potential for improvement. For example, it is widely held that the more favorable the individual's prepsychotic adjustment, the better the prognosis. Also, the more sudden the onset, the more favorable the prognosis. One of the most consistent findings is that process schizophrenics have a much poorer prognosis than reactive schizophrenics. Approximately 55 percent of the process type will remain unimproved, compared with less than 10 percent of the reactive type (Stephens 1970). This prognosis also carries over to the similar distinction on the chronic–acute dimension. Those who have an acute onset (that is, less than six months) have a much better recovery rate than those with a more gradual onset. Stephens (1978) identifies several other factors related to a favorable prognosis:

1. married at one time, especially if there is an existing satisfactory marital relationship
2. at least an average IQ
3. a specific precipitating event
4. period from onset of symptoms to hospitalization less than six months
5. previous work history
6. clear-cut depressive symptoms
7. absence of emotional blunting
8. absence of schizoid (severely withdrawn) personality
9. confusion or perplexity about condition

Stephens predicts the presence of at least five of the nine items were predictive of a favorable outcome.

Schizophrenia is indeed a strange and puzzling disorder, comprising a group of behaviors whose prominent common features include retreat from reality, emotional blunting, and disturbed thinking. These features vary in severity from client to client. It is a serious condition, often involving severe impairment of social, occupational, and personal functioning, loss of contact with reality, and great subjective discomfort.

The estimated incidence of schizophrenia in the United States is about 1 percent of the population, a figure that has been quite stable over time. The actual incidence of the disorder has been estimated at about 150 cases per 100,000 population per year (Crocetti and Lemkau 1967). The number of new cases of schizophrenia is estimated to be between 100,000 and 200,000 persons every year in the United States (Babigan 1975). There are approximately 1 million actively schizophrenic persons in the United States at the present time (Berger 1978) and probably 10 to 15 times more than that who are subject to schizophrenic episodes (Dohrenwend et al. 1980). However, only 600,000 are treated in a typical year. Schizophrenics constitute the largest diagnostic group of patients in psychiatric hospitals. They occupy almost two thirds of the beds in psychiatric hospitals and one quarter of all hospital beds. About one fourth of the patients admitted each year to mental hospitals and clinics are diagnosed as schizophrenic, and since schizophrenic individuals often require prolonged or repeated hospitalization, they usually constitute about half the patient population for all available psychiatric hospital beds (President's Commission on Mental Health 1978).

There appear to be substantial sex differences in the age of onset of schizophrenia: Men are at risk for schizophrenia before age 25, while women are at risk for schizophrenia after age 25 (Lewine 1981, Zigler and Levine 1981). Although schizophrenic disorders sometimes occur during childhood or old age, about three fourths of all first admissions are between the ages of 15 and 45, with a median age of just over 30. Most schizophrenics admitted to the hospital are between 20 and 40 years of age, and the hospitalization rate among persons in the age group between 25 and 34 is strikingly higher than for any other age group (Yolles and Kramer 1969). The incidence is about the same for males and females. First hospitalizations average four to five months and hospitalizations throughout the schizophrenic's life may last 10 years or longer.

It appears that schizophrenic disorders occur in all societies, from the aborigines of the western Australian desert and the remote interior jungles of Malaysia to the most technologically advanced societies. An interesting study is reported by Murphy (1978), however, who found that the prevalence rate of schizophrenia is markedly higher in the Irish Republic than in Northern Ireland. Numerous other studies identify areas of especially high or especially low prevalence rates of schizophrenia throughout the world. Thus, the

oft-quoted 1 percent may be quite misleading (Torrey 1980). Besides the Irish Republic, there are two other areas having well-
documented rates of schizophrenia: a region of Croatia in Yugo-
slavia (Crocetti et al. 1971) and the northern reaches of Sweden
(Book 1979). Among the methodologically sound studies showing
low prevalence rates of schizophrenia are Eaton and Weil's (1955)
well-known survey of the Hutterite communities in the United
States and the study by Torrey and colleagues (1974) of the high-
land dwellers in Papua, New Guinea. By and large, in the studies
noted, the variations from expected rates of prevalence are far
from trivial and cannot readily be accounted for along genetic or
other biological bases. There is evidence, therefore, that certain
cultural factors may operate in some cases to enhance and facilitate
the risk of schizophrenia and in other cases to weaken its expression.

By far the most puzzling and unexpected of epidemiological findings on schizophrenia has been the recent discovery that births of
schizophrenic persons tend to concentrate in certain months of the
year. The findings reviewed by Torrey (1980) are so numerous and
compelling that they cannot be dismissed. It appears that the births
of persons who later become schizophrenic tend statistically to occur in the late winter or spring months.

Babigan (1975) summarized other factors related to the diagnosis
of schizophrenia:

1. The incidence of schizophrenia is higher in lower socioeconomic groups.
2. Schizophrenia is more prevalent in nonwhites compared with
   whites; but the rate in men and women is approximately
   equal.
3. Schizophrenics are at a greater risk of early death than
   "normals."
4. The reproduction rate of schizophrenic persons is lower than
   that of the general population.
5. The total direct and indirect cost of schizophrenia in our society is estimated at $14 billion a year.

Garmezy and Streitman (1974) outlined the antecedents of schizophrenia. The most powerful predictor of schizophrenia is a family

history of the disorder. On the average, 10 percent of persons who have one schizophrenic parent will eventually be diagnosed as schizophrenic. For individuals who have two schizophrenic parents, the chances increase to 35 to 40 percent (Hanson et al. 1977, Rosenthal 1970). Interestingly, as will be discussed later, the unaffected children of schizophrenic parents often appear to be particularly talented and creative (Meehl 1962).

Another predictor of schizophrenia is severe family conflict. Often this centers on extremely poor, disorganized relationships between family members. Marital disharmony and poor communication are quite common in these families (Jacobs 1975, Robbins 1966). A third general predictor is socioeconomic status (Dohrenwend and Dohrenwend 1969, Faris and Dunham 1939, Hollingshead and Redlich 1958). Consistent findings have indicated that the incidence of schizophrenia is highest in the lowest socioeconomic groups.

The schizophrenias are considered the most serious of all psychotic disorders because of their complexity, high rate of incidence, especially during the most productive years of life, and their tendency to recur and/or become chronic. DSM-III specifies a list of criteria for the diagnosis.

DSM-III SYMPTOMS

Before listing the diagnostic criteria for schizophrenia, it is important to note some important diagnostic and methodological considerations. Researchers are required to establish operational definitions of the terms that are incorporated in their diagnostic criteria for mental health. An *operational definition* specifies precisely what *observable* phenomena the term designates. It appears, however, that every researcher's operational definition of *schizophrenia* is simply a matter of his own way of diagnosing clients. There is not much diagnostic agreement among professionals when it comes to schizophrenia. Consider, for example, the finding, published in a recent cross-national study, that schizophrenia is more common in New York than in London, while the affective disorders are more common in London than in New York. A group of investigators (Cooper et al. 1972), guessing that this disparity might have more to do with national diagnostic "favorites" than with an actual difference in the psychic life of Londoners and New Yorkers, decided to test their hypothesis by showing groups of psychiatrists in New York and in London identical videotapes of doctor–patient interviews. The results confirmed the investigators' hypothesis. In cases involving disturbances of both mood and thought, the American psychiatrists tended to attribute more weight to the thought disturbance and were consequently more likely to diagnose the patient as schizophrenic. The British psychiatrists, on the other hand, tended to see the mood disturbance as the primary symptom and therefore to diagnose the patient as either manic or depressed.

Such inconsistencies exist not only from one country to another, but also among professionals. A given patient who has received one diagnosis from one clinician might very well be given a different diagnosis by another. Both Beck and colleagues (1962) and Sandifer and colleagues (1964) found that the percentage of agreement among professionals on a general diagnosis of schizophrenia ranged from only 53 percent to 74 percent. When attempts have been made to specify the subcategory of schizophrenia, the rate of agreement has generally dropped to between 35 percent and 50 percent. This lack of agreement hinders any attempt to make meaningful comparisons between research findings.

In any case, DSM-III, in an attempt to clarify some of the more common symptoms of schizophrenia, lists the following specific criteria for a schizophrenic disorder:

1. At least one of the following during a phase of the illness:
   a. bizarre delusions (content is patently absurd and has no possible basis in fact), such as delusions of being controlled, thought broadcasting, thought insertion, or thought withdrawal
   b. somatic, grandiose, religious, nihilistic, or other delusions without persecutory or jealous content
   c. delusions with persecutory or jealous content if accompanied by hallucinations of any type
   d. auditory hallucinations in which either a voice keeps up a running commentary on the individual's behavior or thoughts, or two or more voices converse with each other

e. auditory hallucinations on several occasions with content of more than one or two words, having no apparent relation to depression or elation

f. incoherence, marked loosening of associations, markedly illogical thinking, or marked poverty of content of speech if associated with at least one of the following:
- blunted, flat, or inappropriate affect
- delusions or hallucinations
- catatonic or other grossly disorganized behavior

2. Deterioration from a previous level of functioning in such areas as work, social relationships, and self-care.

3. Duration: Continuous signs of the illness for at least six months at some time during the person's life, with some signs of the illness at present. The six-month period must include an active phase during which there were symptoms from item 1, with or without a prodromal or residual phase, defined as follows:

Prodromal phase: A clear deterioration in functioning before the active phase of the illness, not due to a disturbance in mood or to a substance use disorder and involving at least two of the symptoms which follow.

Residual phase: Persistence, following the active phase of the illness, of at least two of the symptoms which follow, not due to a disturbance in mood or to a substance use disorder.

Prodromal or Residual Symptoms:

a. social isolation or withdrawal

b. marked impairment in role functioning as wage earner, student, or homemaker

c. markedly peculiar behavior (for example, collecting garbage, talking to self in public, or hoarding food)

d. marked impairment in personal hygiene and grooming

e. blunted, flat, or inappropriate affect

f. digressive, vague, overelaborate, circumstantial, or metaphorical speech

g. odd or bizarre ideation, or magical thinking (for example, superstitiousness, clairvoyance, telepathy, "sixth sense," "others can feel my feelings"), overvalued ideas, ideas of reference

   h. unusual perceptual experiences (for example, recurrent il-
      lusions, sensing the presence of a force or person not actu-
      ally present)
4. The full depressive or manic syndrome (criteria A and B of
   major depressive or manic episode in the DSM-III), if present,
   developed after any psychotic symptoms, or was brief in duration relative to the duration of the psychotic symptoms in 1.
5. Onset of prodromal or active phase of the illness before age
   45.
6. Not due to any organic mental disorder or mental retardation.

Although schizophrenia is often thought of as if it were a unitary
disorder, the differences between the various types of schizophrenia outweigh their similarities. Thus, because of their diversity, it is
increasingly common to speak of the "schizophrenias." The DSM-
III distinguishes between four basic subtypes of schizophrenia.

Paranoid Schizophrenia

The presence of systematized delusions marks this subtype. The
paranoid schizophrenic suffers from remarkably systematized and
complex delusions of persecution or grandeur. This complexity
renders the schizophrenic's experiences comprehensible to himself
but impenetrable to the outsider.

Beyond delusions of persecution or grandeur, paranoid schizophrenics may also experience delusional jealousy, the deep belief
that their sexual partner is unfaithful. Despite the intensity of their
feelings, however, paranoid schizophrenics rarely display severely
disorganized behavior. Rather, their demeanor tends to be extremely formal or quite intense.

According to DSM-III, the diagnostic criteria for paranoid type
are as follows:

A type of schizophrenia dominated by one or more of the following:

1. persecutory delusions
2. grandiose delusions
3. delusional jealousy
4. hallucinations with persecutory or grandiose content

Disorganized Schizophrenia

Formerly called *hebephrenic schizophrenia,* the most striking behavioral characteristic of disorganized schizophrenics is silliness and incoherence. They burst into laughter, grimaces, or giggles without any observable stimulus. Their behavior is jovial; however, it is also quite bizarre and absurd, suggesting extreme sensitivity to internal cues and extreme insensitivity to external ones. Correspondingly, they are voluble, bursting into meaningless conversation for long periods of time.

Disorganized schizophrenics may experience delusions and hallucinations. These are generally not systematized, however. Rather, they tend to be more disorganized and diffuse than those experienced by paranoid schizophrenics, and they often center on their bodies. For example, disorganized schizophrenics may complain that their blood has turned to cement or that their brains have been removed. Their delusions may be quite pleasant and may contribute to the silliness of their behavior.

Disorganized schizophrenics often disregard bathing and grooming. They may not become incontinent, but they may eat their own body products, as well as other dirt. Again, a marked insensitivity is noted, similar to their insensitivity to social surroundings.

The specific criteria cited by DSM-III are as follows:

1. frequent incoherence
2. absence of systematized delusions
3. blunted, inappropriate, or silly affect

Catatonic Schizophrenia

The salient feature of catatonic schizophrenia is motor behavior that is either extremely excited or strikingly frozen, and that may occasionally alternate between the two states. The onset of the disorder is sudden. When behavior is excited, the individual may seem agitated, even wild, strongly resisting any attempts at control. Catatonic individuals' affect is inappropriate, while their agitation is enormously energetic and surprisingly prolonged, commonly yielding only to strong sedation.

Stuporous or frozen behavior is also quite striking in this subtype of schizophrenia. Individuals may be entirely immobile, often adopting quite uncomfortable postures and maintaining them for long periods. If someone moves them, they will freeze in a new position. A kind of statuesque, waxy flexibility is characteristic. After emerging from such a stuporous episode, patients sometimes report that they had been experiencing hallucinations or delusions, sometimes centering on death and destruction and conveying the sense that any movement will provoke an enormous catastrophe.

Some theorists find evidence of negativism among catatonic schizophrenics—so much so that, in addition to the excited and stuporous behavior, they take negativism to define the category (Maher 1966). Forbidden to sit, the catatonic will sit. Told to sit, the catatonic will insist on standing.

The specific symptoms of catatonic schizophrenia as listed in DSM-III are as follows:

1. Catatonic stupor (marked decrease in reactivity to environment and/or reduction of spontaneous movements and activity) or mutism
2. Catatonic negativism (an apparently motiveless resistance to all instructions or attempts to be moved)
3. Catatonic rigidity (maintenance of a rigid posture against efforts to be moved)
4. Catatonic excitement (excited motor activity, apparently purposeless and not influenced by external stimuli)
5. Catatonic posturing (voluntary assumption of inappropriate or bizarre posture)

Undifferentiated Schizophrenia

Along with paranoid schizophrenia, this is a widely applied designation used to categorize individuals who do not otherwise fit neatly into the other classifications. It is a less specific diagnosis for disturbed individuals who present evidence of thought disorder as well as behavioral and affective anomalies, but who are not classifiable under the other subtypes.

The diagnostic criteria for undifferentiated type as listed in DSM-III are as follows:

1. A type of schizophrenia in which there are prominent delusions, hallucinations, incoherence, or grossly disorganized behavior
2. Does not meet the criteria for any of the previously listed types or meets the criteria for more than one

CASE DESCRIPTION

Carrie Z. was a 27-year-old, single, Jewish, white woman who had successfully completed three years of college. However, she was functioning on minimal educational and vocational levels and had progressively deteriorated since her first hospitalization. She had a full head of dark hair streaked with grey, glasses, and an acne-scarred complexion. She sobbed almost constantly, but the crying did not appear to be reactive to sad affect. The patient was referred by her counselor at the transitional living center, an after-care program for psychiatric patients, where she lived with a roommate.

Carrie stated that in order to remain in the transitional living program, she was required to participate in psychotherapy and that she was being forced to seek the services of the clinic. On the other hand, she also admitted through her tears that she hoped her future therapist would give her some motivation. During the intake interview, she avoided eye contact, used copious quantities of tissues, and alternated her tears with angry answers or self-pitying statements.

Carrie was born and raised on Long Island, New York, the youngest of three daughters. She described her mother as loving and strict and her father as domineering and controlling. The only significant childhood event that she recalled was her father's business bankruptcy, which occurred when she was 8 years old. This event had severely limited the family's standard of living. It was later learned that because of his business failure, Mr. Z. had become peripheral to the family. As a result, Carrie no longer felt like the prized and cared-for child. Her early schooling was uneventful, and she said that she did have some friends. She reported that she often "made new friends by crying." Her first year and a half of college was interrupted by the first of many "depressions." She began group psychotherapy at age 19 and experimented with sex and drugs. She dropped out of college by the end of her junior year, after cutting classes and not seriously studying. She spent the next year and a half at her parent's home, "doing nothing." The feeling induced during the interview was that Carrie was often out of touch with events and her surroundings. She also often indulged in fantasies that either were sexual or involved the reliving of angry moments with her family and friends.

Her inpatient history began when she was 23 years old and was hospitalized for three months in a reputable private hospital. She then spent eight months in a day hospital program affiliated with that institution and eventually moved to her own apartment near the hospital. At that point she was being maintained on imipramine hydrochloride (Tofranil) and loxapine succinate (Loxitane). She then returned to college for a while and, believing herself to be well, stopped all medication. She was rehospitalized shortly thereafter, discharged, and rehospitalized later that year. Upon discharge, she moved into an apartment supervised by the transitional living program.

Carrie created so many problems for her roommates that she was moved to a smaller room. The residents were expected to do their own cooking and cleaning. Carrie insisted that she had been forced into the program by her psychiatrist and her parents, and it was characteristic of her to assume little responsibility for any of shopping, cooking, or cleaning unless it was insisted upon by the counselors. She started the intake interview by crying about having eaten her roommate's food, which she said she was unable to resist due to her lack of willpower. She seemed to have been compelled to do so by a force beyond her control.

She was required to do volunteer secretarial work at a nearby hospital, but she often did not go, opting instead to stay in her apartment and sleep late. She reported that she was a chronic liar who often felt suicidal because of the hopelessness of her situation. Referring to all the "shit" that she had been through, Carrie asserted that she wanted the therapist to know nothing more about her. She then fell silent and did not resume talking until the interviewer did.

She was as familiar with psychotherapeutic techniques and themes as the therapist was. She even recounted her diagnoses (schizophrenia, paranoid type; schizophrenia, chronic type; and schizoaffective disorder). She was being medicated with 50 milligrams of amitriptyline hydrochloride (Elavil) three times a day and 50 milligrams of fluphenazine (Prolixin Decanoate), injected intramuscularly, every other week.

Characteristically, Carrie indicated that her self-expectation was just to "shuffle along" in her therapy. She seemed quite taken aback by the therapist's statement that since all the therapists worked hard, they usually expected the same thing of their patients. Carrie was thoroughly socialized into the role of the chronic psychiatric patient and received satisfaction from the hopelessness, pity, and low self-expectations often ascribed to such patients. While not denying the evident and serious pathology in this young woman, the clinic's treatment review team felt that the therapist should avoid the traditional focus on symptoms and unconscious conflicts, and should instead insist that Carrie focus on the "here and now" in her therapy sessions. She was a classic example of an intelligent, alert patient who could discuss her psychodynamics for hours while disowning all responsibility for her behavior.

Carrie experienced a thought disorder when overwhelmed with anxiety stimulated by interpersonal, vocational, and intrapsychic events. She was also subject to extreme variations in affect that often further disorganized her thinking to the point of loosening of associations and tangentiality of thought. Although she seemed intent on convincing the interviewer that she had pulled "things together for herself," the opposite impression was created. Her only clear intention during the interview was to manipulate the interviewer into feeling that she was honest about herself, which her behavior during the remainder of the session then contradicted.

WHAT DOES SCHIZOPHRENIC BEHAVIOR LOOK LIKE?

Bleuler chose the term *schizophrenia* because it described the disorder's central symptom: a lack of association (a split) either among ideas or between ideas and emotions. This lack of coherence in the individual's mind may result in the association of words, not on the basis of any logic whatsoever, but only, for example, because they rhyme. Such a series of rhyming or similar-sounding words is called a *clang association.* Cohen and co-workers (1974) have pointed out that schizophrenic speech is ordinarily quite competent syntactically—that is, subject, predicate, modifiers, and so forth are usually present and in the proper order. Thus, it is not the sentence structure that is incorrect but the meaning of the words themselves.

According to Cohen and coworkers (1974), schizophrenics can make common primary associations to given stimuli about as easily as normal people can. It is the more subtle secondary associations which a schizophrenic cannot make—at least not without becoming confused and incoherent. Cromwell and Dokecki (1968) have suggested that the schizophrenic has difficulty "disattending to" a stimulus after having attended to it. This hypothesis is similar to that presented by Cameron (1938), who saw schizophrenic thought as an overinclusion of stimuli. Like normal persons, the schizophrenic forms many tangential associations to stimuli, including the stimulus of his own speech; unlike normal persons, however, the schizophrenic cannot filter out the irrelevant associations. Thinking and speech may therefore zigzag rapidly from one topic to another without any coherence other than the irresistible associations. In other words, the individual's behavior is filled with many irrelevant items and, as a result, it is difficult to make sense out of the stream of speech.

The elements of schizophrenic incoherence vary from case to case. The speech of some schizophrenics is permeated by *neologisms,* words which are formed by condensing and combining several words. Another common schizophrenic feature is *echolalia,* the constant parroting or repetition of certain words and phrases. Some schizophrenics display *verbigeration*, a senseless repetition of the same words or phrases. *Mutism* may typify schizophrenic language; it represents an extreme form of the schizophrenic's communication deficit and has been observed in some individuals for periods of many years. Part of the schizophrenic's communication deficit is a sharp reduction in the expression of appropriate emotional responses. He frequently appears to be indifferent and at times seems totally apathetic. The *indifference* and seeming apathy are part of his emotional blunting, the shallowness with which he expresses his feelings, and an apparently arbitrary dissociation of feeling and verbal expression. As stated earlier, the schizophrenias are characterized by delusional beliefs and disturbances in thought processes, sensations and perceptions, affect, and motor behavior.

Disorganized Thought Processes

One aspect of the schizophrenic's difficulty in thinking and speaking clearly is a tendency toward loose, disjointed expression. Bleuler (1950) referred to this problem as *derailment of associations*, by which he meant that the schizophrenic becomes distracted by irrelevant associations, cannot suppress them, and as a consequence wanders farther and farther from the subject. The thinking and language of the schizophrenic is often loose, disjointed, tangential, and illogical. This obvious and often bizarre characteristic has been referred to variously as *derailment, associative looseness,* or *cognitive slippage* (Meehl 1962). Schizophrenic thought and language often appears to follow sound patterns rather than logic. A typical clang association might be, "I lack Jack, not black, stabbed in the back."

Schizophrenic speech aberrations range from only slight peculiarity to total disorganization. The combination of words and phrases in what appears to be a completely disorganized and idiosyncratic fashion is referred to as *word salad*. Unlike neologisms, word salad seems to have no communicative value whatsoever. Nor does it appear to reflect thoughts that generalize on the basis of tangential associations. Seemingly devoid not only of logic and meaning but even of associational links, word salad is defined by its total inaccessibility to the listener.

In describing schizophrenic symptomatology, most specialists make little distinction between disorders of thought and disorders of language, reasoning that the confused speech of the schizophrenic is simply the result of confused thinking. However, some writers (Fish 1957, Kleist 1960) have suggested that schizophrenic language disturbances result, not from disordered thought processes, but rather from disorganization and inaccessibility of verbal symbols. Thus the schizophrenic might know what word she wants but might simply be unable to find it. Schizophrenic speech often includes words and phrases not found in even the most comprehensive dictionary. These neologisms are often formed by combining parts of two or more regular words; or, they may simply involve the use of common words in a unique fashion. In either case, what is interesting about neologisms is that while they are sometimes unintelligible, they at other times manage to communicate ideas quite clearly and vividly.

Delusional Belief

A delusion is an irrational belief that an individual holds with great vigor despite overwhelming evidence that it has no basis in reality. A delusion, then, is a belief contrary to social reality that becomes fixed and resistant to change even in the face of strong evidence against it. Delusions are among the most common of the schizophrenic thought disorders. Approximately three quarters of all schizophrenics hold beliefs that others consider to be false or illogical (Lucas et al. 1962). In a sample of 405 schizophrenics, Lucas and colleagues (1962) found 71 percent to be delusional.

Several types of delusions are particularly common: grandeur, persecution, and reference; thought broadcasting, thought blocking, and withdrawal; and thought insertion and control. The individual with *delusions of grandeur* believes that he is a famous or important person, usually a political, military, or religious leader. At the other end of the continuum is the *self-deprecatory delusion* — the belief that one has done some horrible deed. Such beliefs may explain feelings of guilt and a need for punishment.

Delusions of persecution involve the belief that one is being plotted against, spied upon, threatened, interfered with, or otherwise mistreated. People with delusions of persecution believe that they are threatened and persecuted by various persons or groups, and they find confirmation for this delusion by misinterpreting everyday experiences; they might insist, for example, that a group of laughing persons are laughing at them. *Delusions of control* (also called *delusions of influence*) lead one to believe that other persons, animals, or things are controlling their thoughts or actions, often by means of electronic devices which send signals directly to their brains. Persons with delusions of influence believe that they are being controlled by some external agent. Thus, they might believe that a murderous impulse, a sexual fantasy, or an urge to commit suicide is imposed from the outside. The controlling agent may be God, the devil, or some vague "they." The critical difference between a neurotic obsession or compulsion and a delusion of influence is whether the person takes the additional step of interpreting the obsessive idea or compulsive urge as being implanted by an external agent. In contrast to the belief that external agents are inserting thoughts into one's head is the delusion that one's thoughts are being *broadcast* into the external world so that everyone can hear them.

Hypochondriacal delusions are also common. These beliefs differ from neurotic hypochondriacal beliefs in that delusions are generally marked by a bizarre quality. For example, schizophrenics may believe that their insides are rotting or that their brains are full of gelatin. *Delusions of sin and guilt* involve the unfounded belief that one has committed an unpardonable sin or has brought great harm to others. Theorists generally believe that as an extension of an egocentric and autistic orientation, many schizophrenic individuals at some point begin to see personal significance in everyday events, to "read in" intents and meanings that are not there. Personalizations of everyday experiences, or *ideas of reference,* provide a background against which more systematic delusions can develop. Other delusions, such as *delusions of body change,* are beliefs about physical changes in the body; for example, a man may believe that his body is changing from male to female, that his insides are rotting, or that his head is filled with cement.

Disturbances in Sensations and Perception

There is considerable evidence that the schizophrenic's perception of the world is different from that of "normal" people. First, schizophrenics consistently report perceptual dysfunction. Second, these reports are confirmed by standard laboratory perceptual tests, which indicate that schizophrenics perform poorly on such perceptual tasks as size estimation (Strauss et al. 1974), time estimation (Johnson and Petzel 1971, Petzel and Johnson 1972), and proprioceptive discrimination (Ritzler and Rosenbaum 1974). Other tests have shown schizophrenics to be generally deficient in sensory sensitivity (Broen and Nakamura 1972).

To the observer, the most dramatic type of schizophrenic perceptual disorder is the *hallucination,* a sensory perception which occurs in the absence of any appropriate external stimulus. Most of us are able, with varying degrees of vividness, to hear imagined voices, to form pictures "in the mind's eye," and even to re-create experiences of taste, touch, or smell in the absence of any primary stimulation. But we are usually aware that these sensory experiences are the byproducts of our imagination rather than responses to external stimuli. Furthermore, we probably feel that we have control over such experiences. Hallucinations differ from such "normal" imaginings in two respects. First, they are not conjured up or created at will; they occur spontaneously. Second, while many schizophrenics do recognize that the voices they hear exist only in their minds, many others are not sure of whether their hallucinations are real or imagined, and a fair percentage—presumably the more severely psychotic (Buss 1966)—are convinced that their hallucinations are perceptions of objectively real events.

The common clinical observation is that auditory hallucinations are the most frequent, followed by hallucinations involving other senses. These frequencies have been confirmed by Malitz and colleagues (1962), who found that out of a random sample of 100 schizophrenics, 50 percent reported auditory hallucinations, while 9 percent reported visual hallucinations.

Disturbances in Affect

Schizophrenia is characterized by disturbances in affect. The affective abnormalities suffered by the schizophrenic differ from those that typify the affective psychoses in two important respects. First, the affective psychoses involve either deep depression or manic elation, or a combination of the two; in schizophrenia, on the other hand, what is generally seen is either a lack of affect or affect which is inappropriate to the immediate context. Second, the affective psychoses may involve sudden and extreme mood reversals. For example, the manic-depressive psychotic is capable of progressing rapidly from a state of expansive euphoria to a state of bleak despair. In contrast, the schizophrenic is unlikely to undergo such extreme mood shifts.

Three basic types of affective abnormality are common to schizophrenics. The first is *ambivalent affect.* In this case, the schizophrenic may manifest both a strong positive reaction and a strong negative reaction at the same time, which leads to a state of confusion or blocked action. The second abnormality is a constricted emotional responsiveness, often described as *flat affect*. Nothing can elicit any emotional response whatsoever from the person; regardless of what is going on around her, she remains totally apathetic. Finally, many schizophrenics display *inappropriate affect;* that is, their emotional responses are entirely unsuitable to the immediate context. For example, a client may giggle upon hearing of his mother's death, or he may become very angry when given a present.

Disorders of Motor Behavior

The variety of unusual behaviors, including the absence of behavior, manifested by schizophrenics seems to be limited only by the boundaries of the behaviors themselves. In other words, in spite of the wide range of behaviors, both usual and unusual, taking place on the hospital ward, there is one behavior that is strikingly absent: interpersonal interaction or attraction. Rarely do these clients engage in small talk. Rarely do they address one another except to ask for a cigarette or a light. Indeed, one of the most salient characteristics of severely disturbed clients is withdrawal from interpersonal relationships. This is especially true of the chronic schizophrenic.

The question remains, though, is this social withdrawal a response to living year after year amid the unchanging drabness of the institutional ward? Or is it due specifically to an avoidance of interpersonal involvement on the part of schizophrenics? Duke and Mullins (1973), for example, found that chronic schizophrenics preferred greater interpersonal distances than either nonschizophrenic psychiatric clients or a group of "normal" people. They also found that although hospitalization did have some effect upon interpersonal distance, hospitalization alone did not account for the magnitude of interpersonal distance preferred by the schizophrenics. Furthermore, it has been found that schizophrenics tend to look at other people less than do "normal" people, and that they have a tendency to avoid the gaze of anyone looking directly at them (Harris 1968).

HOW DOES THE SCHIZOPHRENIC CLIENT FEEL?

Paranoia

Paranoia is a term borrowed from ancient Greek, in which it means "beside or outside of reason," a fitting description of the delusions of persecution that constitute the most prominent symptom of paranoid schizophrenia. The paranoid individual feels singled out and taken advantage of, mistreated, plotted against, stolen from, spied upon, ignored, or otherwise mistreated by enemies. The delusional system usually centers around one major theme, such as financial matters, a job, or other life affairs. For example, a woman who is failing on the job may insist that her fellow workers and superiors have it in for her because they are jealous of her ability and efficiency. As a result, she may quit her job and go to work elsewhere, only to find similar friction developing and her new job in jeopardy. Now she may become convinced that the first company has written to her present employer in the hope of turning everyone against her so that she would not be given a fair chance. With time, more and more of the environment is integrated into her delusional system as each additional experience is misconstrued and reinterpreted in the light of her delusions.

Although the evidence advanced by paranoid persons to justify their claims may be extremely tenuous and inconclusive, they are unwilling to accept any alternative explanation and are impervious to reason. For example, a husband may be convinced of his spouse's unfaithfulness because when he answered the phone on two occasions, the party on the other end hung up. Argument and logic are futile; in fact, any questioning of the delusions only serves to convince the client that the interrogator has sold out to his enemies.

Although ideas of persecution predominate, many paranoid individuals develop delusions of grandeur, in which they endow themselves with superior or unique ability. Such exalted ideas usually center around messianic missions, political or social reforms, or remarkable inventions. Paranoid persons who are religious may consider themselves appointed by God to save the world and may spend most of their time preaching and crusading. Threats of fire and brimstone, burning in hell, and similar persuasive devices are liberally employed. Many paranoid persons have become attached to extremist movements and are tireless and fanatical crusaders, although they often do their cause more harm than good with their self-righteousness and condemnation of others.

Some paranoid individuals develop remarkable inventions that they have endless trouble patenting or selling. They gradually become convinced that there is a plot against them to steal their invention, or that enemies of the United States are working against them to prevent the country from receiving the benefits of their remarkable talents. Aside from the delusional system, such individuals may appear perfectly normal in conversation, emotionality, and conduct. Hallucinations and other obvious signs of psychopathology are generally not found.

This normal appearance, together with the logical and coherent way in which the delusional ideas are presented, typically make paranoid individuals most convincing and they often fool fledgling professionals. However, the delusional system is apt to be convincing only if one accepts the basic premise or premises upon which it is based. The defense of the premise or hypothesis is based on logically air-tight polarities of thought which defy testing or reasonable argumentation or reasoning. The paranoid premise is often a defense against severe confusion about both self-concept and relationships with others. If the usual derailment of ideas or loss of association of ideas are not present, one would diagnose the individual as having a paranoid psychosis—not paranoid schizophrenia.

Dependency

Schizophrenics have difficulty developing close relationships with other human beings. One probable reason is conflict over dependency. The dependence on parents, which most adolescents begin to resolve, is for the schizophrenic a repetition of the dependency struggle for infancy. The individual fears that closeness will result in a loss of identity—being engulfed or even, symbolically, eaten up alive. On the other hand, he may fear that his own intense wish for closeness and need fulfillment will lead to his eating up his loved one. The schizophrenic wants to be dependent, but at the same time feels this to be dangerous to himself as well as the loved one. Therefore, wishes to be independent cannot be gratified, and closeness is impossible. Because of the pain of this conflict, the person falls out of contact with himself and into a state of no feelings and no felt wishes. He then feels that he has no "I" and no capacity to say "I want" in a relationship.

Rage

Another reason for the difficulty that schizophrenics experience in being close to other human beings is intense rage. Generally, the rage is caused by the injustices psychotic individuals believe have been foisted upon them and by their enormous envy of others for their ability to cope. The world of reality, the world of people, even the parts of the personality that wish to relate to reality are hated by the psychotic and are felt to be the enemy. The external world is perceived as depriving and persecutory. Their withdrawal from others expresses this rage and terror, and rage makes it difficult to satisfy any need. Attacks on people (in terms of their thoughts and fantasies) who are trying to help them are common.

Projection of this anger onto the world causes the individual to see others as hostile and hurtful. *Denial* of large aspects of reality and *projection* of negative feelings onto the outside world are common psychotic defense mechanisms. One of the authors interviewed a patient in a veterans' hospital who appeared to be making a stable adjustment and for whom the staff psychiatrist thought it appropriate to consider discharge. When his thoughts and plans were further assessed, however, it was ascertained that the patient had no intention of shopping for food, cooking, or eating. In fact, his refusal to attend to these aspects of his corporal life is what had led to his hospitalization in the first place. The antipsychotic medication and structured life on the ward, where all his physical requirements were attended to, had not changed his thinking to the extent that he had learned that he had to take care of his own needs. He had simply gone along with the staff's instruction in routines of self-care. He assumed that returning to the world outside of the hospital meant that he no longer had to conform to the routine!

If the schizophrenic approaches any feeling of closeness to another, the result is often a breakdown in the relationship, a state of confusion, and massive anxiety. The desired closeness brings with it intense hatred and the wish to annihilate the loved one and destroy those parts of the personality that seek the closeness. Schizophrenics generally hate their own loving feelings and any person for whom they might experience those feelings. They experience this hate because, for them, interpersonal relationships lead only to overwhelming pain.

Rosenfeld (1965) describes this confused state in a young patient who was beginning to feel some closeness to her therapist. She finally admitted that she was madly in love with him and wanted to marry him. She wanted to approach him in a seductive manner and then strangle him. She stated that he had simultaneously saved her life and driven her mad. The fear of the aggressiveness that is experienced along with love, the intense rage, causes the psychotic patient to turn away from love objects and withdraw from people. Potential love objects are devalued and ridiculed. Contempt is often expressed for the behavior or possessions of others. In fact, contempt is often felt for all reality, and the schizophrenic uses this contempt as a reason to avoid other people, asserting that "no one is good enough for me." Hostile rejection of others, arrogant, omnipotent egocentricity, and angry withdrawal mask enormous pain and the fear of loving.

Feelings of Deadness

Schizophrenics commonly complain of affective deadness. Clients often relate terrifying dreams or fantasies of dying. Some psychotic individuals report that they are really in the grave and that someone else is walking around in their bodies, leaving them with a feeling of nothingness.

It is interesting to speculate about what part of the personality is dead. What is the missing part and how does one find it? The missing part is the feeling of selfness that the person either has had and lost, or has never had. In "normal" people, a sense of identity, of who one is, comes from a subjective feeling of selfness that is responded to by the environment. It is the "I am" feeling to which the environment (mother) responds with food or emotional relatedness (caring). This basic need satisfaction is necessary for the establishment of basic trust in infancy, and later for basic identity formation. If the environment fails to respond to basic needs, or is perceived to be failing (the child is full but not emotionally responded to), and if there is a genetic or biochemical vulnerability, the personality fails to develop and partially or totally deadens itself to any further growth or interpersonal involvement. The client gives up and consequently feels dead. Unlike other individuals, the schizophrenic is unable to integrate ambivalent feelings and must therefore keep himself and the world separate. The schizophrenic has not had the positive relationships needed to temper the pain and rage into ambivalence, a state in which both positive and negative feelings are more acceptable (Kernberg 1965). In this manner, ego splitting may be a way of avoiding the overwhelming pain when there is no nurturing environment, no loving relationship to help with the pain. It is a mechanism used to protect the person from an overwhelming, fearful environment.

Out of fear that the rage may destroy the giving mother, out of terror that the pain will overwhelm and destroy him, and to preserve the feeling of receiving needed emotional supplies, the schizophrenic uses splitting as a defense. This is sometimes thought of as splitting the loved one into the "good mother" and the "bad mother" and the "good self" and the "bad self," but the object splitting results in further regression and fragmentation of the ego to a psychotic level.

Feelings of Terror

When the feelings of unreality become severe, the schizophrenic appears to experience terror. Often these individuals will do anything to regain some sense of reality or feeling of life, including performing self-destructive acts like cutting, hurting, or hitting themselves, screaming, or beating their own heads.

Feelings of Badness

Schizophrenics often feel that evil and badness are at the core of their beings. This extremely painful feeling of badness has been theoretically explained as the result of primitive, guiltlike, self-punitive feelings resulting from envy, greed, and aggressive wishes. The badness may also be seen as pure destructive rage that has not been tempered by loving, positive experiences. The schizophrenic experiences just being alive as bad.

A young man who was interviewed by one of the authors felt that he talked to and was directed by the devil. He tried to fight him off, but the devil succeeded in entering his body. After he had known the interviewer for some time (several sessions), he asked if the interviewer wanted to enter his body also. The therapist would thus be engulfed by the devil and/or the bad self, and then both would be helpless to the patient's rage and self-punitiveness.

Feelings of Pain

The schizophrenic's psychological death — the numbing of feelings and wishes to relate — is extremely painful. The pain, which has been described as grief over the loss of one's self, is made bearable only through the use of primitive defense mechanisms such as delusions, hallucinations, and loss of ego boundaries. Psychological death comes when all wishes for fulfillment of basic needs and all wishes for real intimacy are abandoned as futile. The real self, the feeling self, withdraws inside the fantasied womb, leaving a "false self," a dead self, to function and relate superficially to the world. The pain is locked up within the person, and enormous relief is experienced when it is touched on or shared with another, such as the therapist. The danger remains, however, that the pain can be externalized, displaced or projected on the therapist and can be represented as a struggle from which the patient must escape or avoid by getting rid of the therapist.

Carrie, the "professional patient," was helped by her therapist to feel more alive during sessions. She eventually felt that waking up and getting up out of bed was desirable; however, this behavior also triggered feelings of guilt and conflict about giving up infantile satisfactions like staying in a safe, warm bed, and self-gratifying fantasies about how safe and comfortable she felt. By staying in bed, she also avoided all adult responsibilities. While rushing up the steps to her appointment, she had a self-punitive fantasy of throwing herself down the steps. Better yet, she thought, maybe she would throw the therapist down the steps; after all, wasn't it the therapist who was responsible for her present suffering and pain? Thus, the small degree of success produced by allowing reality to come through was quickly dissipated by displacing the strength onto the therapist, who was the intrusion in her false-comfortable existence. She continually returned to this false self whenever reality intruded too heavily upon her.

Feelings of Rebirth

Often the schizophrenic wishes for a rebirth—to feel, to become alive, to relate to reality, to grow emotionally, to develop creative resources, and to enter into an interpersonal relationship in which she can separate and individuate to develop a unique identity. Although individuating is a crisis for most adolescents, for a schizophrenic, their common fantasy of dying and being reborn demonstrates the extreme of this need to grow.

Creativity

Any comprehensive treatment of schizophrenia must take into account the possible relationship between schizophrenia and creativity. Being related to a schizophrenic may not be all bad; in fact, it may have some distinct advantages. Reporting on a follow-up study of children born to schizophrenic mothers and placed in adoptive or foster homes shortly after birth, Heston and Denney note that the children who did not become schizophrenic were more "spontaneous," "had more colorful life histories," "held more creative jobs," and pursued "more imaginative hobbies . . . " than normals (Heston and Denny 1968, p. 371). Indeed, one study reports that nonparanoid schizophrenics scored higher on a test of creativity than either paranoid schizophrenics or nonparanoid controls (Keefe and Magaro 1980, Magaro 1981).

A study of genetics and schizophrenia in Iceland further supports the connection between creativity and schizophrenia. Karlson reports that the "genetic carriers" of schizophrenia often exhibit "unusual ability" and display a "superior capacity for associative thinking" (Karlson 1966, p. 61). Fascinated by this finding, Karlson proposes that society may even depend upon "persons with a schizophrenic constitution" for its social and scientific progress. He remarks that a disproportionate number of the most creative people in philosophy, physics, music, literature, mathematics, and the fine arts often developed psychiatric disorders. "Superphrenic" is Karlson's term for these people, who are both related to schizophrenics and recognizably outstanding in politics, science, and the arts.

THE CLIENT'S DILEMMA

Carrie experienced an intense sense of failure in both early performance as a college student and later regression and deterioration of
vocational and social skills. She consequently expected that others
would reject and ultimately abandon her. She was thus unable to remain consistently involved in her work and in relationships. She
was hypersensitive to others' responses, both verbal and nonverbal,
and this influenced her to be ever vigilant, suspicious, and defensive. Her dependency was so well entrenched by her repeated failures over the three years since her last hospitalization that she had
little hope that anything would change.

Despite a primary diagnosis of schizophrenia, she had a passive-
aggressive personality structure and readily experienced narcissistic
injury, which could seriously disorganize her thinking. Depressed
affect, at times accompanied by suicidal ideation, was often experienced in response to injuries to self-esteem precipitated by performance difficulties or disappointments in interactions with others. Before she could allow herself to experience disappointment with her
roommates, she would blame and verbally attack them or fail to do
what was expected of her. This would result in her roommates' or
counselors' deciding that she needed to be moved to another apartment or discharged from the program.

She often vascillated between guilt and self-disparaging preoccupations, which later turned to paranoid ideation that others were
picking on her and wouldn't give her a chance. When faced with the
possibility of rejection, her reality testing and judgment became impaired. Carrie's impulse control was poor, as she experienced a high
degree of restlessness and had a need for immediate gratification.
She relied heavily on others for validation and she often chose relationships based on their potential for providing self-indulgence and
immediate need gratification. However, her fear of engulfment in
these relationships overwhelmed her sense of boundaries and blur-
red her self-experiences. Only the ever-present role of the helpless,
deprived, hopeless patient gave her a sense, if somewhat fragile, of
herself.

When she was disturbed, she experienced racing and flooding of thoughts, and her speech was pressured and tangential. Depression, especially when accompanied by varying degrees of suicidal ideation, was frightening to her, as it heightened her sense of vulnerability and brought with it the possible need for another hospitalization. Although Carrie was of above-average intelligence, her emotional lability was so overwhelming at times that it interfered with her cognitive functioning. She was nevertheless able to enter into a therapeutic alliance with her therapist and to use the therapist as an auxiliary ego to sort out thoughts and feelings she experienced as confusing and disorganizing. Her self-esteem improved as she began to experience success in task-focused activities. All of these gains were reversed, however, when she stopped taking her medication. Indeed, consistent use of Loxitane and Imipramine was effective in enabling Carrie to recompensate from an acute psychotic state and helped her to maintain a state of remission. When she took her medication, she was no longer troubled by ideas of reference, persecutory or suicidal ideation, or flooding by disorganized thoughts.

Chapter 10

Theories, Explanations, and Interventions for Schizophrenic Behavior

The etiology of schizophrenia has been a puzzle of central concern to psychologists and psychiatrists for over a century. Behavioral extremes also seem to exert their own influence and fascination. Quite unlike most medical problems, which can be traced to a single microorganism or a single organ dysfunction, schizophrenia appears to be the result of a highly complex interaction of social, psychological, interpersonal, and biological factors, each of which has claimed the attention of a number of theoretical perspectives.

Research on schizophrenia has taken two divergent paths. On the one hand are the medically oriented researchers, who explore genetic heritage and physiological processes. These investigators have discovered many drugs that alleviate some of the symptoms of schizophrenia. The success of drug treatment has emptied many hospital wards and has promoted research into the biochemical roots of psychosis. The second path has been the search for psychological causes, beginning with psychoanalytic researchers working with hospitalized schizophrenics. Their theories initially focused on the internal, intrapsychic life of the schizophrenic; more recently, however, they have also examined the family environment for clues as to the reasons for the schizophrenic's lack of adaptation to reality. Most therapists now believe that the causes of schizophrenia are both biological and psychological. It has been suggested that biochemical weakness or predisposition, intrapsychic difficulties, and life stress resulting from a traumatic or maladaptive family situation probably combine to produce a schizophrenic break.

THE PSYCHOLOGICAL THEORIES

Psychological theories of schizophrenia generally focus on the child's early family life and on how specific types of parent–child relationships can lead to schizophrenia.

Psychoanalytic

According to the psychoanalytic theorists, there is no single psychodynamic formulation of schizophrenia; instead, there are a variety of positions, all of which are basically offshoots of Freud's theories. Orthodox Freudian theory speculated that excessively strong id impulses provoked regression to the earliest stage of development, in which no ego had yet been formed to interact with reality. Although Freud devoted his attention primarily to the neuroses, he did offer an interpretation of psychosis as well, and especially of paranoia. In his earliest psychoanalytic study of psychosis (1911), Freud viewed the development of the disorder as a two-stage process. The first stage involves a complete or partial withdrawal of cathexes (emotional investments) from the object world, the world of people and things. In the second phase, the restitution phase, the individual attempts to regain the lost object world by substituting imaginary events and relationships for the real ones that have been abandoned. Thus, hallucinations can be accounted for as remembered sensory events that the psychotic uses to replace lost object relations.

According to Freud, the schizophrenic's disturbed thinking can be seen as the result of a similar two-stage process. First there is the withdrawal of cathexes from internal forms of object representation—that is, the individual's mental images of the object world. Then, in the restitution phase, the cathexes are redirected toward words that remain in the memory but that are no longer tied to appropriate objects. As a result, the words come out but they are no longer coherent, since they have lost their value as symbols of real things (Freud 1915). Thus, the preschizophrenic child, because of his deficient perceptual apparatus and learning capacity, does not internalize a stable sense of himself from his early experience with his parents. In times of stress, the fragile self does not endure, leaving the schizophrenic selfless and alone. The overwhelming experience leads the schizophrenic to attempt to understand objects that have been distorted (object restitution) in ways that constitute familiar symptoms of schizophrenia (hallucinations and delusions, for example).

Thus, although Freud did not concentrate on schizophrenia, he did attempt to explain it. However, his theory was not a very helpful one. Freud believed that schizophrenics were narcissistic—that they had withdrawn their energies from the outside world and turned inward upon themselves, unable to cathect with the world of objects.

After Freud's elaboration in 1926 of the structural concepts of ego and superego, the psychoanalytic interpretation of psychosis shifted from object decathexis to ego insufficiency or disintegration. According to the latter view, the schizophrenic is a person who, because of inability to cope with unacceptable id impulses, regresses to an early phase of the oral stage. In this phase of infancy, there is not yet a separate ego to exercise the basic cognitive functions of perception, memory, judgment, and so forth. Hence the psychotic's loss of contact with reality, since the phase to which he has regressed provides no developed cognitive apparatus for reality testing.

Whereas regression is the mechanism that has received theoretical emphasis in psychoanalytic accounts of schizophrenia, projection has been viewed as the basic mechanism of paranoia. In all his cases involving paranoia, Freud inferred a connection with repressed homosexuality (Jones 1955). When the ego is threatened by these unacceptable id impulses, the projection mechanism presumably enables the individual to externalize them. That is, the source of the threat is no longer seen as within oneself, but rather as coming from someone else — "It is not my own desires that are threatening me; it's that person over there who is threatening me." Hence the development of delusions of persecution.

Most psychoanalytic investigators feel that schizophrenia reflects an *impaired or defective ego structure.* There are those, such as Hartmann (1953) and Jacobson (1964), who attribute the defectiveness of the schizophrenic ego to constitutional defects and vulnerabilities and/or environmental trauma. For the ego to develop properly — that is, to develop a boundary between internal and external reality — it is thought that there must first be a "good-enough" self with no basic deficits and then what Winnicott (1958) has called "good-enough mothering." Normally the good-enough mothering becomes internalized, imparting a basic sense of trust and security. Without one or both of these factors, the probability of schizophrenia is increased.

Mahler (1975) and others see schizophrenia as difficulty with the early childhood phases of separation-individuation. Mahler stresses the central role of separation and individuation in normal and pathological development. She believes that parental unresponsiveness to the infant's needs, or withdrawal of emotional supplies when the baby initially attempts separation and individuation, leads to what is called a *developmental standstill,* or a retreat to an undifferentiated state. She noted that there are normally occurring autistic and symbiotic phases in the infant's relationship to the mother. During such phases, the infant has a poor sense of herself as independent from the mother. It is only through a gradual process of separation that the formation of a stable sense of self is possible. This process is seen as largely dependent upon the libidinal gratification available from the mother. Masterson (1972) suggests that when there is a problem, the difficulty is due to the lack of emotional supplies and support necessary for the unfolding of the individual's personality.

British psychoanalyst Melanie Klein (1946), who has influenced many American analysts, believes that the newborn's psyche is sufficiently organized to experience anxiety, to build defense mechanisms, and to make fantasy- as well as reality-based relations to people and things. In order to defend against overwhelming anxiety, the infant learns to introject (take in psychologically) and project (put outside the self psychologically). During the first six months of life, she believes, the infant takes a paranoid-schizoid position, in which he feels persecutory anxiety because "bad parts of the self" are projected into the environment. In most cases, the infant then moves into the depressive position, in which the bad parts of the self are accepted as part of the self. If things do not proceed normally, however, the infant (who may become schizophrenic) remains or returns to the paranoid-schizoid position.

Grotstein (1977) feels that schizophrenia is the "result of a defective development of the ego caused by either heredity or early environmental circumstance. The resultant infantile maldevelopment is due to everdefensive attacks by one part of the psyche upon other aspects which can sense and perceive its needs." This attack on one's own sensations and thinking takes place to avoid the "nameless dread"—being absolutely overwhelmed with internal and external stimuli. The child's infantile self is unable to cope and deadens itself as its only defense. Since the immature, vulnerable personality cannot perceive and integrate stressful stimuli, it attacks and deadens itself to protect itself. Such patients are thus literally and figuratively out of contact with themselves, unable to differentiate between external reality and sensory impressions which tell them of their own subjective needs. Schizophrenia, then, according to these theorists, is an undifferentiated process that results in the experience of a lack of boundaries between sensations and thought, which then results in feelings of psychological deadness.

Gunderson and Mosher (1975) describe schizophrenia as a disorder of ego functioning which is caused by negative parent–child experiences and possibly, too, by biological-constitutional elements. They suggest that the schizophrenic's inability to develop and maintain accurate internal representations of the outside world causes the production of restitutional symptoms such as delusions and hallucinations. These symptoms become prominent when the individual is confronted with the stresses of developing independent, mature, trusting relationships.

The neo-Freudians view schizophrenia as a developmental disorder (White and Watt 1973). The child, having experienced relationships with others as painful and hostile, withdraws into a world of fantasy, a withdrawal which he expresses in behavior. Having withdrawn from others, the child never develops appropriate social behaviors, which results in further unpleasantness and consequently in further withdrawal. Such continually negative social experience severely damages the child's self-esteem. While young, the child may manage to cope with his world of unhappiness. At some point later in life, however, he may experience such negative social encounters that the resulting anxiety, pain, and withdrawal cause a general breakdown in functioning—a schizophrenic break.

From a psychodynamic perspective, then, the irrational thoughts and bizarre behavior of the schizophrenic are caused by unconsciousness of urges and ideas that usually remain inaccessible. These thoughts break through to awareness when the individual undergoes a regression brought about by his/her generalized fear of the world. According to psychodynamic thought, the schizophrenic's fearfulness was originally created by profoundly frustrating interpersonal relationships in the early years of life, during which he had no expectation of support and warmth from the social environment. As a result, the infant regards others as not only uninterested in him, but dangerous and threatening as well. Especially dangerous are sexual, aggressive, and dependent relationships. These theorists feel that the onset of schizophrenic symptoms do not represent a new problem, but rather are signs of a life crisis in which previously controlled thoughts and fantasies are given overt expression. The maladaptive behavior generally becomes noticeable during the postadolescent period, because it is then that the individual is expected to become independent and to cope successfully with the environment. Schizophrenic postadolescents have no faith in their ability to accomplish anything of value in the social environment. Thus, they continue to live within themselves. As their terrible fear of people causes them to lose contact with the environment, schizophrenics struggle to provide a new environment to which they can adjust.

Cameron (1963) believes that the *pseudocommunity,* a device attributed to paranoia, is also applicable to most varieties of schizophrenic reactions. He defines a pseudocommunity as a reconstruction of reality containing both real and imagined individuals. The purpose of the development of the schizophrenic's pseudocommunity is not so much to achieve rapprochement with reality, but rather to establish a world that will minimize the experience of anxiety. According to Cameron, the premorbid schizophrenic, like all other prepsychotic personalities with basic ego defects, seems especially vulnerable to five general situations: loss or threatened loss of a major source of gratification; loss or threatened loss of basic security; upsurge of erotic or hostile impulses; sudden increase in guilt (conscious, preconscious, or unconscious); and reduced general effectiveness of ego adaptation or defense.

The schizophrenic person — whose conscious and preconscious psyche is flooded with infantile impulses, fantasies, conflicts, and fears — meets adult demands with archaic forms of defense, such as massive projection, introjection, or denial. The loss of reality adaptation renders this person unable to control the environment or to negotiate the various aspects of daily living. Cameron then describes schizophrenia as a thought disorder that has two basic aspects: (1) the inability to think and communicate in conventional terms due to social isolation, and (2) the use of unrealistic thought as a defense against anxiety (and in the case of the schizophrenic, the development of a pseudo-community).

According to Arieti (1955, 1969), two cognitive principles are especially needed to interpret schizophrenic thought. One of them, the *principle of active concretization,* states that although the schizophrenic is capable of thinking in abstract terms, she is not able to sustain this process when the situation is too anxiety provoking. With an increase in anxiety, the schizophrenic immediately and unconsciously shifts to a concrete mode of thought. The Von Domarus principle states that while normal persons interpret events on the basis of their objective features, schizophrenics interpret events in an idiosyncratic and unrealistic way (Von Domarus 1944).

Interpersonal

The interpersonal perspective focuses primarily on the individual's interactions in an effort to determine what kind of interpersonal relationships could possibly bring about schizophrenia. According to Sullivan (1931), normal human beings have all sorts of skills that they are inclined to take very much for granted. They need these skills to function every day, and they continually monitor their behavior to guard against unfortunate mistakes. Sullivan called these "monitoring systems" or "supervisory patterns" and remarked that they are really like imaginary people who are always with one, carrying on a helpful dialogue.

With the schizophrenic, however, these supervisory patterns break down; Sullivan feels it very likely that they were not too firmly established in the first place. In any case, deprived of the capacity to monitor their own behavior and thoughts, schizophrenics have a great deal of difficulty determining what is appropriate and what is inappropriate. Indeed, what is left of their own supervisory patterns seems to have acquired an almost independent existence or dissociative phenomenon. Therefore, what most persons experience as a part of themselves becomes strange and alien to schizophrenics. They do not have imaginary listeners or spectators. They may actually hear voices correcting them or commenting on their behavior. They may actually see other people watching them (Linn 1977).

Because schizophrenics cannot regulate their own behavior very effectively, their ability to communicate with others is likely to be severely impaired. They are thus increasingly thrown back into a strange, often frightening, world. It is a world populated by their own private symbols and words, concepts that cannot be readily shared with anyone else. Consequently, schizophrenics often sound as though they are speaking some exotic foreign language. Generally speaking, the more disturbed the client, the more unintelligible his speech and ideas (Sullivan 1962).

Social Learning

A substantial and persuasive body of research indicates that schizophrenics have difficulty maintaining selective attention (Neucherlein 1977), such as in reaction-time tasks, which require the person to respond as quickly as possible when cued to do so. The question, though, is what causes these deficits in the first place. They may be due to high distractibility (Chapman and McGhie 1962), slow processing of sensory input (Yates 1966), or interfering factors such as increased anxiety (Mednick 1958). Ullman and Krasner (1975) have focused more on environmental controls over attention and believe that such deficits may be caused by a lack of reinforcement; attention, like any other response, requires sufficient reinforcement in order to be maintained.

If one stops attending to important social cues, one is likely to be defined as socially inappropriate or bizarre. This is likely to lead to a certain degree of isolation, since others tend to avoid contact with anyone who appears to be so "strange." This may lead to a loss of social relationships and further withdrawal from social situations. Stated somewhat simplistically, this is the basic premise of the social-learning perspective.

Mednick (1958) and Ullmann and Krasner (1975) have also proposed that schizophrenic behavior is caused and maintained by reinforcement from various sources. Mednick's theory focuses on internal sources of reinforcement, whereas Ullmann and Krasner speak in terms of external sources.

Ullmann and Krasner (1975) believe that everyone is crazy to some extent, but that most of us either are not reinforced or are punished for our bizarre behavior. If individuals who otherwise received very little attention from others were to act in a strange way, however, the attention they received might reinforce the behavior. This could lead to an increase in the frequency or magnitude of the behavior such that, if it continued to be reinforced, it might be maintained from various sources, eventually causing the person to behave in a schizophrenic way.

Ullman and Krasner's interpretation of schizophrenia is within the behaviorist tradition. According to these investigators, the schizophrenic is subject to the same principles of learning and behavior as are "normal" people; however, because of a failure of reinforcement, the schizophrenic has ceased to attend to the social stimuli to which most of us respond. Instead, he attends to his own idiosyncratic cues, and as a result, his behavior seems odd or bizarre to the "normal" observer. As Ullman and Krasner point out, "Attention responses require effort. When they do not pay off, they decrease in emission" (1975, p. 357). And this, they believe, is what happened to the schizophrenic. Furthermore, the following behavioral cycle may be instituted: When an individual ceases responding to certain accepted social cues, he may become the target of disciplinary action and social rejection, leading to deeper feelings of alienation and adding to the belief that others are out to get him. Hence, his behavior becomes even more strange. In addition, other sources may begin providing reinforcement for his deviant behavior, in the form of either social attention or any of the other advantages one gains from being "sick." Once reinforced, these behaviors will, of course, increase in frequency.

In support of their argument that schizophrenia is a learned behavior, Ullman and Krasner cite two basic lines of evidence. First, there is good reason to believe that schizophrenics know what they are doing. For instance, their bizarre behaviors are not equally distributed across situations; rather, like other learned behaviors, they are often responses to specific stimuli. Schizophrenics have also been found to engage in *impression management*—that is, they can look "healthy" or "sick," depending on the advantages or disadvantages of each. Moreover, schizophrenics appear to be much more socially sensitive than one would expect. Ullman and Krasner point out, for example, that schizophrenic inpatients have been able to predict the posthospital adjustment of other patients as well as staff could.

Ullman and Krasner's second line of evidence has to do with the demonstrated ability of schizophrenics to unlearn their maladaptive behaviors. It has been shown that when the advantages of acting out the schizophrenic role are withdrawn and instead socially valued behaviors are reinforced, schizophrenics can quite readily give up many of their bizarre behavior patterns. Ullman and Krasner (1975) believe, then, that the basic process involved in schizophrenia is the extinction of attending to typical social stimuli.

Humanistic-Existential

Most humanistic and existential theorists direct their attention primarily to the neuroses, but a few systematic attempts have been made to apply the humanistic-existential model of behavior to the problem of psychosis. The writer who has contributed the most in this area is R. D. Laing, a British existential psychiatrist. Laing's interpretation may be reduced to two central arguments. The first is that mental illness is largely a matter of perspective. His second point is that schizophrenia is simply "a special sort of strategy that a person invents in order to live in an unlivable situation" (1964, p. 187). Laing argues that the schizophrenic may be more sane than the society which labels him mad. According to his theory, schizophrenia is not insanity, but rather *hypersanity,* an exploration from our own insane reality into another reality in the existential search for autonomy and meaning.

One of the most extreme existential views put forth by Laing (1967) is that schizophrenia is a positive growth experience used by the person to cope with an insane world. He also believes that psychosis is caused by the parental definition of a child's being a certain way when he cannot possibly fulfill that definition. Psychiatrists, Laing argues, have no right to interfere with the schizophrenic's quest: "Can we not see that this voyage is not what we need to be cured of, but that it is itself a natural way of healing our own appalling state of alienation called normality?" (1967, p. 116).

In his defense of the schizophrenic experience against the presumptions of conventional psychiatry, Laing is supported by a group of writers whose major contention is that the state called "insanity" is simply a label fabricated by society to justify the exploitation of persons so labeled. This group, which includes Thomas Szasz and a number of other eminent writers, along with Laing, sees the schizophrenic virtually as a victim of an Establishment plot. These psychiatrists, psychologists, and sociologists would like to do away with conventional psychiatry and to redefine psychosis as a disruption of social or interpersonal relationships. Szasz (1976) insists that the disorder is nothing more than a "political" label. He believes that schizophrenia is the result of a deficiency in introjected objects; the schizophrenic has so few internal objects that he has few models to use in living.

Mosher (1974) lists four major criticisms raised by this group of traditional views and treatment of the persons labeled schizophrenic. First, they argue that by classifying so-called schizophrenics as mentally ill or diseased, society justifies the detention of these individuals in distant, dehumanizing, impersonal institutions and also sanctions treatment methods that do no more than persuade deviant individuals to conform more closely to society's norms. Second, these critics point out the adverse social consequences of the labeling process; for example, a person who has at any time been labeled schizophrenic will probably have difficulty for the rest of his life both in establishing social relationships and in getting a job. Scheff (1970) in particular believes that the labeling process is the single most important cause of continuing deviance.

A third source of criticism is psychiatry's preoccupation with finding out what kind of "disease" the person has, to the neglect of the person himself. And fourth, these writers object to the traditional doctor–patient relationship, which, they feel, enables the physician to have unlimited power to manipulate — often for the satisfaction of his own needs — the submissive, dependent patient. By its very nature, they believe, this relationship destroys any possibility of patients' achieving the independence they are supposed to achieve.

Family Environment

The following family patterns have been theorized as responsible for schizophrenia: problematic parenting, disturbed marital relationships, and communication problems. The schizophrenogenic parent — usually thought to be the mother — has been described as domineering, rejecting, cold, and immature. Initially, then, the family environmental theories focused on the overcontrolling mother as responsible for the development of schizophrenia in the child. It was believed that the mother's behavior tended to foster dependency and in so doing made the child prone to schizophrenia.

The terms *symbiotic union* and *overcontrolling mother* have also been applied to this parenting pattern. A number of studies have suggested that there is a high frequency of symbiotic unions between parents and children who later become schizophrenic. In symbiotic unions, mothers usually encourage their children to form extremely strong dependencies on them. Often the mother will continue to treat the child as if he were still an infant (for example, mothers may continue to bathe their adolescent sons).

The notion of symbiotic unions is quite similar to the overcontrolling patterns seen in the mothers of schizophrenics. McCord and co-workers (1962) found that 67 percent of schizophrenics had what they determined to be overcontrolling mothers, in contrast to only 8 percent of the mothers of matched control subjects.

In 1948, Freida Fromm-Reichmann coined the term *schizophrenogenic mother* to describe the type of mother who was capable of inducing schizophrenia in her children. Such mothers were characterized as cold, domineering, rejecting, and yet overprotective. The father, meanwhile, was faulted mainly for his passivity in not interfering in the pernicious mother–child relationship.

Bateson and colleagues (1956) believed that the communication pattern between the mother and child was a critical factor in the development of schizophrenia. This emphasis on the mother as the principle culprit in producing schizophrenia was not new when they wrote their now-famous article. During the 1950s, Bateson and his associates advanced a rather specific hypothesis concerning the development of schizophrenia: the theory of the double bind. In the double-bind situation, the mother gives the child mutually contradictory messages, meanwhile implicitly forbidding the child to point out the contradiction. The child is caught in the middle; no matter which alternative he chooses, he is the loser. In short, the child is in a double bind, a no-win situation.

Bateson and colleagues proposed that the type of mother most likely to engage in double-bind communication is one who finds closeness with her child intolerable but who at the same time finds it intolerable to admit this to herself. In other words, she pushes the child away and the child senses this "push," but when the child withdraws, the mother accuses the child of not loving her. Bateson and co-workers suggested that people who become schizophrenic were repeatedly confronted with "impossible" situations during childhood. No matter how they behaved, their parents make them feel "damned if they did" and also "damned if they didn't."

Potential schizophrenics are, in short, constantly subjected to demands that are both arbitrary and contradictory. Bateson and colleagues propose that children who are continuously placed in such a situation will not be able to relate to others. The parent's incompatible messages to the child almost certainly evoke in the child a state of overwhelming anxiety and frustration—overwhelming enough to cause some people (especially those who had remained very dependent upon their parents) to break down.

Research on the role of double-bind communication in the development of schizophrenia has been largely anecdotal and very scanty. Consequently, there does not seem to be much support for considering the double bind as a major factor in the etiology of schizophrenia. However, other more general communication problems, such as unclear and inaccurate communication, have been found more frequently in families of schizophrenics than in families of normal controls (Jacobs 1975).

Lidz (1973) suggests that schizophrenia is related to difficulty in the establishment of preverbal mutuality between the mother and child. Before the child can speak, or when he can say only single words, the mother must be able to fulfill his needs by intimately knowing the child and his behavior patterns. According to Lidz, the mothers of most schizophrenics are so profoundly egocentric that they respond to their own needs rather than the needs of the child. He has proposed the notion of schizophrenogenic families in which there is a delusion that pervades all family relationships. Recent investigations (e.g., Caputo 1968), however, have suggested that the fathers are as responsible as the mothers for the hostile, aggressive atmosphere that seems to permeate the homes of many schizophrenic children. In fact, the trend of recent studies has been to focus attention on the communication patterns among *all* members of the family (Mishler and Waxler 1968).

The data on family systems suggest that there may be some factors—such as severe family conflict, or inaccurate or distorted communications—that are in some way related to schizophrenia. It is generally agreed that the family has a greater impact on the individual's psychosocial development than any other element in society.

Searles (1959) describes the following six ways in which parents can undermine their child's confidence to differentiate her own emotional reactions and perceptions of reality: (1) The parent repeatedly calls attention to areas of the child's personality that are different from the areas that the child feels are important to defining her identity. (2) The parent simultaneously exposes the child to stimulation and frustration or rapidly alternates stimulation and frustration. (3) The parent switches from one topic to the next while maintaining the same emotional feeling, so that matters of life and death are spoken of as if unimportant. (4) The parent switches emotions while discussing a single specific topic. (5) The parent stimulates the child sexually in areas in which it would be disastrous to find gratification. (6) The parent relates to the child simultaneously on different levels. Searles feels that these processes, which can literally drive a person insane, are unconscious, but are nonetheless the ingredients of the pathogenic relationships of psychotic families.

Bowen (1960) hypothesizes that one child may be selected as the focal point toward which both parents direct their emotional immaturity. This in turn helps them to achieve a fragile stabilization of their own relationship. In addition, Mosher, Pollin, and Stabenau (1971) suggest that such a focal child may be selected from among the others because he is weaker, less intelligent, or otherwise constitutionally inferior to his siblings. Similarly, Waring and Ricks (1965) found a higher frequency of what they termed *emotional divorces* in the parents of schizophrenics. Although the parents were not actually separated or divorced, they were living in their own separate worlds, with very few positive interactions taking place between them.

Lidz (1973) claims that a great number of schizophrenic children come from families that fall into one of two categories: the *schismatic family,* in which parental discord has divided the family into opposing factions, and the *skewed family,* which remains reasonably calm, but only because one spouse is totally dominated by the pathology of the other. In the marital schism, there is open conflict between the parents, who attempt to control each other in various power plays. These parents are divided into two antagonistic and competing factions. *Marital skew* describes the situation in which the dominant partner is seriously disturbed, and the spouse passively submits to the will of the disturbed partner. In both situations the child is denied the emotional support necessary for a sense of security and self-worth, the ingredients necessary for emotional growth.

Lidz, then, views schizophrenia as an outcome of disturbed family communication patterns which negate the "selfness" of the person that will eventually be labeled schizophrenic. In such a chaotic setting, the children have inevitably received very faulty training in reality testing and have grown up riddled with insecurities. It is therefore almost impossible for them to achieve a firm sense of identity, and at least some of them eventually break down and develop schizophrenia. Both patterns may have negative effects on the children who grow up with poor examples of how parents relate to one another.

He also believed that mothers of schizophrenics are so egocentric that they cannot respond to the child's preverbal needs. The mother can respond only to her own needs. Arieti (1974b) sees the schizophrenic's family milieu as one in which the child is deprived of all security and is surrounded by anxiety and hostility in most, if not all, family interactions. In setting the tone of such interactions, the relationship of the parents is particularly decisive. Although the data do indicate that disturbed marital and family relationships are associated with later schizophrenia, it is not clear that these conflicts are necessary or sufficient causes of schizophrenia.

Concern with specific forms of family deviance implicated by the earlier investigators, such as "double binding," "pseudomutuality," and the "transmission of irrationality," seems to have given way to broader concepts of overall communication deficiency. Thus, Singer and colleagues (1978) employed the concept of communication of deviance to refer to 32 categories of peculiarities in Rorschach responding found to differentiate between the parents of schizophrenic (including borderline) persons and those of neurotic or normal persons. Interestingly, the actively schizophrenic offspring turned out to have lower communication deviance scores than their parents, perhaps suggesting a parent-to-child directional effect.

Important work by these same investigators has also shown it to be possible to predict later development of schizophrenia from parent communication deviance measured at a point before breakdown but during serious adolescent disturbance (Goldstein et al. 1978). Vaughn and Leff's (1976, 1981) studies related relapse rates in schizophrenia to a certain pattern of noxious communication in families, termed "expressed emotion"; the study by Scott (1976) related outcome after a schizophrenic break to patterns of reciprocal perceptions of each other held by patient and family members; and Waxler (1974) and Liem (1974) employed the strategy of "artificial" families — triads consisting of a patient and two (unrelated) parents. They found that the cognitive performance of schizophrenic persons improved when they communicated with normal parents, whereas Liem demonstrated a deterioration in the performance of normal parents when communicating with a schizophrenic son. She also found that parents communicated better with their own schizophrenic sons than with strangers' schizophrenic sons. Evidence of circularity notwithstanding, it is probably fair to say that the available findings strongly implicate family communication patterns as having at least some etiological significance in schizophrenia.

It should be noted, however, that while many investigators accept the correlation between schizophrenia and disordered family relationships, drawing etiological conclusions from studies of the families of schizophrenic children is always hazardous. In the first place, there is the chicken-egg problem: It is not clear whether the family disruptions are causing the child's disorder or whether the presence of an abnormal child produces abnormal relationships among family members (Gunderson et al. 1974). Furthermore, there is the third variable problem. For example, it is possible that both the child's disturbance *and* the abnormal family interactions are the result of yet another factor, such as shared genetic defect (Reiss 1974). In any case, studies of the families of schizophrenics are extremely difficult to conduct, both because of the multitude of uncontrollable variables and because of ethical problems—for example, the invasion of the family's privacy or the implication that the parents are to blame for the child's deviance. Nevertheless, recent developments in family study methodology, particularly the high-risk family studies, are making it increasingly possible for investigators to address the critical questions in this area.

BIOLOGICAL FACTORS

The idea that insanity is an inherited trait became particularly popular in the latter half of the eighteenth century and was shared by Kraeplin and Bleuler. It is only within the last two decades, however, that studies have been conducted that are sophisticated enough to provide what appears to be evidence in support of a genetic hypothesis.

The Diathesis-Stress Model

There remains a great deal of disagreement over the particular mode of genetic transmission. Early researchers tended to hold to the monogenetic biochemical theory: that a single gene—dominant, recessive, or intermediate—was responsible for a specific metabolic dysfunction which in turn then produced the behavioral manifestations of schizophrenia. Within the past few years, however, there has been a stronger movement toward a diathesis-stress position. According to this theory, what is inherited is a diathesis, or predisposition, toward schizophrenia, and the schizophrenia itself will develop only if certain life stresses are encountered.

The most widely known diathesis-stress model is that proposed by Paul Meehl (1962). Meehl postulates that the phenotypic consequence of the genetic abnormality is a neural defect which he labels *schizotaxia*. The normal stresses and strains of any social learning environment produce in schizotaxic individuals a somewhat peculiar personality organization which Meehl calls *schizotypy*. If schizotypes have the good fortune to be reared in a favorable social milieu, then they will remain fairly normal, though perhaps slightly eccentric. But if their milieu is stressful—if, for example, the mother has engaged in double-bind communication—then it is more likely that they will develop clinical schizophrenia. Thus, as long as schizotypes do not encounter severe stress in their lives, they will not become schizophrenic, even though they may seem a bit odd. Under sufficient stress, however, they will not be able to cope adequately and might develop a full-blown schizophrenic behavior pattern. In contrast, those who have not inherited the schizotaxia will be relatively immune to a schizophrenic pattern even under considerable stress.

The diathesis-stress model of Meehl seems to be a step in the right direction since it takes into account both genetic and environmental factors. Here, a predisposition, or diathesis, is inherited, but only if sufficient stress is encountered is the person likely to develop the disorder. This model implies that the primary predisposing factor is genetically determined, is permanent, and with sufficient stress will result in a relatively enduring schizophrenic behavior pattern. A somewhat more flexible approach that is quite similar to the views of Meehl is the vulnerability model recently described by Zubin and Spring (1977).

The Vulnerability Model

The vulnerability model proposes that each individual has a certain degree of vulnerability that under certain conditions will lead to a schizophrenic episode. Although this view is similar to the diathesis-stress model, some distinctions are made. First, the origins of vulnerability can be diverse and are not limited to genetic causation. Vulnerability could be due to a combination of biological and psychological factors. There will be debate as to how much is contributed by each factor, but the essential feature is that nonbiological factors can also influence vulnerability. Thus, some of the components of vulnerability are inherited, but some are acquired. Zubin and Spring (1977) note that the potential stressors, which they refer to as "challenging events," will call for some forms of adaptation or coping. If the stress is above the person's threshold, there is likely to be an episode of maladaptive behavior, in this case a schizophrenic episode. However, if the stress can be reduced to a level below the threshold, the maladaptive behavior is likely to resolve.

Family Studies

If a disorder is genetically transmitted, then relatives of an affected individual are more likely to have the predisposing gene that are persons in the general population. If the incidence of the disorder among the relatives is significantly higher than among the general population, then a genetic contribution to the etiology is suspected. Thus, a disorder that shows a pattern of transmission from unaffected mothers to 50 percent of their sons suggests that an X-chromosome-linked mode of inheritance is involved (Karon and Vandenbos 1981). If both parents and children manifest a disorder, the gene suspected of causing the condition must be dominant. When 25 percent of the children of unaffected parents manifest a disorder, the responsible gene is considered to be recessive. Schizophrenia, however, does not appear to fall into any of these categories (Kessler 1980, Lidz 1973).

Recent studies have found that for all siblings of a schizophrenic, the risk of schizophrenia is higher than for individuals in the general population. These rates vary from 2 to 46 times higher than the risk for schizophrenia in the average population (e.g. Rosenthal et al. 1975). Among first-degree relatives of the patient, the average risk for schizophrenia is roughly 8 to 10 percent. The risk for relatives is graded, so that relatives who share comparatively few genes with an affected individual show a lower rate of schizophrenia than do those who have more genes in common.

Family studies of the genetics of schizophrenia clearly indicate that the more closely one is related to a schizophrenic, the more likely one is to develop schizophrenia. The child of a schizophrenic parent has a 16.4 percent chance of developing schizophrenia, and the child of two schizophrenic parents has a 68 percent chance of becoming schizophrenic, as compared to an incidence of less than 1 percent in the general population. However, because some families tend to share the same environment as well as the same genes, it is nearly impossible in family studies to determine whether correlations are the function of genetic or environmental influences.

Twin Studies

Many researchers have compared identical twins (monozygotic twins) with fraternal twins (dizygotic) on the concordance for diagnoses of schizophrenia. Higher concordance rates among monozygotic twins, who have the same genetic material, and dizygotic twins, who share roughly 50 percent of the same genes, as would any pair of siblings, provide strong evidence of genetic factors in the transmission of schizophrenia. Kallman (1941) conducted two important studies of the genetics of schizophrenia. The first was on brothers and sisters of 1,000 patients of a Berlin psychiatric hospital, and the second was on 953 twins from New York psychiatric hospitals. Kallman found full siblings of patients to have a higher expectancy for the disorder than half siblings. The highest incidence of schizophrenia was among the children of schizophrenic parents and among monozygotic (identical) twins.

Book (1960) also showed that the incidence of schizophrenia was higher in the families of schizophrenics than in the general population. Slater (1968) showed that schizophrenia was present in 14 percent of schizophrenic dizygotic (fraternal) twins and 76 percent of monozygotic twins. Although many of the data on schizophrenia have been questioned on the basis of faulty statistical techniques, these studies appear to confirm the belief held for centuries that schizophrenia is likely to run in families. However, these early studies were not well controlled and tended to find higher concordance rates in identical twins than in fraternal twins. More recent and better controlled twin studies have found much lower concordance rates than the earlier studies, but they have consistently shown that identical twins are more concordant than fraternal twins.

In the twin studies conducted over the past 50 years, then, the mean concordance rates for schizophrenia in monozygotic twins comes to 43.9 percent, approximately five times as great as the mean concordance rate of 8.8 percent for dizygotic twins (Ban 1973, Rosenthal 1970). As more recent studies have improved in research methodology, the concordance rates have tended to diminish for both monozygotic and dizygotic twins (Allen et al. 1972, Mosher and Gunderson 1973). Nevertheless, the monozygotic and dizygotic concordance ratios found in these stuudies usually lie between 3:1 and 6:1.

Adoption Studies

The adoption studies come even closer to separating the influence of heredity and environment. Most adoption studies follow this procedure: A group of adopted children, preferably infants, who were born to schizophrenic parents are compared to a control group of adopted children born to nonschizophrenic, or normal, parents. Assuming the adopting parents were normal, certain findings would then be expected, depending upon how important the genetic influence was. If genetic transmission is occurring, adopted children of schizophrenics should be more likely to become schizophrenic than children of normal parents. And this is indeed what many adoption studies have found.

Heston (1966) completed one of the most methodologically sound adoption studies. He was able to gather very detailed information on 47 individuals who had been removed very shortly after birth from their schizophrenic mothers, who were hospitalized in psychiatric institutions. These infants had been placed either in foster homes or with relatives and were raised without any contact with their biological mothers. A control group included individuals who had been raised in the same foster or adoptive home settings in which the experimental subjects had been placed. Independent ratings by two psychiatrists were rendered on these individuals following interviews and testing. Heston found that 5 of the 47 children of the schizophrenic mothers (10.6 percent) were diagnosed as schizophrenic, whereas none of the control-group subjects were. When Heston made age corrections, which means that he took into consideration the statistical chances of developing schizophrenia at a later age, the rate increased to 16.6 percent.

An important result of Heston's work is emphasized by those who favor a genetic model of schizophrenia (Gottesman and Shields 1976). It should be pointed out that his 16.6 percent age-corrected incidence of schizophrenia in adopted children is almost identical to Kallman's (1953) rate of 16.4 percent for children raised with one schizophrenic parent. From an environmental viewpoint, one would expect that children raised away from their schizophrenic parents should be less likely to develop schizophrenic behavior patterns than children raised with their parents.

Most of the adoption studies first identify a group of psychotic parents and then study the offspring. However, another approach would be to identify any adoptees who become schizophrenic and then study their biological and adoptive families. With this strategy in mind, Kety and colleagues (1975) used the Danish registry to find adopted individuals who had been diagnosed as schizophrenic and a matched control group. The biological and adoptive families were then compared. For the control group there was no difference in the rate of schizophrenia in biological and adoptive families. As would be expected from a genetic viewpoint, however, the biological families of adoptees who became schizophrenic had a much higher incidence of the disorder than did the adoptive families that raised these individuals.

Probably one of the most interesting studies that has attempted to sort out the influence of genetic and environmental factors was reported by Wender and colleagues (1974), who also used the Danish registry to obtain their subjects. In addition to the typical comparisons of adoptees born to schizophrenic parents and those born to normal parents, Wender and coworkers were also able to study a unique group of adoptees. Subjects in their group were born to normal parents but were adopted and raised by families in which at least one of the adopting parents was eventually considered schizophrenic, or at least borderline schizophrenic. They found that adoptees born to normal parents but raised by a schizophrenic parent were no more likely to be considered disturbed than those raised by normal adoptive parents. Once again, the group most likely to be diagnosed schizophrenic were those who were born to schizophrenics.

It seems somewhat clear that genetics does have some influence on the development of schizophrenia. The real question is not whether there is an influence, but rather how much of an influence is contributed by genetics. The process-reactive distinction provides some clues in determining the relative degree of genetic involvement. Garmezy (1970) proposed that there is a greater genetic involvement in process schizophrenia than there is in reactive schizophrenia. Some support for this view was provided by Kringlen (1968), who found that the concordance rate for process schizophrenia in monozygotic twins was higher than for reactive schizophrenia.

The adoption studies have not gone unchallenged. Sarbin and Mancuso (1980) have delivered a highly detailed critique of the findings and conclusions thus far reported. Thus, although the genetic case is impressive, it is not yet definitively settled.

BIOCHEMICAL THEORIES

Protein Abnormalities

In the late 1950s, Heath isolated a factor in the blood serum of schizophrenics that he believed disturbed neural functioning in the brain, thus causing schizophrenia. This factor was a simple protein. Heath (1960) called the protein *taraxin*, from the Greek word meaning "to disturb." When Heath injected taraxin into monkeys, marked changes in behavior and in electroencephalogram (EEG) tracings were observed. In addition, prison volunteers who were injected with the substance showed a number of characteristically schizophrenic symptoms, such as severely disorganized thought processes, withdrawal, and feelings of depersonalization. These startling findings received a great deal of attention at the time of publication, but because some investigators found it difficult to replicate Heath's work (Siegel et al. 1959), further investigation is necessary before any firm conclusions can be drawn.

Other researchers are convinced that schizophrenia is due to biochemical changes in the brain, which may or may not have a hereditary link. Metabolic or allergic causes for some schizophrenias are based on the finding of an abnormal protein called *traxein* in the blood of schizophrenics. Kety (1972) showed that the serum of schizophrenics is toxic for tadpoles and rats. Other experimenters have demonstrated that extracts of the urine of schizophrenics change the behavior of rats and disturb spiders' ability to construct webs. Early researchers showed that schizophrenics have a deficiency in their ability to take in oxygen. Also, the carbohydrate metabolism of schizophrenics is different from that of normal people. Liver insufficiency is claimed by Buscaino (1952). Others report a high concentration of aromatic compounds in the urine of schizophrenics.

Schizophrenic patients are widely reported to exude an unusual odor and to have oily skin. Perhaps the odoriferous substance is a clue to the schizophrenic metabolism; however, the schizophrenics studied had been hospitalized for years, and hospital living plus poor personal habits may have accounted for the odor. Sines (1959) report that both trained rats and a human odor-testing panel were able to discriminate between the sweat of schizophrenics and normal controls. However, Kety, one of the foremost researchers in this area, argues that many biochemical studies have not been confirmed (Arieti 1974a). Horwitt (1956) notes that the various biochemical theories of schizophrenia render the schizophrenic a sorry specimen, with his liver, brain, kidneys, and circulatory system impaired, deficiencies of every vitamin, and enzymes and hormones out of balance.

It is important to note that emotional activity does require biochemical processes, which means that the emotions of schizophrenics may be correlated with, but not caused by, biochemical processes. Thus, one does not know whether disturbed thoughts cause disturbed biochemistry or whether disturbed biochemistry causes disturbed thoughts (or whether a third factor causes both). All that is known now is that biochemistry and thoughts may be statistically associated.

If there is a genetic factor in schizophrenia, the question becomes, what is the phenotypic mechanism that translates the genetic abnormality into behavioral abnormality? Many investigators today believe that this mechanism has to do with body chemicals, but for the reason mentioned earlier in this chapter — specifically, interference by third variables such as hospitalizations, drugs, diet, and exercise — the progress in biochemical research has been slow and has suffered setbacks.

Transmethylation

The transmission of nerve impulses in the brain is dependent upon several different neurotransmitters that chemically bridge the gaps between neural synapses. Interestingly, many of these transmitters are structurally similar to hallucinogenic substances that cause distorted perceptual experiences, such as LSD or mescaline. Osmond and Smythies (1952) suggested the transmethylation hypothesis, which holds that, through some metabolic error, the carbon-oxygen molecule methyl is added to the neurotransmitters, rendering them even more similar to hallucinogens. In other words, individuals predisposed to schizophrenia appear to have a built-in supply of substances that can dramatically alter their behavior.

The research supporting the transmethylation hypothesis has taken two different approaches. In one line of research, substances that increase the supply of methyl molecules were administered to schizophrenic individuals (Park et al. 1965). As predicted, these substances were found to exacerbate the schizophrenic's behavior problems. Conversely, Hoffer and Osmond (1962, 1968) showed that high doses of niacin (nicotinic acid, or Vitamin B-3), which decreases methyl levels, resulted in improvements in the treated individuals. The transmethylation hypothesis has received some support; however, there have also been failures to replicate some of the positive findings.

What we are left with, then, are some interesting hypotheses whose confirmation has proved extremely elusive. As a consequence, investigators seem to have turned much of their attention to other things.

Dopamine

Various lines of evidence have also suggested that one particular neurotransmitter, dopamine, may be related to schizophrenia (Meltzer and Stahl 1976, Snyder 1974). The first line of evidence is related to the action of the phenothiazines, which are a group of drugs that are relatively effective in decreasing schizophrenic symptoms such as disturbed thought processes and hallucinations. Research suggests that phenothiazines block the receptor sites of nerves that respond to dopamine in the dopamine tract. This tract of nerve fibers is located in the midbrain and limbic system and may be closely related to arousal and attention processes (Ungerstedt 1971). Thus, the phenothiazines can be thought of as decreasing various symptoms by decreasing the activity of dopamine.

A related piece of evidence is that many schizophrenics who are treated with phenothiazines develop various Parkinsonian symptoms, which resemble the motor dysfunctions seen in Parkinson's disease. A very effective chemical treatment of Parkinson's disease is levodopa, which increases the supply of dopamine. Thus, the Parkinsonian symptoms in the schizophrenic on phenothiazines may be due to too much of a decrease in dopamine activity.

The dopamine hypothesis has also been supported by various findings with amphetamine drugs, a group of powerful stimulants. Many types of amphetamines are available. Some have been used by dieters because of the diminished appetite produced by these drugs, and others, like dextroamphetamine, or "speed," have been used extensively by drug abusers. It has been found that many individuals who used high doses of amphetamines for long periods of time develop what appears to be paranoid schizophrenia, or amphetamine psychosis (Griffith et al. 1972). Furthermore, small doses of amphetamines seem to aggravate the behavior problems of schizophrenic individuals. As a result, Snyder (1974) has argued that amphetamines produce a schizophrenic-like disorder. Supporting this view is the fact that phenothiazines seem to be the best treatment for amphetamine psychosis.

Davis (1978) has noted several temporal factors that do not fit. For example, dopamine receptors are blocked quite rapidly with the ingestion, in clinical doses, of a neuroleptic drug. However, the clinical effect in terms of a lessening of schizophrenic-like symptoms normally develops gradually over a period of weeks, during a time in which many patients are actually acquiring a tolerance to dopamine blockade. In response to these problems, Davis offered a *two-factor theory* of schizophrenia, in which dopamine plays a distinctly secondary role; the first factor (unspecific) actually gets the schizophrenia going, while the dopaminergic activity simply turns up the speed. What this amounts to, of course, is a rejection of dopamine's alleged etiological significance in schizophrenia.

The biochemical theories most popularly held today are all based on the hypothesis that schizophrenia is caused by substances known as *methylated amines*, which are produced by the body and act as hallucinogens (like LSD or mescaline), causing hallucinations and disorganized thinking. In one line of research, a group of neurotransmitters known as the indolamines, principally sertotonin and tryptamine, are believed to be chemically altered (methylated) in an abnormal way to form hallucinogenic compounds. For example, Mandell and colleagues (1972) have reported that under certain circumstances, an enzyme in the brain known as indolamine-N-methyltransferase can convert serotonin and tryptamine into a hallucinogenic compound.

Another group of neurotransmitters that has gained attention are the *catecholamines*, principally epinephrine, norepinephrine, and dopamine. It has been proposed that in the schizophrenic, these catecholamines are abnormally methylated into a mescaline-like compound. For example, Friedhoff (cited in Mosher and Gunderson 1973) has demonstrated that the human organism is able to synthesize, from dopamine, compounds that are similar to the dimethoxy hallucinogens, of which mescaline is one.

Somewhat conversely to these positions, it has been suggested by other researchers that schizophrenia is caused, not by the production of abnormal methylated amines, but rather by an inability to demethylate normally present hallucinogenic amines, and thus to prevent their accumulation.

THE PHYSIOLOGICAL APPROACH

Studies in the physiological aspects of schizophrenia do not necessarily compete with genetic or biochemical views. Rather, by concentrating on the functions and processes of the body rather than on qualitative biological differences between individuals, they tend to complement the other views, adding another side to what may be a many-faceted organically based condition. It should be kept in mind, however, that a physiological abnormality, similar to a biochemical abnormality, may well be the result, rather than the cause, of schizophrenia. Or, as in the earlier situation, both the abnormality and the schizophrenia may be the result of a third variable.

Neurophysiological Dysfunction

Studies show that autonomic arousal patterns among schizophrenics are different from those observed in normal people (Fenz and Velner 1970). What researchers have discovered is that in resting states, the arousal level of schizophrenics is higher than normal, but in situations that call for a reaction to some stimulus, the arousal level of schizophrenics is lower than normal. In sum, the schizophrenic is overreactive in situations that require a resting state and underreactive in situations that call for an alert state (Buss 1966). To account for this apparent contradiction, it has been suggested that faulty metabolism of neurotransmitters are what produces the autonomic overactivity of schizophrenics, and that the low level of reactivity is simply a normal reaction of the nervous system to high resting levels. For example, it has been shown in normal subjects that at extremely high resting levels of autonomic arousal, a stimulus will generally not elicit further arousal; rather, a paradoxical decrease in arousal may be effected (Lacey 1956). Thus, the lower reactivity of schizophrenics may be not a primary characteristic but rather a secondary one, reflecting the "normal" functioning of a hyperactive nervous system (Buss 1966).

Low Stress Tolerance

Investigators have also suggested that the schizophrenic does not have a store of adaptive energy that may be mobilized in order to cope with the stresses of everyday life. Such a deficiency, they feel, might be genetic. On the other hand, some researchers have suggested that it might be a physiological consequence of the strains imposed on the body by a prolonged schizophrenic condition (Beckett et al. 1963, Luby et al. 1962). One study has shown, for example, that during acute schizophrenic episodes, certain steroids are excreted at abnormally high levels (Sachar et al. 1970). It is possible that a series of such episodes might eventually simply exhaust the adrenal glands, which would then cease to secrete the hormones necessary to deal with stress.

SOCIOLOGICAL THEORIES

Rosenhan's (1973) well-known study provides little assurance that professional diagnosticians are routinely capable of detecting "malingering." In an article entitled "The Art of Being Schizophrenic," Haley was the first to take the suggestion explicitly. Braginsky and colleagues (1969) demonstrated that a group of hospitalized mental patients, most diagnosed schizophrenics, were actively engaged in impression management and in controlling the diagnoses and other assessments made of them by the professional staff. Shimkunas (1972), Ritchie (1975), and Levy (1976) presented experimental evidence that certain behaviors that are definable of schizophrenia (delusional verbalizations, for example) are variably emitted by persons diagnosed as schizophrenic. The chief value of these studies is in demonstrating that schizophrenia, viewed as a class of behaviors, seems to present itself and disappear according to the characteristics of the interpersonal situation confronting the patient.

Drake and Wallach (1979) presented evidence that hospital stays of "functionally psychotic" patients are determined primarily by preferences for hospital versus community living, not by severity of the disorder. Most of the severely disturbed patients were the ones who gained discharge from the hospital!

Sociological researchers have suggested that the passive, apathetic, and bizarre behavior of long-term hospitalized schizophrenics may be the result not only of the effects of their psychological difficulty, but also of their treatment within the hospital setting. Goffman (1961) spent a year observing patients in a large state hospital and found that their behavior was very similar to that of other inmates in what he called "total institutions" — jails, reform schools, and so on, which regulate every aspect of a person's life. Goffman feels that the behavior of mental patients is similar to that of prisoners, sanatorium inmates, prisoners of war, preparatory school students, and armed forces recruits. People in each of these groups are depersonalized by their environments. They lose their individuality and personality as they come under the total control of bureaucratic authorities who demand complete adherence to a rigid set of rules. Though the position somewhat oversimplifies the situation, Goffman feels that the passive, uninvolved behavior of chronic mental patients is a result of living in an environment that is dull and boring and makes no allowance for individualized behavior. In addition, hospital staff expect little of their chronic patients and do not get involved with them. Their expectations thus become a self-fulfilling prophecy.

Some attempts to alter the treatment patterns of chronic schizophrenics have been successful, and the behavior of certain individuals has been changed. Ayllon and Azrin (1965) note that when hospital staff expect responsible behavior from their chronic patients, they do in fact get it. Some treatment programs for such patients have focused, not on the causes or treatment of their disorders, but on teaching socially useful, adaptive behavior and creating environments in which such behavior is rewarded. It has been theorized that people become chronic patients when they do not have the social skills to survive in the outside world. As Goffman notes, the hospital environment does little to foster such adaptive, socially appropriate behavior.

The High-Risk Strategy

The high-risk strategy in its usual form capitalizes on the actuarial fact that a substantial proportion of children born to schizophrenic parents will become schizophrenic. Pioneered by Fish (1957) and Sobel (1961), high-risk research has proliferated at a very rapid rate in recent years. Mednick and Schulsinger (1973) found that the following were among the factors differentiating the schizophrenic from other high-risk subjects: (1) Their (schizophrenic) mothers' disorders and first hospitalizations occurred at a younger age, suggesting greater severity. (2) Obstetrical complications, including long labor, occurred more often in their births. (3) Teachers judged their school behavior as erratic, disturbing, persistently upset, aggressive, and violent. (4) In a more recent study, Mednick and colleagues (1973), employing path analysis, discovered that for males (but not for females), the age of the mothers' onset of disorder apparently contributed to a schizophrenic outcome only indirectly, through enhancing the likelihood of parent–child separation. (5) This analysis also showed that for males (but not for females), schizophrenia was predicted by autonomic nervous system anomaly, which was, in turn, well predicted by complications in the mother's pregnancy or the subject's birth.

PRACTICE TECHNIQUES

Members of the mental health profession are generally called upon to identify high-risk populations and to offer preventative, as well as therapeutic and palliative, services. They generally participate as part of the hospital interdisciplinary team in treatment planning and implementation for the psychiatrically ill patient and are responsible for treatment planning and implementation in outpatient and community care facilities. They often see the patient or the patient's family, or both, in an outpatient facility, such as a halfway house or community mental health center. Schizophrenic patients require ongoing support if they are to remain in the community, and their families need help and education to adjust to the disorder. Mental health professionals can develop family and patient self-help groups, set up supervised residences and sheltered workshops, and make necessary referrals.

The administrative structure of community mental health services is unwieldy and does not facilitate care of the chronic patient. Responsibility for such patients is divided among state, county, and voluntary agencies. Mental health professionals can help to coordinate community facilities and evaluate both the need for care and the agencies' ability and willingness to meet the community's identified mental health needs. By initiating joint planning on the part of hospitals, public health facilities, welfare agencies, and voluntary agencies, mental health professionals can make efficient the now-fragmented mental health service system, much to the benefit of the chronically mentally ill.

Equally important, mental health professionals must identify vulnerable persons and facilitate their entry into treatment before they develop an illness that overwhelms both the family and the patient. To this end, it is necessary to develop new resources, organize natural support networks, and establish linkages and networks between people and resources. It is also necessary to help patients overcome their resistance to utilizing these resources.

Until the mid-1950s, treatment of schizophrenia was primarily custodial. Patients were warehoused for long periods of time in environments that were both unstimulating and hopeless. The disorder and the hospital environment often interacted to bring about behavior that required physical restraint.

There are as many approaches to treating schizophrenic behavior as there are theories of its etiology. Nearly any form of therapy that one could imagine has been tried, sometimes to the dismay of the schizophrenic individuals being treated. Numerous biological forms of therapy have been used, including electroconvulsive shock, insulin shock, psychosurgery, numerous types of chemotherapy, massive doses of vitamins (orthomolecular therapy), brain pacemakers, and kidney dialysis. Psychologically oriented approaches to therapy have included many types of individual, family, and group therapy from various theoretical orientations. Institutional approaches for dealing with schizophrenia have involved standard hospital care, milieu therapy, token economies, and halfway houses. The most recent endeavors have taken place in

community-based mental health centers which use a variety of therapeutic interventions to keep and treat the individuals in their own
communities.

Since schizophrenics are so commonly treated with drugs, it is
difficult to find research on drug-free individuals who receive only
psychological treatment (May 1975). Nevertheless, there are some
general findings that are relatively consistent for the different
forms of psychological therapy.

The treatment of schizophrenia depends on the stage of the disorder, the depth of the regression, the grasp on reality that remains,
and the patient's desire for therapy and ability to establish a relationship with the therapist. It is necessary from the outset to help
these patients move from their regressed state to a more integrated
level of functioning.

1. First and foremost, establish a positive therapeutic alliance with
the patient.

In the case of Carrie, mentioned in Chapter 9, although her orientation to person, place, and time appeared appropriate, her ca-
thexis to reality was quite tenuous. Attending weekly sessions and
talking at great length about her feelings and her past was not a sign
of her motivation to help herself. In fact, the therapist could easily
have assumed that her life outside the sessions was going quite well,
since Carrie hardly ever mentioned it. However, frequent complaints from her counselors and roommates led the therapist to explore with her the reality of her life as she lived it outside the therapist's office. It then became clear that a hornet's nest of turmoil and
problems in daily living existed for her.

Frequent bouts of hysterical crying with her counselors at the
transitional-living quarters occurred daily, often with the client
blaming her roommates for their lack of cooperation and hostility.
She avoided caring for her room, cooking, and shopping for food.
When she was confronted with this, she would temporarily conform and then feel entitled to eat her roommate's food without asking permission. Beneath the superficial surface of the conforming,
compliant patient was an angry, negativistic, rebellious woman

who felt entitled to be cared for by others and who was bent on coercing others to provide this care. Her attendance at weekly therapy sessions was not a sign of motivation; instead, it was a defense against revealing her feelings about what was happening and her adamant resistance to change.

Carrie viewed the therapist's attempt to establish a caring, supportive relationship with her as a hostile, exploitative act, no doubt a collusion on the part of the therapist and counselors to judge her efforts at cooperating with her roommates inadequate. She experienced the therapist's gentle inquiries into the events of her life as a hostile effort to deprive her of her right to lead her own life. The therapist's attempts to clarify the reality of the situation often led to Carrie's ruminating about her problems and bemoaning her fate as a hopeless, unwanted patient. It was therefore very important for the therapist to help Carrie distinguish between her own feelings and those of the therapist.

2. Identify the hidden thoughts that evoke the client's emotional responses.

Treatment of schizophrenics requires considerable patience and constant awareness of and reasonable response to their feelings. The client's emotional responses are appropriate to his inner experience, which he may successfully hide from the therapist. Schizophrenic clients tend to exhibit low frustration tolerance, suspiciousness of the therapist's motives, and projection onto the therapist of their own prejudices and fears.

After several sessions with her male therapist, Carrie asked her therapist if he had noticed that she sat with her legs crossed. When the therapist did not reply affirmatively, she stated that she did this because she did not want him to enter her through her vagina, which she knew was what he wanted to do. Interpretation of the desire for sexual fusion does not appear to be indicated for this client; instead, recognition of her anxiety and positive reinforcement of her desire for a firmer sense of self and clearer ego boundaries were more appropriate interventions.

Since these clients feel incapable of dealing with real life, they may resent the therapist's intrusion into their fantasy lives of withdrawal and safety from a turbulent existence. Although they are aware that the therapist's goal is to return them to the real world, this prospect holds untold terrors for them. Often, this anxiety may provoke a temporary regression that interrupts therapy. These clients may also erupt with hostile or violent reactions when they feel that their retreat is being threatened by the efficacy of treatment.

Fromm-Reichman (1959) explained that the therapist must be engaged in an ongoing sympathetic and understanding relationship with the schizophrenic client; intellectual comprehension of the illness is secondary. Wolberg (1954) emphasized that the therapist must continuously analyze his own reactions because his sense of frustration may arouse the client's aggression and interfere with treatment. Wolberg cautioned that the therapist must provide unlimited warmth, understanding, protection, and assistance.

Carrie was often troublesome, frustrating, belligerent, and overwhelming in her demands for instant attention and understanding. However, it was important for the therapist to guard against careless and impulsive expression of frustration. Instead, a reasonable and measured reaction to the client's confusion and poor reality testing often enabled her to become more reasonable and self-contained.

"The chief emphasis in treatment must be on the creation of a human relationship with the patient that has pleasure value for him. Only by this means will he relinquish the safety and gratification of regression and, utilizing the therapist as a bridge, return to reality" (Wolberg 1954, p. 63). In Carrie's dreams, a benevolent, bearded male figure (which were the physical characteristics of her therapist) appeared to carry her to a peaceful land. This dream occurred well before Carrie could express any pleasure or trust in her male therapist, who was, she felt, only out to use her.

Since the ego of schizophrenic clients is very immature, their reactions to people are unstable and ambivalent. Carrie often felt rejected and frustrated for insufficient reasons; her concept of reality was distorted and unreliable, so that her inner mental processes were often confused with external reality. Such patients may react with hostility if the therapist does not grant what they wish. On several occasions when Carrie was involved in group treatment with another therapist, she would storm out of the room spewing vulgar accusations if the group did not pay immediate attention to her demands or complaints.

3. Pay attention to clients' strange gestures; they constitute important nonverbal communications.

The schizophrenic client may choose to remain silent throughout the treatment hour. When the client finally feels safe and trusting enough to communicate with the therapist, however, he will often reveal all that was absorbed during the silence. It is helpful to remember that symptoms express the patient's feelings.

The first step in resolving schizophrenic symptoms, then, is to establish emotional contact with the client. Making an accurate interpretation or spontaneous clarification of what the client is communicating may make him feel secure enough to relinquish some of his psychotic manifestations.

Identifying the major difficulties in coping with each developmental task are of critical importance to the therapist, whose task is to strengthen the client's capacity to deal with the exigencies of the environment. Clarifying the client's problem and identifying stressors related to certain events in the life cycle are of essential value in treatment. The first manifestation of Carrie's problems appeared while she was away at school. Subsequent attempts to gain independence were often acted out by stopping her medication, running away from treatment, and returning to the school where her problems first occurred in an attempt to recapture the freedom from anxiety she had felt as a student.

Individual Psychotherapy

In order to treat the schizophrenic client, the psychoanalytically oriented therapist often has to combine the principles of psychoanalysis with principles from other schools of thought, such as the behaviorist's emphasis on reinforcement and the humanist's concern for personal autonomy. In treating the schizophrenic, psychodynamically oriented therapists proceed in many respects as they would with a neurotic. With the schizophrenic, however, much more attention is given to creating a warm, nurturant therapeutic relationship (Arieti 1974b). Through this relationship and through analysis of the transference, the therapist aims to heal the psychic wounds left over from childhood and to reorient the schizophrenic toward interpersonal relationships. In short, the therapist becomes a sort of second parent, providing the sympathy, support, and esteem that the patient needs in order to rediscover the sources of value and pleasure in himself and others.

Individual psychodynamic psychotherapy has not been found effective in treating schizophrenia, however (Feinsilver and Gunderson 1972, May 1975). There are few well-controlled studies of psychotherapy with schizophrenics (Feinsilver and Gunderson 1972); in general, the results have not been impressive and suggest that psychodynamically oriented psychotherapy adds very little to pharmacotherapy and hospital care.

Special countertransference issues arise in therapy with schizophrenics. Most notably, the basic dependency needs of the schizophrenic client have not been adequately gratified; hence the severity of the symptoms. If the therapist can gratify the patient's needs in a practical and realistic way, however, the results can be surprisingly positive.

Generally, patients suffering from severe forms of schizophrenia benefit most from learning basic trust and self-acceptance through the therapeutic alliance. The schizophrenic client fears experiencing warm and positive feelings, which, in any case, are sporadic. The therapist should utilize her own optimistic and encouraging approach to generate an affective relationship with the patient.

While the schizophrenic has a fear of becoming close, there is also a wish to become a part of others in order to make himself feel whole. Establishing and maintaining emotional support is of utmost importance in the therapeutic relationship. It is only when the schizophrenic client is able to have a satisfying experience with someone who does not encompass and overwhelm him that he can begin to trust in and benefit from the relationship.

If the patient is listless and withdrawn, the therapist should attempt to stimulate his interest in the environment. The patient's withdrawal is an attempt to deal with frustration and hopelessness, and he needs great encouragement to give up his coping mechanism. While often ambivalent about giving up his isolation and social withdrawal and attempting to cope with life, the schizophrenic also wishes that someone would care enough about him to help him do so. Withdrawal is also a way to prevent rejection, and the schizophrenic client may make it clear that he will accept pleasant experiences only on his own terms. The therapist should then accept the client's limitations while providing consistent interest. It is of great importance to follow the client's lead in maintaining an emotional distance with which he feels comfortable.

Even though schizophrenic clients are often preoccupied with fantasy material, it is best to postpone direct exploration of this material until they are better integrated. At the same time, MacKinnon (1969) suggests that therapists pay close attention to their own responses to the schizophrenic client's distorted thinking. If the therapist cannot understand the client, the therapist might say that she is having difficulty following what the client is saying. In this way, the therapist can both ascertain whether the client is able to present material in another way and learn what the client wishes to communicate. The schizophrenic client also needs the therapist's active assistance in defining problems and focusing on issues. The therapist should direct attention to the client's strengths (while not discounting problems), thereby furnishing positive feedback. Any bit of progress is very significant to these clients, so the therapist should be sure to acknowledge each one.

There is agreement that rage commonly underlies the schizophrenic client's inhibition. Schizophrenics withdraw from contact with the world for fear that if they expressed themselves, they might lose control of their aggressive, destructive impulses.

Family Therapy

A variety of techniques have been used to alter interactions in the families of schizophrenic individuals. Although it seems that family therapy would be useful because of the potential involvement of the family in the schizophrenic's behavior, relatively few adequate studies have examined this issue. In their review of recent types of family interventions, Massie and Beels (1972) concluded that even though some poorly designed studies indicate the potential effectiveness of family therapy, there remains a clear need for systematic evaluation.

Among the most interesting of the uncontrolled studies in this area is the one reported by Jackson and Weakland (1961). After periods of 3 to 41 months in treatment, 6 out of 7 hospitalized patient-members of treated families had returned to the community, and a comparable proportion of outpatients had also significantly benefited in terms of similar criteria. These authors also reported the significant deterioration of some nonpatient members of the treated families, an observation that contributed to the idea of family homeostasis. Among the more controlled studies of family intervention is that of Ro-Trock and co-workers (1977), in which individual and family therapies were competitively compared. The outcome measures were complex and difficult to interpret, but on the important dimension of rehospitalization, family therapy was the winner by a substantial margin. It is obvious that family therapy is difficult to research on many dimensions, among them that of isolating what is therapeutic, what is neutral, and what is destructive.

Family therapy with schizophrenics focuses on correcting family role relationships and skewed and schismatic family patterns. A popular treatment approach, it usually involves patient, parents, and/or spouses. Other relatives central in the patient's life may also be included. Family therapy can help family members better understand each other's point of view. This can modify a family's attitude and behavior, which may be related to the development and maintenance of the patient's illness.

It is probable that the failure of parents to preserve appropriate age and sex boundaries between family members plays a role in the etiology of schizophrenia. Sometimes the parent turns to a child rather than the spouse to gratify emotional needs. Or, children are obliged to assume the parenting role. In some families, communication is disordered. Since researchers have produced the strongest and most consistent evidence for links between patterns of maladaptive family interaction and schizophrenia, it is essential that both individual and family therapy be employed in the treatment of adolescents and young adults who are schizophrenic.

Lidz (1973) suggested that family pathology is often extensive and forms a pathogenic environment for the patient. Therefore, it is usually unwise for the patient to return to his environment. Although making alternate living arrangements usually requires considerable work with the parents and the patient, the outcome of treatment may depend on taking this step. The mental health professional working with schizophrenic clients should consider family therapy.

Family therapy was initiated early in the initial hospitalization of the Z. case. Mr. and Mrs. Z. both acknowledged a wish to work on their difficulties, as they had a long history of marital conflict. They needed help in dealing with their feelings of rage and guilt in relation to their daughter and her psychiatric illness. They insisted that they wanted her to function on an adult, responsible level and live apart from them; it was obvious, however, that her illness played a significant role in keeping them together. Both parents experienced frustration, disappointment, and a lack of support in not having their needs met by one another. With difficulty, they made efforts to change their interactions with Carrie so as not to infantilize her and to support differentiation and autonomous functioning.

Family sessions were held at one point in the treatment with the patient's individual hospital therapist, the parents, the client, and her sister. It emerged that dependency was of concern to all members, as was the patient's illness and its impact on family interactions. These issues particularly concerned the parents, who devoted a great deal of energy to being with the patient and trying to help her, to the exclusion or minimization of interaction with other family members or friends. They needed help in dealing with their own fears around the unpredictability of their daughter's responses. The opportunity to deal with one another directly helped to diminish distortions.

It was important for family members to see that, in the course of a session, Carrie could move from a depressed, angry position to one in which she was composed and able to express herself clearly and with relevance. They began to trust that dealing directly with each other could enhance feelings of hopefulness and diminish their collective sense of helplessness, inadequacy, and incompetence.

Despite this gain, Mr. Z. withdrew from sessions in the autumn of his daughter's hospitalization, leaving the client and her mother in joint sessions. His absence was ostensibly related to work pressures, but his withdrawal came at a time when there was a beginning shift in family functioning as members took greater responsibility for themselves as separate individuals and began to move away from a hypervigilant response to Carrie. The father's behavior also resembled Carrie's first withdrawal and unavailability to the family when they had experienced financial difficulties. It was at that time that Carrie first felt that she was no longer special to her father. Thus, the semblance of family cooperation and strength soon evaporated into mistrust and turbulent anger.

Mr. Z. was concerned that confronting their marriage of accommodation would create stress for him and his wife. He was not prepared to deal openly with his extramarital relationship. Both Mr. and Mrs. Z. expressed a desire to maintain the avoidance pattern of dealing with their difficulties, recognizing that they would remain in a superficially caring relationship. It was agreed that each needed time for self-reflection before resuming joint treatment. Family therapy was then modified to focus on discharge planning and on the sibling relationship. Carrie and her sister found it difficult to examine their relationship because of long-standing hurt, anger, and defensiveness, which characterized the entire family system. By the time of Carrie's discharge, Mr. and Mrs. Z. were able to express disappointment over the daughter's slow progress, but they had developed more realistic expectations and were less critical. Carrie was able to tolerate other family member's feelings about her without becoming defensive.

Carrie retained her wish to be pseudoindependent and autonomous, and she had had great difficulty accepting help from a hospital program that she felt stigmatized her. She also had minimal ability to adapt to separations and transitions; despite numerous hospitalizations, she had not been in any sustained treatment. She attempted to impress her therapists with abstractions and intellectualizations, presenting herself as a passive-aggressive individual who resented the dependent patient role. She was indecisive and lacked insight. At times loose and tangential, she could organize her thoughts and remain goal oriented when asked to do so.

Carrie sensed her parents' disappointment and embarrassment about their pathetic, strange child who was so obviously ill. As the youngest of several females, she was forced to compete for her father's attentions by being "cute, seductive, and smart." Failure was not tolerated in this materialistic, success-oriented family, whose central concern was with the community's evaluation of them. Mr. and Mrs. Z. indeed offered scant nurturance or support. Mr. Z. was seductive and superficial, while Mrs. Z. was hysterical and labile. The patient's tendency to fall apart and become overwhelmed by small setbacks resembled the mother's behavior.

Group Therapy

Group therapy is widely used in the treatment of schizophrenics, especially following discharge from hospitals. More research is needed, but a number of studies have found posthospital group therapy to be somewhat effective (May 1975). In general, the research comparing group and individual therapy has found group therapy to be more effective. For example, O'Brien and colleagues (1972) found that after 2 years, 40 percent of individual therapy patients had to be rehospitalized, but only 24 percent of group patients had to return to the hosptial. The efficacy of group therapy is not surprising, since group-oriented programs "force" a certain amount of social interaction and may thereby prevent social isolation common among schizophrenics.

In our experience in an outpatient setting, group modality, in conjunction with individual therapy and chemotherapy, is extremely effective in preventing further regressive behavior and rehospitalization. Clients were referred by their individual therapists for screening by the group therapist. Criteria were established for participation in the group. These criteria included: the absence of severely interfering hallucinations or delusions, the absense of extreme paranoid trends that could be disruptive to the group, and willingness to participate in group activities.

The group initially focused on "safe topics": daily routine, preparation for holidays and the attendant increased contact with family members, and the discussion of psychotropic medication. Later, these "veterans of multiple hospitalizations" would recount their "battle experiences." The group established its own norms about the need for medication, increasing the probability that members would be medication compliant.

As the group became more cohesive and less deferential to the group leader, the members began to explore painful feelings around setting lower standards of functioning for themselves, "losing the dream" of finally getting well, and modifying their unrealistic ambitions and wishes. Finally, the group discussed adjusting to the prospect of limited achievement and the possibilities of feeling comfortable with their limitations. The group developed its own climate of support and nurturance and provided its own parenting and problem solving to help members through interpersonal conflicts.

The group members socialized with each other after group sessions, and planned and supported each other in attending community events that would have paralyzed them if they were to have attended on their own. Members who dropped out of the ongoing two-year group were more apt to discontinue their medication, become socially isolated, regress, and, finally, require rehospitalization.

Several conclusions regarding group therapy for schizophrenics were also noted in O'Brien's (1975) review.

1. Group therapy may be advantageous for schizophrenic outpatients.
2. Group therapy is less effective and may be detrimental for acutely psychotic clients.
3. For withdrawn schizophrenics, the therapist's primary task is to promote social interaction among group members.
4. Group therapy can be effectively combined with other treatment modalities.

Thus, the primary aim of group psychotherapy is to facilitate the patient's awareness into personal and interpersonal problems and to provide a supportive environment in which patients can develop appropriate social skills. Group treatment helps schizophrenic clients develop social skills and establish supportive friendships.

Social-Learning Therapy

The utility of therapeutic efforts based on learning-theory principles has been demonstrated in a number of large studies (O'Leary and Wilson 1975). Rather than trying to change the whole schizophrenic syndrome, social-learning techniques usually focus on target behaviors that are interfering with the client's functioning. Various techniques have been successfully used to increase appropriate behaviors and to improve interpersonal skills (Hersen and Bellak 1976). Other interventions have been successful in eliminating or decreasing inappropriate behaviors such as delusional speech, reported hallucinations, mutism, bizarre verbalizations, destructiveness, noncompliance, and apathy (Liberman et al. 1974).

Individually tailored behavior therapy involves considerable therapist-time costs. Thus, the more comprehensive behavioral treatment programs are usually established in institutional settings, where many problem behaviors can be treated simultaneously. This has been found to be more feasible and effective and less expensive than standard hospital care.

Many of these programs systematically build in reinforcement contingencies that will teach new adaptive skills, rather than merely provide custodial care. Such programs are often termed *token economies* (Atthowe and Krasner 1968, Ayllon and Azrin 1965). The basic components of a token economy include the following:

1. Delineation of the adaptive behaviors that are to be reinforced.
2. Specification of a number of back-up reinforcers that clients can work for. (These reinforcers might include either tangible items, such as food or cigarettes, or privileges, such as going on a pass, watching a movie, or extra television time.)
3. A specific medium of exchange (that is, the actual tokens — perhaps poker chips or paper money) which would be used like "real money" to purchase the available reinforcers.
4. A set of exchange rules which indicate how many tokens each reinforcer will cost.

The token economy is structured so that the behaviors to be learned will be reinforced with tokens that can in turn be spent in any way the client wishes. Behaviors that are considered maladaptive might be "fined" in order to extinguish them. When a hospital discharge is a possibility, it is often assumed that a long-term client will have to first learn how to function in the hospital's artifical token economy in order to function successfully within the monetary system of our society.

One of the most impressive studies comparing comprehensive token economy methods with other procedures was carried out by Paul and Lentz (1977). The results of this complex and important study have important implications for the treatment of chronic psychiatric clients. In this project, which took over six years to complete, Paul and Lentz compared two psychological approaches to standard hospital care — a social-learning program which included a token economy and a milieu therapy program. Milieu therapy attempts to incorporate all staff members and clients into a total therapeutic community. The two methods shared similar comprehensive objectives, which included the following:

1. resocialization (teaching self-care, interpersonal, and communication skills)
2. teaching vocational and housekeeping skills
3. reduction in bizarre behavior
4. provision of aftercare support in the community

The milieu training program emphasized communication of expectations, group support and cohesiveness, group pressure, and group problem-solving efforts. This was consistent with most milieu approaches, which generally maintain a democratic philosophy in which the client is more of an equal participant than a dependent patient.

The social-learning program used a token economy with a heavy emphasis on reinforcement for appropriate behavior, modeling of correct behavior, extinction of undesirable behavior, and skills-training groups. The standard hospital program was primarily a maintenance program, providing physical care, medications, and routine patient activities.

The subjects included in this study were the most severely disturbed schizophrenics with the least chance of recovery—they had been hospitalized for an average of over 14 years. The findings indicated that although both psychological programs were more effective than standard care on most measures of treatment success, the social-learning approach was consistently the most effective method. Probably the most impressive finding was that over 90 percent of the released social-learning patients were able to remain continuously in the community in some type of treatment setting through the final 18-month follow-up evaluation.

Community-Based Programs

Over the past 20 years, there has been a steady decline in the number of schizophrenic persons treated in residential psychiatric institutions and a decline in the average stay in such facilities. These declines have come about for four basic reasons: the advent of major tranquilizers; the belief, generally based on fact, that psychiatric hospitals are a bad place for anyone to live; the belief that clients can be more appropriately and effectively treated in their own communities; and perhaps most importantly the fact that outpatient treatment facilities are simply less expensive than long-term inpatient treatment care. Collectively, this movement has been referred to as *deinstitutionalization*. Since the 1960s, therefore, federal and local governments have funded two kinds of community facilities: community mental health centers, designed to provide local treatment, and half-way houses or group homes, designed to ease the transition from psychiatric hospitals back to the community.

Psychiatric hospitals, or psychiatric units of general hospitals, provide a temporary protective environment in which the client can be helped through the initial period of acute disturbance. He can then be transferred to an outpatient community facility. However, long-term hospitalization may offer the best therapeutic results in some cases and should be available as a referral source.

After clients emerge from the initial crisis, they need help adjusting to life in the community. Occupational therapy, vocational counseling, job training, art therapy, and social clubs are appropriate supportive services. Community-centered treatment of schizophrenic clients can provide them with the social and vocational skills they need to lead productive and meaningful lives outside the hospital.

Chemotherapy

Before this section ends, a word must be said about the various antipsychotic drugs that are prescribed to modify the effects of the supposed biological abnormalities that have been discussed in this chapter. Lehmann (1974) lists three principal uses of these drugs: (1) to bring the client out of an acute schizophrenic crisis; (2) to facilitate management and control of clients; and (3) to prevent the recurrence of schizophrenic symptoms. That chemotherapy makes it possible to realize these goals in a large number of cases is beyond dispute. The question that remains, however, is whether such effects are due to the chemicals themselves or to the expectations of the clients and the staff.

The drug *chlorpromazine* (Thorazine) revolutionized the treatment of schizophrenia. In 1955, there were about 560,000 patients in American psychiatric hospitals, and 1 out of every 2 hospital beds was devoted to psychiatric care. It was then estimated that by 1971, some 750,000 beds would be required to care for the growing psychiatric population. In fact, there were only 308,000 patients in psychiatric hospitals in 1971, less than half the projected estimate, and about 40 percent fewer than were hospitalized in 1955. By 1977, the patient census had declined to less than 160,000. Such is the power of major tranquilizers.

Of the major tranquilizers, chlorpromazine (Thorazine) and haloperidol (Haldol) are two of the most commonly used. Their most striking effect is the degree to which they "tranquilize," make peaceful, even sedate. Could it be that these drugs are no different from barbiturates, whose sedative action produces no greater improvements for schizophrenics than placebo? Some evidence suggests that this is not the case (Klein 1968). The major psychotropic medications including phenothiazines, chlorpromazines and haloperidol seem to have specific ameliorating effects on schizophrenic symptoms, beyond their sedative effects and even beyond their impact on anxiety. Thought disorder, hallucinations, flattened affect, and withdrawal—all of these are affected by these drugs. Equally important, these drugs have virtually no effect on psychiatric symptoms that are not associated with schizophrenia (Casey et al. 1960, Klein 1968). Subjective emotional experiences, such as guilt and depression, continue unabated despite a course of drug treatment.

Just how the phenothiazines achieve their effects on schizophrenic symptoms is not yet clear. Nevertheless, the average hospital stay for a schizophrenic client has declined to fewer than 13 days, whereas it formerly was months, years, even a lifetime. Phenothiazines have, nearly single-handedly, been responsible for a revolution in psychiatric care.

Unfortunately, the antipsychotic drugs have a variety of unpleasant side effects that often lead clients to discontinue using them. Side effects of chlorpromazine, for example, frequently include dryness of the mouth and throat, drowsiness, visual disturbances, weight gain or loss, menstrual disturbances, constipation, and depression. For most patients these are relatively minor problems; for others, however, they are annoying enough to induce them to discontinue medications after discharge.

One class of more serious side effects, called extrapyramidal, or Parkinson-like, effects, appears to arise because, as previously noted, antipsychotic medications affect the dopamine receptors, which are implicated in Parkinson's disease. These drugs do not cause Parkinson's disease, but they do induce analogous symptoms, including stiffness of muscles and consequent difficulty moving; freezing of facial muscles, which results in a glum or sour look as well as an inability to smile; tremors of the extremities as well as spasms of limbs and body; and akathesia, a peculiar "itchiness" in the muscles which results in an inability to sit still and an urge to pace continuously and energetically (Snyder 1974). Other drugs can control these side effects, but no phenothiazine has yet been produced which avoids them.

Even more serious is the neurological disorder called *tardive dyskinesia.* Its symptoms consist of sucking, lip-smacking, and vermicular tongue movements. Tardive dyskinesia is not reversible. Conservative estimates are that it affects 18 percent of hospitalized schizophrenics, and the figure rises with clients' age and length of time on antipsychotic medication (Klein 1968).

In sum, schizophrenia can at this time be neither prevented nor cured. Nevertheless, substantial numbers of clients recover sufficiently to lead rewarding and functional lives in the community. Schizophrenics are treatable by a combination of medication, therapy, and other modalities. However, it is critical to identify the person in psychological trouble before personality change, withdrawal, and interpersonal difficulties become pronounced. Effective treatment cannot be provided if necessary resources do not exist or remain underutilized by various social and ethnic groups. Mental health professionals have an invaluable role to play in comprehensive treatment of the schizophrenic client.

WHEN DO YOU REFER THE CLIENT?

1. Schizophrenic clients should be referred if they are showing increased signs of psychotic defenses such as hallucinations or delusions or anxiety despite the therapist's efforts to help them contain it. Schizophrenic clients should be referred to a psychiatrist if their medication is ineffective. They need psychiatric evaluation in order to determine whether increasing the dosage of the present medication or changing the medication is advisable. Schizophrenic clients should also be referred if, along with the anxiety, the initial symptoms of the illness reappear.

2. If, despite every effort to help the client, he is unable to reality test or to control destructive impulses, then a psychiatric emergency exists. The client's judgment is impaired. Immersion in his delusional system adds to his feeling of being out of control. Most state hospitals and general hospitals have psychiatric emergency units in which the client's need for hospitalization can be evaluated. Alternatively, an attempt to tranquilize the client can be made in the emergency unit.

3. Referral to a day hospital is appropriate if the family environment seems to exacerbate the client's symptoms.
4. For clients who are able to return to their stable functioning, vocational evaluation and socialization groups are necessary referrals. At this point in treatment, the client will need additional stimulation and positive reinforcement in order to remain actively engaged in the external social environment. Many mental health centers and hospital outpatient departments provide groups for previously hospitalized clients where friendships can be formed, social skills can be practiced, and feelings can be shared. A transitional-living referral may be necessary in order to remove the client from the isolated, dependency-inducing environment of the psychiatric hospital.
5. If the therapist should become the personification of the bad parent to the client, the malevolent force in the client's life, then termination of treatment or referral to another therapist is necessary. This decision can be discussed with the client and, if appropriate, the family, and it can be explained that continuation of treatment under this circumstance would be unproductive and perhaps dangerous. It should be noted that some degree of transference to the therapist as the malevolent parent can be helpful for working through the client's negative attitudes about herself, but a therapeutic alliance needs to be formed if this is to occur. The client would then be able to recognize that her reactions and feelings are being induced by the treatment process and that she is not just a victim of the therapist's neglect, abuse, or evil intent.

Chapter 11

The Three Phases of Treatment

THE BEGINNING PHASE

This chapter illustrates many of the points made in previous chapters. Treatment strategies and basic psychotherapeutic techniques and issues are explored through the three phases of treatment:

1. Listen actively.

Active listening refers to intense focus on the client, hearing what the client is saying rather than thinking about treatment strategies, plans, diagnoses, and psychodynamics. Inattentiveness will be picked up by clients and experienced as evidence of lack of caring, a rejection, or devaluation. Active listening refers to continuous attention; it is not passive. It is an active process of listening without making judgments or becoming defensive about what the client is saying.

Try to picture what the client is feeling or is anxious about. Imagine a scenario of your own that relates to what the client is saying. Focus at all times on the client's verbal and nonverbal cues. Before beginning each session, tune out personal issues and tune in to the client. Maintain a blank screen that will receive what the client places on it.

2. Check out ambiguous messages. Help clients to articulate their problems.

Explore the client's ambiguous messages. Use of statements or questions like "I'm not clear on that," or "Could you elaborate?" not only evoke clarification, but also serve to assure the client of your interest. Trying to fully understand another human being is both exhilarating and frightening. You can expand your understanding of how the client feels by placing yourself in the client's situation.

It is sometimes frightening to be that close to the client's feelings; you may also feel overwhelmed and anxious about having your ego boundaries crossed. For therapists who are secure about their identity and boundaries, temporarily experiencing another person's view of reality is like taking a trip into another world that is perhaps not as orderly or consistent or stable. In your efforts to seek a clear understanding of the client's perceptions and situation, it is important not to read clarity into frightening, dissociating, or fragmented aspects of the client's life.

When clients appear for the first session, they are usually anxious and often do not know what to expect. They may articulate confusing half thoughts. If you are uncertain at all about what the client is really saying, use clarifying questions like "Do you mean . . ?" Other useful techniques include questioning, paraphrasing, and interpreting. If you can help clients see that their stories have certain human and understandable aspects despite their anger and fear, then the recounting becomes rewarding in itself. Too much questioning and intruding into the client's self-account can disturb a growing sense of autonomy and mastery, however. You will then be directing and controlling the client in a way that probably diminishes *your* anxiety rather than the client's.

3. Take into account racial, subcultural, religious, socioeconomic, age, and language factors.

Although opinions differ with regard to this principle, it is often best to match therapist with client in a like-to-like manner; that is, treatment may be facilitated if the therapist has had experiences similar to those of the client. This is not always possible, however. It is therefore important for the mental health professional to be aware of certain statements, preferences, emotions, or behaviors that might be racially, culturally, or religiously based so that the client's problem can be viewed in a more objective manner. Minority-group clients, particularly of those of low socioeconomic standing, are oriented more toward symptom relief and situational change than they are toward understanding their own psychodynamics.

Be aware of the status differential between yourself and the client. At the least, you represent an authority figure to the client. Minimize some of the differences so that the client can relax and be comfortable.

Speak on the client's level. Use language that the client understands and is comfortable with. This is not to say that you should use incorrect or inappropriate language. But omit the professional diagnoses and jargon. It can intimidate, separate you from the client, and create further feelings of loss of control on the client's part. Use appropriate language in an easy-to-understand way. You will be a more effective therapist if you focus on the human bond between you and the client and on the fact that you can both understand the client's plight. Status differential can create a relationship in which the client feels manipulated. A reciprocal and caring relationship is one in which the understanding and exploration of feelings and problems are understood by both, regardless of who initiates the understanding.

Be conscious of age differences. Use language that is relevant to the age group with which you are dealing. If you are working with a child, for example, use language that a child can understand.

4. Partialize; break the problem down into more manageable parts.

Many clients feel overwhelmed when they begin therapy. This feeling is often the precipitating factor that brings them into the helping situation. One technique to alleviate this feeling of helplessness is to break the problem into manageable parts. For example, the client may report feeling depressed because *everything* has gone wrong. Statements such as, "I understand that you feel that everything has gone wrong with your life," or, "You feel completely helpless, but is there one thing in particular that makes you feel sad or hopeless?" Upon further questioning, the counselor will be able to elicit specifically which things have gone wrong. The all-encompassing feeling of depression is thus broken into smaller concrete issues or situations. Clarifying the purpose of the session often helps, as does clarifying the role of the therapist. For example, "Last time we spoke about your relationship with your children, which you said made you feel ashamed and worthless. Can we pursue that further? Perhaps it would be helpful to see how things got so terribly out of hand."

5. Tune into the client's self-perception and affective state.

This technique is related to active listening and specifically addresses the issue of unconscious needs and empathy. It refers to getting in touch with the client's feelings and responses. For example, "When you are having a panic attack, it feels like the whole world is swallowing you up. You don't seem to be able to think logically and sequentially because the little girl in you is lost and confused. Just keeping your wits about you is often the best you can do."

6. Separate and identify the client's level of response.

Ascertain the client's level of response (perceptual, cognitive, affective, or behavioral) and respond appropriately to that level. For example, if the client is talking about a specific behavior or incident, it would not be necessary for you to express your own feeling and affective state about the incident. Rather allow and elicit the client's feelings. This helps clients see their reactions in perspective and helps them become aware of their own feelings about the situation.

Focus on the client's here-and-now physical and emotional state. Be aware that most of the presenting problems you will hear in the course of your professional career have been shaped by the client's past experiences, but do not dwell on these past occurrences. Focus instead on the client's present emotional state. Is the client crying? Does she seem nervous? It is usually wise to focus on alleviating a problem rather than on the problem's etiology, which the client may be unable to explore or integrate.

7. Examine your own feelings present during the initial phases and understand that these feelings are also present to varying and distorted degrees in the client.

Examine such feelings as apprehensiveness, awkwardness, hope, curiosity, fear, anticipation, anxiety, excitement, inadequacy, confidence, protectiveness, and interest. The client may try to elicit guilt and protectiveness in you so that he can protect his self-image as a helpless, dependent person who is unable to direct and understand his own life.

8. Negotiate a contract.

A contract is a blueprint for your work. It identifies what you are going to work on and the methods you will use, and it gives both therapist and client a sense of direction. The contract is an agreement between therapist and client about what is to happen in therapy. It anchors both individuals by forcing them back to square one if things go awry. The contract can always be renegotiated.

9. Create a productive climate for growth.

Perhaps the most essential and difficult technique, this one incorporates all the others. Create an environment for the client that is accepting, nurturing, empathetic, genuine, and sincere. This therapeutic climate will facilitate psychological growth and positive change. Let the client know that you respect her opinions and feelings and then support them. If the client's previously repressed and disowned feelings and experiences can be explored, understood, and accepted within the therapeutic relationship, then the client can learn self-acceptance. What has been kept from the self can now be understood and accepted by another — the therapist.

CASE DESCRIPTION

Josephine G. is a 37-year-old housewife married to Carmine G., a 42-year-old accountant. They have three sons, ages 15, 13, and 6. Two of the sons, the 13-year-old and the 6-year-old, suffer from thalassemia and sickle cell anemia. Medical testing revealed that the thalassemia gene is carried by the mother and the sickle cell gene by the father. A fourth son died 18 years ago at age 18 months. No autopsy was performed, so the cause of death remains unknown; however, the family's physician believes that, based on the medical record, the boy probably also had the two disorders.

Along with coping on a day-to-day basis with her sons' illnesses (frequent hospital visits, tranfusions for the boys on a weekly basis, frequent bouts of pneumonia and severe pain crises requiring hospitalization), Josephine also suffers from severe panic attacks. Her symptoms include hyperventilation, buzzing and ringing in her ears, heart palpitations, dissociation of feelings, and a sense of impending horror and doom. She has been thoroughly examined by various medical professionals, and they have concluded that her symptoms are psychologically based.

Her relationship with her husband is also of concern to her. She feels that he does not understand the severity of the boys' diseases, nor does he provide her with any nurturance or understanding with regard to her panic attacks. She also believes that Marty, their 15-year-old son, is overly rebellious, continually testing and rejecting authority. The family has recently moved to an upper-class community, which Josephine believes has added to her problems, as she has no friends. Josephine frequently mentions that she would feel better if her mother were still alive because then she would have someone to talk to. She seems to be conforming her life and relationships to previous relationships with which she feels comfortable.

Josephine has been in private therapy for approximately eight years, with three different therapists. Her presenting problem was the panic attacks.

Preengagement

Because the panic attacks were of major concern to Josephine, the therapist planned to work on these first. They were especially frightening to her at night because she would wake up at 3:00 A.M. and be unable to fall back to sleep because she was in such a state of terror. This contributed to her feeling that she was losing her mind.

Carmine G. attended the second session alone. He corroborated Josephine's panic symptoms and much of her definition of the boys' illnesses. On the basis of that session, the therapist felt that they probably held the same perception of the bases of their problems.

During the third session, Josephine was taught Jacobson's deep muscle relaxation techniques. (For a detailed description of one deep muscle relaxation technique, please refer to the end of this chapter.) She was also given a tape describing the procedure to be used along with these exercises. The tape enabled her to pace her own exercises and facilitate relaxation. The physiological basis (Wolpe's theory) for the exercises' effect was explained to her.

Josephine has been able to control her panic attacks since she started practicing the deep muscle relaxation techniques. She still wakes up in the middle of the night; but she puts on the tape, does the exercises, she then goes right back to sleep. Josephine is very pleased with the results but fears that the effects may be short-lived and that at any time she may be unable to control the attacks. Based upon this fear, the therapist believed that it would be useful for Josephine to speak with Leslie S., age 39, who has been free of panic attacks since starting the relaxation exercises three years ago.

The following process is based on Josephine G.'s fifth therapy session, attended by the therapist, Josephine, and Leslie S.

Therapist: Leslie, why don't you explain to Josephine how you felt when you first came to see me 3 years ago.

Leslie: Well, I had been in therapy for about 15 years. I had a lot of problems with my mother as an adolescent, and I hadn't resolved them. It was a situation of constant fighting. I started getting anxiety attacks when I was about 15 years old, but they were very infrequent and sporadic. It was then that I started therapy with a woman therapist in Lindenhurst. We never dealt with the panic attacks specifically. All we ever talked about was my relationship with my mother and father. Over time, the panic attacks started to happen more frequently and started to get more severe. Finally, I decided to change therapists.

I guess I stayed in therapy that long primarily because I didn't know any better. I guess I felt that even though the therapy did not help my panic attacks, it may have helped in other areas. I felt I couldn't go any further with this therapist and decided to quit. Then I got married and remained out of therapy for the next 5 or 6 years. I was still having the panic attacks and they were very debilitating. I felt that I couldn't work or go anywhere alone because they might happen at any time.

Therapist: Leslie, why don't you describe some of the feelings that you used to have when you were having a panic attack.

Leslie: Well, I felt like I couldn't breathe, like my throat was closing up. My heart would start to pound and I thought it would jump out of my chest. I would feel totally out of control of my body. I would feel like I wasn't in me — like I was watching me from some outside place (*Notice here that the client's ego is dissociating the self from her experiences and affect.*) I would feel terrified but I didn't know of what.

Therapist: Josephine, is that the way you feel when you get panic attacks?

Josephine: It's *exactly* what I feel! I can't believe you're saying this. I never met anyone before who has ever had the same thing. I felt like I was going crazy — like I was the only person in the world who could be experiencing these things.

Therapist: Leslie, would you describe to Josephine what happened when you started to do the exercises?

Leslie: Sure. Well, at first I was leary of the whole method. After all, I thought, I was in therapy for a long time and nothing helped me, so why should these exercises? I decided to do them anyway. Once I started doing them, the panic attacks would subside. At first I didn't believe it and would almost test it. In other words, I let the anxiety attack begin to happen, and then do the exercises, almost challenging the anxiety attack to win out over the exercise. But it didn't. I still mistrusted the exercises . . . felt they wouldn't last. (*It was not only the exercises that she mistrusted but also those aspects of herself which could have quelled the anxiety and allowed her to feel good about herself.*) But the exercises did work, and after about 3 months the attacks stopped happening. It was almost like once I knew I could control them, they didn't have to happen, because they were only there if I thought I couldn't control them. I haven't had a panic attack now for over 2½ years.

Impressions

The therapist believed that the session was effective for several reasons:

1. Josephine was able to see and talk with someone who had felt and understood panic attacks, someone who had felt out of control to the point of experiencing herself as outside of her body, an observer in her own experiences.
2. Josephine was able to see that she was not the only person in the world who suffered from panic attacks. She was not the only person who felt helpless and unable to overcome her overwhelming affect and mistrust of her self-control.
3. She was able to see that the attacks could be mastered by practicing the exercises and that they could be controlled or eliminated for long periods of time. She had a chance to speak to a person who had felt removed and detached from her self and now feels so much a part of her life experiences.
4. By returning for another session, Leslie was made aware of her progress and her own contribution to it. She was now completing her bachelor's degree on a part-time basis and working as a full-time secretary. She had not been able to do these things, she believed, while she was having her panic at-

tacks. Leslie also said that she felt good about herself because she believed she had helped Josephine.

Plans

Individual counseling with Josephine should be expanded beyond dealing with her panic attacks. Counseling could focus on the following areas: Josephine has expressed an interest in returning to school for a nursing degree, but she is afraid she will fail. She wants to make new friends, but when faced with opportunity, she rejects it. Her mother has been dead for eight years, yet she still dwells on the negative and detrimental aspects of their relationship. It is as if she has neither purpose nor direction in life without her attachment to her dead mother.

The therapist recommended marriage counseling in addition to Josephine's individual counseling. Although the husband and wife are operating from the same perceptual base, the husband seems to be denying the severity of his children's diseases, saying "So what? Other kids get sick." (It is likely that two of his sons will die by age 30, which does not happen to most other kids!)

It is important for Carmine to become aware of and verbalize his anxiety about his children's impending deaths. Carmine's denial of the severity of their illnesses places the burden of their pain and distress almost exclusively on Josephine's shoulders. Her consequent anger toward him and about their situation needs to be explored further in therapy. Both Josephine and Carmine could benefit from learning communication techniques. They have both indicated that they often play "games" with each other and attack and blame each other. Learning to openly communicate and risk vulnerability with each other would help them to comfort each other in times of crisis. Sexual dysfunction symptoms are also evident: Josephine states that she hates sex; "It feels dead down there." Thus, counseling in the area of sexuality and emotional intimacy is also indicated. Some preparation for the impending death of their sons is needed, in order to facilitate the grieving process. They could be referred to a group for parents who are dealing with similar issues.

In order to deal with the problems of Marty G., the 15-year-old son, family counseling would be helpful.

THE MIDDLE PHASE

1. Tune in to each session.

At the beginning of each session, it is necessary to reestablish where the client is and what he is experiencing. For example, if the client is in a different place than he was during the previous session, you might say, "Last week you had a different opinion on the matter. Have you changed your mind?" In asking such a question, you indicate to the client that (1) you remember what went on during the last session, (2) you have noticed a change, and (3) you are curious about why the change occurred. It may imply that the client needs to reevaluate his opinions and feelings. A statement like, "It must be confusing to have contrasting opinions about what you are going through," would be appropriate.

2. Contract for each session.

It may be necessary to restate the initially established goals during each session. This need not be done formally; rather, it could be just a casual reminder of goals earlier agreed upon by the therapist and the client. The client may decide that, for the time being, working on something else is more important than pursuing the original contract.

3. Elaborate on skills.

Expand on concerns that are articulated within the session and point out the client's options and strengths. With Josephine, for example, you might say, "You don't seem to feel that you can manage your situation without the understanding and help of your husband. You have managed your boys through several crises without his being there for you. It would be more helpful if he were there because then you wouldn't feel so helpless and alone." At some other point in treatment, it would be helpful for her to see that she has options—neighbors, friends, support groups—so that she won't be so dependent and alone. A statement like, "You could take better care of yourself by using such people and help . . . unless it feels more gratifying for you to complain about what your husband is not giving you."

4. Demand work.

This technique is appropriate when the client has not been accomplishing what she said she wanted to accomplish. Such a confrontation can range from gentle prodding to a need to renegotiate a contract.

5. Point out obstacles and dysfunctional patterns of behavior.

It is sometimes necessary during the middle phase of therapy to point out obstacles the client may have set up; "Each one of your boy friends seems to have made you feel bad about yourself. Do you see any pattern that could be causing this to happen?"

6. Share knowledge and skills.

It is sometimes helpful if the therapist offers the client information he has learned from research or the literature. It was useful and comforting for Josephine, for example, to hear about the incidence and symptomatology of panic attacks in women.

Management of Resistance, Transference, and Countertransference

Nelsen (1983) defines resistance as follows: "Resistance has to do with clients holding back, disengaging, or in some way subverting change efforts whether knowingly or not, without open discussion . . . Workers rather than clients must be responsible for noticing resistance and seeking to deal with it" (p. 19). According to Wilsnack

(1983), " . . . it covers any and all of a client's defenses against treatment" (p. 31).

"In order to help the client work through resistance, Hepworth (1983) suggests (1) enhancing the commitment of the client to carry out a specific task, (2) planning the specific details of carrying out the task, (3) analyzing obstacles that may be encountered, (4) modeling and rehearsing the behaviors embodied in carrying out the task, (5) summarizing the plan for the implementation of the task and conveying encouragement along with the expectation that the client will carry out the task" (p. 118).

An example of the use of these principles occurred in sessions with the G. family. After the initial few sessions, Josephine came alone because she felt that the most pressing problem in their lives was her panic attacks. Once her panic attacks were alleviated, Carmine came in for a session, during which he stated that Josephine's panic attacks were *her* problem. It had nothing to do with him, was disruptive to the entire family, and was the basis for all their problems. The therapist suggested that although this might be the case, it would be very helpful if he would be part of the helping process. He was not going to be made the target of the family's problems. He needed to see himself as removed and detached from Josephine's overwhelming anxiety and dread. But he agreed to help and consented to attend future sessions with Josephine.

The therapist thought at this point that his resistance had been handled beautifully. However, the therapist never saw him again! When the therapist called him, he reiterated that Josephine was the one creating all the problems, that he himself had none. He was not experiencing anxiety and accepted the situation as it was. He may also have felt that an alliance existed between the therapist and his wife to challenge his invulnerability. Or, he was unconsciously colluding with Josephine to maintain her as the troubled one, the one stirring up family turmoil. He was probably also frightened by any change that might occur in the family system or in himself.

There is a difference between the way resistance is handled in the beginning phase versus the middle phase. In the beginning phase, it is wise for the therapist to allow the resistance to persist, at least until some sort of a trust has been established between therapist and client. Otherwise, there is the risk of alienating the client. More confrontive techniques can be used in the middle phase, however. Carmine placed the therapist in a double-bind situation; she lost whether she confronted him or not.

As a result of the increasing intensity of the interaction during the later stages of therapy, clients experience a wide range of feelings toward therapists, from admiration and affection to anger and rejection. Some reactions may be provoked by specific aspects of the therapist's personality; however, it is more than likely that *transference* is taking place. Feelings once felt toward a significant person from the past are now projected onto the therapist. For example, a client may see his father symbolically in the therapist, who now has a position of some authority and power, and react to the therapist in a manner similar to his childhood response to his father. By *transference* is meant, "the feelings, wishes, fears, and other defenses of the client deriving from reactions to significant others in the past (parents, siblings, extended family, teachers) that influence his current perceptions of the social worker" (Shulman 1979, p. 76).

Similar feelings may be experienced by the therapist. In the therapist, these feelings are known as *countertransference* feelings. For example, the therapist may see the client as an ungrateful child. A clear definition of countertransference is given by Shulman (1979): *Countertransference* similarly refers to aspects of the social worker's history of feelings, wishes, fears, and so on, all of which influence his perception of the client. Scanlon (1983) defines countertransference as "distorted thoughts, feelings, and attitudes toward the client" (p. 216).

An example of countertransference in the therapy with Josephine G. was the therapist's feelings about the impending death of Josephine's sons. It was very difficult for the therapist to separate out her own feelings in order to assess and evaluate how to help Josephine. (The therapist's child was approximately the same age as one of Josephine's sons.) However, *awareness* was the first step. Initially, then, the therapist needs to have a certain level of *self*-awareness. Once this has been achieved, it will become easier for the therapist to *sort out* feelings.

In order to attain self-awareness, the therapist needs to *examine and reflect* on the issue that is eliciting the particular disturbing emotional response. What responses and emotions are preventing the therapist from assessing the situation objectively? The next step in the process is *objectification.* The problem being presented by the client must be *objectified;* the issue must be devoid of the therapist's distortions of the reality of the client's situation.

In the beginning phase of treatment, lack of awareness may hinder negotiation of a workable contract and the setting of appropriate goals. In the middle phase, countertransference can hinder the therapist's ability to help the client achieve the negotiated goals or create obstacles in renegotiating the contract when the client is either ready to move on or needs to set different goals.

Transference and countertransference are crucial to therapeutic progress. During a middle-phase session with Josephine, the therapist's telephone (which was usually unplugged) began to ring. Since no one answered the telephone, the therapist decided to pick it up quickly and arrange to return the call later. The therapist noticed that Josephine was very angry. Her face was red and her answers were curt and nasty. The therapist asked whether Josephine was angry at something, which launched a tirade about how she couldn't believe that the therapist "could do such a thing." Upon further exploration and questioning, it became clear that Josephine's mother liked to talk on the telephone. Josephine hated this because she was then unable to get her mother's attention. Her reaction was clearly transferential; she had tranferred her anger at her mother's seeming indifference onto the therapist. The therapist, however, was not indifferent to Josephine's plight.

In the initial phases of therapy, both therapist and client are unknown entities to each other. It is difficult at this point for the therapist to distinguish countertransference feelings. Countertransference feelings come from one's past, and are not simply a reaction to the client's present situation; they generally are induced by the client to otain some sort of gratification. Induced feelings can help to clarify the client's unconscious psychodynamics. For example, Josephine's quick reaction to the therapist as being uncaring and indifferent reflected her own unresolved ambivalence toward her mother. Part of her could care for herself and her ill sons without needing a kindly parental figure to support and understand her. The other part would do anything, even become terrified, helpless, and immobilized, in order to get a mother to care for her again. If her sons should die, in spite of how well she had cared for them, who would she have? She would then be abandoned both by her own mother and by the mother in her who could provide for her family. She would be alone, without meaning or purpose.

Critical Analysis of Interventions

Levels of Analysis

A facet of this issue is explored by Perlman (1962): "Cognitive and affective ego functions- thought and feeling affect the executive function-action. And turned about, action affects thought and feeling." In a therapy situation, it is not always clear when it is appropriate to focus on thoughts and feelings or action. The basic initial question for the practitioner is, When does one deal with the specific problem presented and when does one deal with the underlying dynamic? In the case presented here, is Josephine's real issue her anxiety attacks, or are the anxiety attacks a symptom of some underlying conflict? The symptom model tends to complicate things at times. On the other hand, to deal with only the presented problem is sometimes simplistic.

Human behavior is superbly complex. To underestimate its complexity by dealing only with the obvious is to eliminate some of the richness of the human condition. The symptom, then, is not always necessarily the real issue. In Josephine's case, the symptom could be a manifestation of something much more complex. If the presenting problem were solved, another problem might quickly take its place because there is energy here that is being directed negatively. *Negative energy* is defined in this case as behavior that is dysfunctional for the client, behavior that makes the person unhappy. In Josephine's case, then, the verbalized content is almost irrelevant; it would be more useful to focus on enabling Josephine to manifest her negative energy in more positive directions. Thus, as Perlman points out, the "answer" is multifaceted and complex.

Honesty: How Much Should the Therapist Tell the Client?

While all therapists would probably say that they feel it is important to be honest with clients, they might also admit that they are often confused as to which level of analysis is appropriate when offering explanations. Some clients are well versed in psychological jargon and expect the therapist to relate on that level. For other clients, dealing on a concrete level is more comfortable and appropriate. For example, if a client requests information about their diagnosis, it is probably not necessary to go into DSM-III terminology although some more psychologically sophisticated clients may require more in-depth information.

Directive versus Nondirective

Almost all clients may at some point in treatment — while they are in crisis or feeling vulnerable — need to draw on the therapist's ego in order to get through a trying time. At such a time, the client may need the therapist to be directive — sometimes even tough. The client will be operating from a child-like state of emotionality and may need a nurturing parent's reassurance and direction. For example, the therapist might suggest to a client who is paralyzed by depression that she go to the movies. Once the client regains strength, the therapist can draw on the evidence of that strength to help the client nurture even more strength.

TERMINATION

A therapeutic relationship may be terminated in a variety of ways, and therapists must develop techniques to deal with termination. Termination is indicated when the client has progressed as far as he wants to in gaining awareness and changing behavior patterns. Termination may be precipitated by an unexpected development, such as a move out of town or a shift in working hours. When circumstances such as these are out of the client's control, it is important that the client experience *closure* on the relationship, even if he has not accomplished his goals. This is obviously a time when the client and therapist may be somewhat hesitant about terminating because they will not have completed their work together.

Termination is indicated when the presenting problem has been significantly resolved and there are indications that the old behavior patterns are no longer operating to a dysfunctional degree. Or, termination might be indicated when no progress occurs or if a maladaptive behavior is accelerating during the treatment process. In some cases, it may be necessary for the therapist to refer the client to another therapist through termination.

Usually, termination comes when the client feels that he has arrived at a decision, has learned something, or is coping adequately with the presenting problem. Clients may indicate that they do not need the counseling any longer. The therapist must consider the client's reasons for wishing to terminate and assess the appropriateness of the decision. It is not uncommon for a feeling of friendship and goodwill to develop between therapist and client. After developing a meaningful helping relationship, it is difficult to separate suddenly.

Ward (1962) notes two points about termination. First, there is a strong tendency to avoid issues of loss by not acknowledging or dealing with them. This results in the loss of an opportunity to develop a model for productively working with such issues. Second, theorists and educators have primarily emphasized facilitative therapeutic techniques and strategies; they have been less interested in closing the relationship. It is essential that termination be considered a crucial part of the therapeutic process.

Ward notes that the termination stage has three primary functions: (1) to assess the client's readiness to end the counseling process and consolidate learning; (2) to resolve the remaining affective issues and bring the relationship between the client and therapist to a close; and (3) to maximize the client's transfer of learning and increase his self-reliance and confidence in his ability to maintain the changes.

Turner (1978) discusses therapy as a transitional process. Initially the client relinquishes some responsibility but later reclaims it as she proceeds with less tension and anxiety and greater ability to define and fulfill herself. Therefore, if therapy is successful, termination can proceed with the full knowledge that the client is now ready to take on responsibilities and use the gains realized in therapy.

Termination does not preclude future contact with the counselor. It is the closure of a unique interpersonal relationship that may be resumed or applied to real-life interpersonal relationships. Termination in the therapeutic process may be complicated. There may be feelings of ambivalence about it. The client may both desire to leave and yet feel anxious about it. A client may recognize that he is handling a problem adequately and may broach the topic of termination to the therapist. The therapist's exploration of the idea with the client communicates the therapist's confidence in the client. Furthermore, it removes any concern the client may have about the therapist's feelings of rejection.

The client should be asked to summarize what he feels he has accomplished in therapy. Referral may be indicated if the client feels a sense of incompleteness but the therapist wishes to discontinue the relationship. Leaving the opportunity for the client to return if he feels it necessary may make him more comfortable. Follow-up may make the termination less abrupt. Therapists should keep in mind, however, that if the therapeutic stages have proceeded successfully, termination need not be a problem. Termination is an important aspect of therapy, and the process is not limited to the time of discontinuation of the relationship. In each therapy session and series of sessions, there is a need to bring closure to aspects of the client–therapist interaction.

Before termination actually occurs, it sometimes becomes necessary to temporarily discontinue the therapeutic relationship. Seligman (1975) presents a model for helping clients deal with intervals in counseling relationships during which the therapist must be absent. She emphasizes the importance of informing clients in advance so they can anticipate the temporary break in the relationship. She uses four weekly sessions for preparation. In the first session, the client is informed of a trip or vacation and assured that a plan for their continuing growth will be developed and referrals provided if necessary. In the second session, although time is allowed for the client's own issues, more extensive discussion of the client's reactions to the therapist's absence takes place, and an interim plan is presented. Most of the third session is used to generate goals and plans and to discuss the separation. In the fourth session, the client's plans are completed and put into writing, and time is spent processing the client's feelings about the separation.

Seligman's plan includes a written outline of five variables. The client and therapist work together to develop appropriate goals and a plan for achieving them in the period during which they are not meeting. The therapist may recommend that the client continue communicating by writing to the therapist during the separation. Even if a client chooses not to accept a referral to another counselor, he should be given the names of two counselors he could contact if it became necessary. Before the separation period begins, it is appropriate for the therapist and client to assess the client's progress toward established goals. Emphasizing the client's gains can serve to reinforce the client's self-confidence. The remaining task is to establish a date and time for the next appointment, in order to provide a sense of continuity and reassure the client that the therapeutic relationship will resume.

Thus, the steps used to close a series of counseling sessions are somewhat parallel to those used in termination. First some preparatory steps should be taken; the therapist should not wait until the last minute to indicate that the relationship is to be discontinued. The therapist provides, or encourages the client to provide, a summary of their work. Because of the complexity of the relationship, it is often necessary for both client and therapist to be involved in summarizing and clarifying. The counselor must avoid leaving the client in an ambiguous or defenseless position. The counselor must either offer further counseling or be certain that the client can function without assistance.

Appendix

Relaxation Skills

Sit comfortably and close your eyes. Take a moment to note the way in which you have arranged yourself in the chair. Sense the relationship of limbs, torso, and head. Reflect upon the effort quality you are utilizing to maintain this relationship of limbs, torso, and head. The following cues will help you maintain a comfortable posture throughout the session. Focus on the two "sit bones" beneath your buttocks. Bring your weight over these two bones, placing your hips towards the back of the chair. Sense your weight equally distributed over both halves of your body. Allow your spine to rest back into the chair, and your arms and hands to rest either in your lap or on the chair's arms. Place both feet flat on the floor in front of you, with a space between your thighs. Focus on the placement of your head. Do you sense the head falling to one side or the other? Try to imagine the head floating on the tip of the spine so that the top of the skull reaches up and away from the body. This placement will create length at the back of your neck. Remember, you are reaching up and outward through the top of the skull, *not* the chin!

Focus on your breathing. What are you aware of? Are you holding your breath, causing tension in the muscles of your body? Observe the flow of your breath as it passes in and out of your nostrils.
In your mind's eye, watch the in flow and watch the out flow of
your breath. Observe this flow just like a doorman would observe
the number of people passing through a building. Shift your attention from both nostrils to the left nostril and watch the flow of
breath through it. Watch the in flow and watch the out flow. Shift
your attention to the right nostril and watch the flow of breath pass
through it. Watch the in flow and watch the out flow. Bring your attention back to both nostrils and sense the release of tension as you
exhale. If your mind wanders, do not be annoyed. Simply bring
your attention back to the flow of your breath. Allow the breath to
soothe you, to relax you, to calm you. Begin to follow your breath
down your throat, through the chest and diaphragm, and deep into
the pelvis. Place your fingertips lightly over your lower abdomen
and sense the movement of the abdomen against your fingertips. In
the mind's eye, watch this movement. Sense the trunk expanding,
growing, pressing into the fingertips. As you inhale and as you exhale, watch the abdomen shrink and contract from your fingertips.
Allow the breath to massage all your internal organs. Remember,
we are three-dimensional beings. Perceive all your organs, bones,
and muscles three-dimensionally. Note the growing and shrinking
of the trunk on all sides and experience the depth of your trunk. Focus on the distance from navel to spine. Watch your breath fill this
space and, as you exhale, watch your breath leave this space. Relax
your hands from your abdomen. Now, as you inhale, try to imagine
drawing the breath in through your fingertips, up the arms, and
through the trunk and skull. As you exhale, watch the breath travel
down the trunk, through the hips and legs, and finally out your
toetips. Continue to inhale through the fingertips and exhale
through the toetips. Allow the breath to pass through every space
within the body, touching every cell, nerve, and tissue. Let all impu-
rities, all tension leave the body. We will now shift our attention
back to the skeletal-muscular system.

Perceive the head three-dimensionally. Note all sides, all surfaces
of the skull. How clearly is the shape of your skull defined within
your own body image? Focus on the inner spaces of the skull. Note

the distance from ear to ear, from back to front, from top to bottom. Locate and identify any tension within or around the skull. Visualize this tension as a bubble and watch the bubble pop, allowing all the tension to leave your skull. Bring your attention to your face. Identify any unnecessary muscular binding across the forehead, the eyes, the bridge of the nose, the cheeks and jaws, mouth and tongue, and chin and throat. Slowly, open and close the lower jaw. Repeat this motion several times. Sense the tension leaving your face. When you close your mouth, allow the lips to touch slightly, teeth apart. Sense the head floating on the tip of the spine, freeing the neck's musculature. See the tension in the neck and then see it relax. Watch the tension bubbles pop. Bring your attention to the shoulder girth. Note the top, sides, front, and back of the shoulders. Allow the shoulders to hang naturally. Allow the muscles supporting the shoulders to be limp, heavy. Focus on the back surface of your body. Define the width of your trunk across the shoulders and hips. Note the length of your spine from one end to the other. Take some time to explore the back surface of your body. Identify any tension and then watch the tension relax. Feel your muscles become limp as the tension bubbles within your back pop, freeing the flow of your energy. Pay particular attention to the space between your shoulder blades and at the small of your back. Come down to your hips. Watch your hips melt into the chair as the muscles of your buttocks become limp. Travel over your pelvic arches. Stop at your abdomen. Relax the abdomen and feel the muscles expand. See your breath swell from within. Again, sense the depth of your trunk as you free your energy flow. Travel around the ribcage. Focus on the chest. See any tension in the muscles of the chest and watch your tension bubbles pop. Draw your attention inward behind your sternum. Listen to the beat of your heart. As you listen to the rhythm of your heart, watch a pendulum swing easily from side to side. Bring the rhythm of your heart and the motion of the pendulum into synchrony. Allow the rhythm to soothe you, to calm you, to relax you. Bring your attention to the left arm. Sense the weight of the arm. Give in to the pull of gravity acting upon you. Visualize any tension in the arm and free your energy as you watch the tension bubbles pop. Watch the tension leave your arm through your fingertips. All five fingers. Bring your attention to your right to relax you. Bring your attention to the left arm. Sense the weight of the arm. Give in to the pull of gravity acting upon you. Visualize any tension in the arm and free your energy as you watch the tension bubbles pop. Watch the tension leave your arm through your fingertips. All five fingers. Bring your attention to your right arm. Sense the weight of your arm. Give in to the pull of gravity acting upon you. Visualize any tension in the arm and free your energy as you watch your tension bubbles pop. Watch the tension leave your arm through your fingertips. All five fingers. Come down to your legs. Sense the weight of your left thigh resting on the chair. Watch the thigh melt into the chair. Allow your tension bubbles to pop, freeing your energy. Travel down the leg, watching the muscles of the lower leg relax until you sense all tension leaving your left leg through your toetips. All five toes. Sense the weight of your right thigh resting on the chair. Watch the thigh melt into the chair. Allow your tension bubbles to pop, freeing your energy. Travel down the leg, watching the muscles of the lower leg relax until you sense all tension leaving your right leg through your toetips. All five toes.

Sit quietly and breathe easily. Visualize yourself lying on the beach, settling deep into the sand. Feel the warmth of the sun upon you penetrating deep into your muscles. Now, watch the tide roll in and watch the tide roll out. Bring the flow of your breath and the motion of the ocean into unison. Stay with this image as long as you like.

References

Adler, A. (1943). Neuropsychiatric complications in victims of Boston's Cocoanut Grove disaster. *Journal of the American Medical Association 123*:1098–1101.

Agras, S., Sylvester, D., and Oliveau, D. (1969). The epidemiology of common fears and phobias. Unpublished manuscript.

Akiskal, H. S., and McKinney, W. T. (1975). Overview of recent research in depression. *Archives of General Psychiatry 32*:285–305.

Allen, M. G., Cohen, S., and Pollin, W. (1972). Schizophrenia in veteran twins: a diagnostic review. *American Journal of Psychiatry 128*:939–947.

American Psychiatric Association (1968). *Diagnostic and Statistical Manual of Mental Disorders*. 2nd ed. Washington, D.C.: Author.

_____ (1980). *Diagnostic and statistical manual of mental disorders*. 3rd ed. Washington, D.C.: Author.

Anderson, B. L. (1983). Primary orgasmic dysfunction: diagnostic considerations and review of treatment. *Psychological Bulletin 93*(1):105–136.

Arieti, S. (1955). *Interpretation of Schizophrenia*. New York: Brunner/Mazel.

_____ (1969). The meeting of the inner and the external world: in schizophrenia, everyday life and creativity. *American Journal of Psychoanalysis, 29*:115–130.

_____ (1974a). An overview of schizophrenia from a predominantly psychological approach. *The American Journal of Psychiatry, 131*(3):241–249.

_____ (1974b). *Interpretation of Schizophrenia.* rev. ed. New York: Basic Books.

Atkeson, B. M., Calhoun, K. S., Resick, P. A., and Ellis, E. M. (1982). Victims of rape: repeated assessment of depressive symptoms. *Journal of Consulting and Clinical Psychology 50*:96–102.

Atthowe, J. M., and Krasner, L. (1968). Preliminary report on the application of contingent reinforcement procedures (token economy) on a "chronic" psychiatric ward. *Journal of Abnormal Psychology 73*:37–43.

Atwood, J. (1985). Techniques to open sexual communication. In *Marriage and Family Living.* St. Meinard, Ind.: Abbey Press.

Auerback, S. M., and Kilmann, P. R. (1977). Crisis intervention: a review of outcome research. *Psychological Bulletin 84*:1189–1197.

Austin, G. A., ed. (1978). *Perspectives on the history of psychoactive substance abuse* (Research Issues #24 of the National Institute of Drug Abuse). Washington, D.C.: U.S. Government Printing Office.

Ayllon, T., and Azrin, N. H. (1965). The measurement and reinforcement of behavior of psychotics. *Journal of the Experimental Analysis of Behavior 8*: 357–384.

Babigan, H. M. (1975). Schizophrenia: epidemiology. In *Comprehensive Textbook of Psychiatry, vol. 2,* ed. A. M. Freedman, H. I. Kaplan, and J. J. Sadock, 2nd ed. Baltimore: Williams and Wilkins.

Baekland, F., Lundwall, L., Kissin, B., and Shanahan, T. (1971). Correlates of outcome in disulfiram treatment of alcoholism. *The Journal of Nervous and Mental Disease 11*: 365–382.

Ban, T. (1973). *Recent Advances in the Biology of Schizophrenia.* Springfield, Ill.: Charles C. Thomas.

Bandura, A. (1969). *Principles of Behavior Modification.* New York: Holt, Rinehart & Winston.

Bandura, A., and Barab, P. (1973). Processes governing disinhibitory effects through symbolic modeling. *Journal of Abnormal Psychology 82*:1–9.

Barchas, J. D., Patrick, R. L., Raese, J., and Berger, P. A. (1977). Neuropharmacological aspects of affective disorders. In *Depression: Clinical, Biological, and Psychological Perspectives.* ed. G. Usdin. New York: Brunner/Mazel.

Bateson, G., Jackson, D., and Weakland, J. (1956). Toward a theory of schizophrenia. *Behavioral Science 1*: 251–264.

Beck, A. T. (1972). *Depression.* Philadelphia: University of Pennsylvania Press.

_____ (1976). *Cognitive Therapy and the Emotional Disorders.* New York: International Universities Press.

Beck, A. T., Rush, A. J., Shaw, B., and Emery, G. (1979). *Cognitive Therapy of Depression: A Treatment Manual.* New York: Guilford.

Beck, A. T., Ward, C. H., Mendelson, M., et al. (1962). Reliability of psychiatric diagnosis, II: a study of consistency of clinical judgments and ratings. *American Journal of Psychiatry 119*:351–357.

Becker, J. V. (1984). Sexual problems of sexual assault survivors. *Women and Health* 9(4):5–20.

Becker, S. S., Horowitz, M. J., and Campbell, L. (1973). Cognitive responses to stress: effects of change in demand and sex. *Journal of Abnormal Psychology 82*:519–522.

Beckett, P. G., Senf, R., Frohman, C. E., and Gottlieb, J. S. (1963). Energy production and premorbid history in schizophrenia. *Archives of General Psychiatry 8*:155–162.

Bellak, L. (1980). Introduction: an idiosyncratic overview. In *Disorders of the Schizophrenic Syndrome,* ed. L. Bellak. New York: Basic Books.

Bemis, K. M. (1978). Current approaches to the etiology and treatment of anorexia nervosa. *Psychological Bulletin 85*:593–617.

Benson, H. (1975). *The Relaxation Response.* New York: Morrow.

Berger, P. A. (1978). Medical treatment of mental illness. *Science 200*:974–981.

Berne, E. (1964). *Games People Play.* New York: Grove.

Bibring, E. (1953). The mechanisms of depression. In *Affective Disorders,* ed. P. Greenacre. New York: International Universities Press.

Blanck, G., and Blanck, R. (1974). *Ego Psychology: Theory and Practice.* New York: Columbia University Press.

Bleuler, E. (1950). *Dementia Praecox, or the Group of Schizophrenias.* New York: International Universities Press (original work published 1911).

Book, J. A. (1960). Genetical aspects of schizophrenic psychosis. In *The Etiology of Schizophrenia,* ed. D. D. Jackson. New York: Basic Books.

Boskland-Lodahl, M. (1976). Cinderella's stepsisters: a feminist perspective on anorexia nervosa and bulimia. *Signs* 2(2);342–356.

Bosse, J. J., Croghan, L. M., Greenstein, M. B., et al. (1975). Frequency of depression in the freshman year as measured in a random sample by a retrospective version of the Beck Depression Inventory. *Journal of Consulting and Clinical Psychology 43*:746–747.

Bourne, P. G. (1969). Military psychiatry and the Viet Nam war in perspective. In *The Psychology and Physiology of Stress,* ed. P. G. Bourne. New York: Academic.

Bowen, M. A. (1960). A family concept of schizophrenia. In *The Etiology of Schizophrenia,* ed. D. D. Jackson. New York: Basic Books.

Bowers, M. K. (1961). Theoretical considerations in the use of hypnosis in the treatment of schizophrenia. *International Journal of Clinical and Experimental Hypnosis 9*:39–46.

Braginsky, B. M., Braginsky, D. D., and Ring, K. (1969). *Methods of Madness: the Mental Hospital as a Last Resort.* New York: Holt, Rinehart, & Winston.

Brandsma, J. M., Maultsby, M. C., and Welsh, R. J. (1980). *Outpatient Treatment of Alcoholism: A Review and Comparative Study.* Baltimore: University Park Press.

Braucht, G. N., Barkarsh, D., Follingstad, D., and Berry, K. L. (1973). Deviant drug use in adolescence: a review of psychological correlates. *Psychology Bulletin 79*(2):92–106.

Briddell, D. W., Rimm, D. C., Caddy, G. R., et al. (1978). The effects of alcohol and expectancy set on male sexual arousal. *Journal of Abnormal Psychology 2*:31–40.

Broen, W. E., Jr., and Nakamura, C. Y. (1972). Reduced range of sensory sensitivity in chronic nonparanoid schizophrenics. *Journal of Abnormal Psychology 79*(1):106–111.

Bruch, H. (1973). *Eating Disorders: Obesity, Anorexia Nervosa, and the Person Within*. New York: Basic Books.

———— (1978). *The Golden Cage: The Enigma of Anorexia Nervosa*. New York: Vintage.

Burgess, A. W., and Holmstrom, L. L. (1974). Rape trauma syndrome. *American Journal of Psychiatry 133*:981–986.

———— (1976). Coping behavior of the rape victim. *American Journal of Psychiatry 133*:413–418.

———— (1978). Recovery from rape and prior life stress. *Research in Nursing and Health 1*:165–174.

———— (1979). Rape: sexual disruption and recovery. *American Journal of Orthopsychiatry 49*:658–669.

Buscaino, V. M. (1952). Extraneural pathology of schizophrenia (liver, digestive tract, reticuloendothelial system). In *Proceeding of the First International Congress of Neuropathology*. Turin, Italy: Rosenberg & Sellier.

Buss, A. A. (1966). *Psychopathology*. New York: Wiley.

Butcher, J. N., and Maudal, G. R. (1976). Crisis intervention. In *Clinical methods in psychology,* ed. I. B. Weiner. New York: Wiley.

Cahalan, D. (1978). Subcultural differences in drinking behavior in U.S. National surveys and selected European studies. In *Alcoholism: New Directions in Behavioral Research and Treatment,* ed. P. E. Nathan, G. A. Marlatt, and T. Loberg. New York: Plenum.

Cameron, N. (1938). Reasoning, regression and communication in schizophrenia. *Psychological Monographs 50,* (no. 221).

———— (1963). *Personality Development and Psychopathology: A Dynamic Approach*. Boston: Houghton Mifflin.

Cannon, W. B. (1929). *Bodily Changes in Pain, Hunger, Fear, and Rage*. New York: Appleton-Century-Crofts.

———— (1932). *The Wisdom of the Body*. New York: Appleton-Century-Crofts.

Cappell, H., and Herman, C. P. (1972). Alcohol and tension reduction: a review. *Quarterly Journal of Studies on Alcohol 33*:33–64.

Caputo, D. V. (1968). The parents of the schizophrenic. In *Family Processes and Schizophrenia,* ed. E. G. Mishler and N. E. Waxler. New York: Science House.

Carson, R. C. (1983). The schizophrenias. In *Comprehensive Handbook of Psychopathology*, ed. H. E. Adams and P. B. Sutker. New York: Plenum.

Casey, J. F., Bennett, I. F., Lindley, C. J., et al. (1960). Drug therapy and schizophrenia: a controlled study of the effectiveness of chlorpromazine, promazine, phenobarbital and placebo. *Archives of General Psychiatry 2*:210–220.

Cassel, J. (1970). Physical illness in response to stress. In *Social Stress,* ed. S. Levine and N. A. Scotch. Chicago: Aldine.

Cautela, J. R. (1967). Covert sensitization. *Psychological Reports 20*:459–468.

Chapman, L. J., and McGhie, A. (1962). A comparative study of disordered attention of schizophrenia. *Journal of Mental Science 108*:487–500.

Claeson, L. E., and Malm, U. (1973). Electro-aversion therapy of chronic alcoholism. *Behavior Research and Therapy 11*(4):663–665.

Clopton, J. R., and Risbrough, R. F. (1973). Use of meditation as a behavioral technique. *Behavior Therapy 4*:743–744.

Cohen, B. D., Nachmani, G., and Rosenberg, S. (1974). Referent communication disturbances in acute schizophrenia. *Journal of Abnormal Psychology 83*(1):1–13.

Cooper, J. E., Kendell, R. E., Gurland, et al. (1972). *Psychiatric Diagnosis in New York and London: A Comparative Study of Mental Hospital Admissions.* New York: Oxford University Press.

Crisp, A. H. (1977). The prevalence of anorexia nervosa and some of its associations in the general population. In *Advances in Psychosomatic Medicine: Epidemiologic Studies in Psychosomatic Medicine,* vol. 9, ed. S. Kasl and F. Reichman, pp. 38–47. Basel, Switzerland: S. Karger.

Crisp, A. H., Harding, B., and McGuinness, B. (1974). Anorexia nervosa: psychoneurotic characteristics of parents: relationship to progress. *Journal of Psychosomatic Research 18*:167–173.

Crisp, A. H., Hsu, L. K., Harding, B., and Hartshorn, J. (1980). Clinical features of anorexia nervosa: a study of a consecutive series of 102 female patients. *Journal of Psychosomatic Research 24*(3–4):179–191.

Crisp, A. H., Palmer, R. L., and Kalury, R. S. (1976). How common is anorexia nervosa? A prevalence study. *British Journal of Psychiatry, 218*:519–554.

Crocetti, G. M., and Lemkau, P. V. (1967). Schizophrenia: epidemiology. In *Comprehensive Textbook of Psychiatry*, ed. A. M. Freeman, H. I. Kaplan, and J. J. Sadock, pp. 599–603. Baltimore: Williams & Wilkins.

Crocetti, G., Spiro, H. R., and Siassi, I. (1971). Are the ranks closed? Attitudinal social distance and mental illness. *American Journal of Psychiatry 127*(9): 1121–1127.

Cromwell, R. L., and Dokecki, P. R. (1968). Schizophrenia language: a disattention interpretation. In *Developments in Applied Psycholinguistics Research,* ed. S. Rosenberg and J. H. Koplin. New York: Macmillan.

Davidson, R. J. (1978). Specificity and patterning in biobehavioral systems: implications for behavior change. *American Psychologist 33*:430–436.

Davidson, W. S. (1974). Studies of aversive conditioning for alcoholics: a critical review of theory and research methodology. *Psychological Bulletin 81*(9): 571–581.

Davis, J. M. (1978). Dopamine theory of schizophrenia: a two-factor theory. In *The Nature of Schizophrenia: New Approaches to Research and Treatment,* ed. L. C. Wynne, R. L. Cromell, and S. Matthysse. New York: Wiley.

Ditman, K. S. (1967). Review and evaluation of current drug therapies in alcoholism. *International Journal of Psychiatry 3*(4):248–266.

Dohrenwend, B. P., Dohrenwend, B. S., Gould, M. S., et al. (1980). *Mental Illness in the United States: Epidemiological Estimates.* New York: Praeger.

Dohrenwend, B. S., and Dohrenwend, B. P. (1969). *Social Status and Psychological Disorder.* New York: Wiley.

Drake, R. E., and Wallach, M. A. (1979). Will mental patients stay in the community? A social psychological perspective. *Journal of Clinical and Consulting Psychology 47*(2):285–294.

Dubos, R. (1965). *Man Adapting.* New Haven: Yale University Press.

Duke, M. P., and Mullins, M. C. (1973). Preferred interpersonal distance as a function of locus of control orientation in chronic schizophrenics, nonschizophrenic patients, and normals. *Journal of Consulting and Clinical Psychology 41*(2):230–234.

Eaton, J., and Weil, R. J. (1955). *Culture and Mental Disorders.* Glencoe, Ill.: Free Press.

Eisenstein, V. W. (1956). *Neurotic Interaction in Marriage.* New York: Basic Books.

Ellis, A. (1962). *Reason and Emotion in Psychotherapy.* New York: Lyle-Stuart.

———— (1970). *The Essence of Rational Psychotherapy: A Comprehensive Approach to Treatment.* New York: Institute for Rational Living.

Erikson, E. H. (1950). *Childhood and Society.* New York: Norton.

———— (1968). *Identity: Youth and Crisis.* New York: Norton.

Ersner-Hershfield, R., and Kopel, S. (1979). Group treatment of preorgasmic women: evaluation of partner involvement and spacing of sessions. *Journal of Consulting and Clinical Psychology 47*:750–759.

Ewing, J. A., Rouse, B. A., and Pellizzari, E. D. (1974). Alcohol sensitivity and ethnic background. *American Journal of Psychiatry 131*:206–210.

Faris, E. L., and Dunham, H. W. (1939). *Mental Disorders in Urban Areas: An Ecological Study of Schizophrenia and Other Psychoses.* Chicago: University of Chicago Press.

Feinsilver, D., and Gunderson, J. (1972). Psychotherapy for schizophrenics: is it indicated? A review of relevant literature. *Schizophrenia Bulletin 6*:11–23.

Feldman-Summers, S., and Linder, K. (1979). Perceptions of victims and defendants in criminal assault cases. *Criminal Justice and Behavior 3*:135–149.

Fenichel, O. (1947). *The Psychoanalytic Theory of Neurosis.* New York: Norton.

Fenz, W. D., and Velner, J. (1970). Psychological concomitants of behavioral indexes in schizophrenia. *Journal of Abnormal Psychology 76*(1):27–35.

Fish, J. F. (1957). The classification of schizophrenia. *Journal of Mental Science 103*:443–465.

Fox, J. H., Ramsey, R. G., Huckman, M. S., and Proske, A. E. (1976). *Journal of the American Medical Association 236*:365–377.

Frank, G. H. (1970). On the nature of borderline personality: A review. *Journal of General Psychology 83*(1):61–77.

Frank, E., Anderson, C., and Rubenstein, D. N. (1978). Frequency of sexual dysfunction in normal couples. *New England Journal of Medicine 299*(3): 111–115.

Fraser, M. (1973). *Children in Conflict*. London: Secker & Warburg.

Freud, S. (1925). Psychoanalytic notes upon an autobiographical account of a case of paranoia (dementia paranoides). In *Collected Papers*, vol. 3. London: Hogarth Press (original work published in 1911).

_____ (1947). *The Ego and the Id*. London: Hogarth Press (original work published in 1923).

_____ (1950). The unconscious. In *Collected Papers,* vol. 4. London: Hogarth Press (original work published in 1915).

_____ (1953). Three essays on sexuality. In *The Standard Edition of the Complete Psychological Works of Sigmund Freud,* vol. 7, London: Hogarth Press (original work published in 1905).

_____ (1957). Mourning and melancholia. In *The Standard Edition of the Complete Psychological Works of Sigmund Freud,* vol. 14, London: Hogarth Press (original work published in 1917).

Fromm-Reichmann, F. (1948). Notes on the development of treatment of schizophrenia by psychoanalytic psychotherapy. *Psychiatry 11*:263–273.

_____ (1959). Loneliness. *Psychiatry 22*:1–15.

Garmezy, N. (1970). Process and reactive schizophrenia: some conceptions and issues. *Schizophrenia Bulletin 2*:30–67.

Garmezy, N. and Streitman, S. (1974). Children at risk: the search for the antecedents of schizophrenia. Part 1: conceptual models and research methods. *Schizophrenia Bulletin 8*:14–90.

Glass, D. C., and Singer, J. E. (1972). *Urban Stress: Experiments on Noise and Social Stresses*. New York: Academic.

Goffman, E. (1961). *Asylums*. New York: Anchor Books.

Goldfried, M. R., and Trier, C. S. (1974). Effectiveness of relaxation as an active coping skill. *Journal of Abnormal Psychology 83*(4):348–355.

Goldstein, A. J., and Chambless, D. L. (1978). A reanalysis of agoraphobia. *Behavior Therapy 9*:47–57.

Goldstein, M. J., Rodnick, E. H., Jones, J. E., et al. (1978). Familial precursors of schizophrenia: spectrum disorders. In *The Nature of Schizophrenia: New Approaches to Research and Treatment,* ed. L. C. Wynne, R. L. Cromwell, and S. Matthyse. New York: Wiley.

Golin, S. (1974). Effects of stress on the performance of normally anxious and high-anxious subjects under chance and skill conditions. *Journal of Abnormal Psychology 83*:466–472.

Gomberg, E. S. (1974). Women and alcoholism. In *Women and Therapy: New Psychotherapies for a Changing Society,* ed. V. Franks and V. Burtle. New York: Brunner/Mazel.

Goodwin, D. W., Schulsinger, F., Hermansen, L., et al. (1973). Alcohol problems in adoptees raised apart from alcoholic biological parents. *Archives of General Psychiatry 28*:238–243.

Goodwin, D. W., Schulsinger, F., Moller, N., et al. (1974). Drinking problems in adopted and nonadopted sons of alcoholics. *Archives of General Psychiatry 31*(2):164–169.

Gorad, S. L. (1971). The alcoholic and his wife: their personal styles of communication and interaction. *Dissertation Abstracts International 32*(B-4):2395–2396.

Gottesman, I. I., and Sheilds, J. (1976). A critical review of recent adoption, twin, and family studies of schizophrenia: behavioral genetics perspectives. *Schizophrenia Bulletin 3*:360–378.

Gottheil, E., Thorton, C. C., Skoloda, T. E., and Alterman, A. I. (1982). Follow-up of abstinent and non-abstinent alcoholics. *American Journal of Psychiatry 139*(5):560–565.

Griffith, J. D., Cavanaugh, J., Held, N. N., and Oates, J. A. (1972). Dexatroamphetamine: evaluation of psychomimetic properties in man. *Archives in General Psychiatry 15*:240–244.

Gross, M. M., and Lewis, C. (1973). Observations on the prevalence of the signs and symptoms associated with withdrawal during continuous observation of experimental intoxication and withdrawal in humans. In *Alcohol Intoxication and Withdrawal: Experimental Studies,* ed. M. M. Gross. New York: Plenum.

Grotstein, J. S. (1972). A theoretical rationale for psychoanalytic treatment of schizophrenia. In *Psychotherapy of Schizophrenia,* ed. J. Gunderson and L. Mosher. New York: Jason Aronson.

Gunderson, J. G., Autry, J. H., and Mosher, L. R. (1974). Special report: schizophrenia. *Schizophrenia Bulletin 9*:15–54.

Gunderson, J. G., and Mosher, L. (1975). *Psychotherapy of Schizophrenia.* New York: Jason Aronson.

Habif, V., and Lahey, B. B. (1979). Vulnerability to depression: social support as a moderator of the life stress–depression relationship. Unpublished manuscript, University of Georgia.

Haley, J. (1965). The art of being schizophrenic. *Voices 1*:133–142.

Hanson, D. R., Gottesman, I. I., and Meehl, P. E. (1977). Genetic theories and the validation of psychiatric diagnoses: implications for the study of children of schizophrenics. *Journal of Abnormal Psychology 86*(6):575–588.

Harris, S. E. (1968). Schizophrenics' mutual glance patterns. *Dissertation Abstracts 298*:2202–2203.

Hartmann, H. (1939). *Ego Psychology and the Problem of Adaptation.* New York: International Universities Press.

_____ (1953). Contributions to the metapsychology of schizophrenia. In *Psychoanalytic Study of the Child,* vol. 8, pp. 177–198. New York: International Universities Press.

Hays, V., and Waddell, K. (1976). Extinguishing ineffective communication behavior: an innovative video-tape-feedback procedure. *Behavioral Engineering* 3(3):8D.

Heath, R. G. (1960). A biochemical hypothesis on the etiology of schizophrenia. In *The Etiology of Schizophrenia,* ed. D. D. Jackson, pp. 146–156. New York: Basic Books.

Hepworth, D. (1983). Early removal of resistance in task-centered case work. In *Handbook.* New York: Adelphi University Press.

Hersen, M., and Bellack, A. S. (1976). Social skills training for chronic psychiatric patients: rationale, research findings, and future directions. *Comprehensive Psychiatry* 17:559–580.

Heston, L. L. (1966). Psychiatric disorders in foster home reared children of schizophrenic mothers. *British Journal of Psychiatry* 112:819–825.

Heston, L. L., and Denny, D. (1968). Interactors between early life experience and the biological factors in schizophrenia. In *The Transmission of Schizophrenia,* ed. D. Rosenthal and S. S. Kety. Elmsford, N.Y.: Pergamon.

Higgins, R. L., and Marlatt, G. A. (1974). The effects of anxiety arousal upon the consumption of alcohol by alcoholics and social drinkers. *Journal of Consulting and Clinical Psychology* 41:426–433.

Hoffer, A., and Osmond, H. (1962). Nicotinamide adenine dinucleotide in the treatment of chronic schizophrenic patients. *British Journal of Psychiatry* 114:915–917.

_____ (1968). Some schizophrenic recoveries. *Diseases of the Nervous System* 23:204–210.

Hollingshead, A. B., and Redlich, F. C. (1958). *Social Class and Mental Illness: A Community Study.* New York: Wiley.

Hollon, S., and Beck, A. T. (1978). Psychotherapy and drug therapy: comparisons and combinations. In *Handbook of Psychotherapy and Behavior Change,* ed. S. L. Garfield and A. E. Bergin. New York: Wiley.

Holmes, T. H., and Rahe, R. H. (1967). The social readjustment rating scale. *Journal of Psychosomatic Research* 11:213–218.

Horowitz, M. J. (1976). *Stress Response Syndromes.* New York: Jason Aronson.

Horowitz, M. J., Becker, S. S., and Malone, P. (1973). Stress: different effects on patients and nonpatients. *Journal of Abnormal Psychology* 82:547–551.

Horwitt, M. K. (1956). Fact and artifact in the biology of schizophrenia. *Science* 124:429–433.

Hsu, L. K. G. (1980). Outcome of anorexia nervosa. *Archives of General Psychiatry* 37:1041–1049.

Ingalls, Z. (1978 October 16). On campus, the biggest drug problem is alcohol. *Chronicle of Higher Education,* pp. 3–5.

Jackson, D. D., and Weakland, J. H. (1961). Conjoint family therapy: some considerations on theory, technique, and results. *Psychiatry 24*(2): 30–45.

Jacobs, T. (1975). Family interaction in disturbed and normal families: a methodological and substantive review. *Psychological Bulletin 82*:33–65.

Jacobson, E. (1938). *Progressive Relaxation.* Chicago: University of Chicago Press.

——— (1964). *The Self and the Object World.* New York: International Universities Press.

Jellinek, E. M. (1952). Phases of alcohol addiction. *Quarterly Journal of Studies on Alcohol 13*:673.

——— (1971). Phases of alcohol addiction. In *Studies in Abnormal Behavior,* ed. G. D. Shean, pp. 86–98. Chicago: Rand McNally.

Johnson, C., and Larson, R. (1982). Bulimia: an analysis of mood and behavior. *Psychosomatic Medicine 44*(4):341–351.

Johnson, J. E., and Petzel, T. P. (1971). Temporal orientation and time estimation in chronic schizophrenics. *Journal of Clinical Psychology 27*(2):194–196.

Jones, M. (1955). Social psychiatry. *Digest of Neurological Psychiatry 23*:245–253.

Kallman, F. J. (1941). Knowledge about the significance of psychopathology in family relations. *Marriage and Family Living 3*:81–82.

——— (1953). *Heredity in Health and Mental Disorder.* New York: W. W. Norton.

Kaplan, H. S. (1974a). The classification of female sexual dysfunctions. *Journal of Sex and Marital Therapy 1*(2):124–138.

——— (1974b). *The New Sex Therapy.* New York: Brunner/Mazel.

Kardiner, A., and Speigel, H. (1947). *War Stress and Neurotic Illness.* New York: Harper & Row.

Karlson, J. L. (1966). *The Biological Basis for Schizophrenia.* Springfield, Ill.: Charles C Thomas.

Karon, B. P., and Vandenbos, G. R. (1981). *Psychotherapy of Schizophrenia: Treatment of Choice.* New York: Jason Aronson.

Katz, S., and Mazur, M. (1979). *Understanding the Rape Victim: A Synthesis of Research Findings.* New York: Wiley.

Keefe, J. A., and Magaro, P. A. (1980). Creativity and schizophrenia: an equivalence of cognitive processing. *Journal of Abnormal Psychology 89*(3):390–398.

Kendler, K. S., and Davis, K. L. (1981). The genetics and biochemistry of paranoid schizophrenia and other paranoid psychoses. *Schizophrenia Bulletin 1*:689–709.

Kendler, K. S. and Tsuang, M. T. (1981). Nosology of paranoid schizophrenia and other paranoid psychoses. *Schizophrenia Bulletin 7*:594–610.

Kernberg, O. (1965). Notes on countertransference. *Journal of the American Psychoanalytic Association 13*(1):38–56.

Kessler, S. (1980). The genetics of schizophrenia: a review. *Schizophrenia Bulletin 6*(3):404–416.

Kety, S. S. (1972). Toward hypothesis for a biochemical component in the vulnerability to schizophrenia. *Seminars in Psychiatry 4*:233–242.

Kety, S. S., Rosenthal, D., Wender, P. H., et al. (1975). Mental illness in the biological and adoptive families of adopted individuals who have become schizophrenic. In *Genetic Research in Psychiatry,* ed. R. R. Fieve, D. Rosenthal, and H. Brill. Baltimore: Johns Hopkins University Press.

Khatchadourian, H. A., and Lunde, D. T. (1972). *Fundamentals of Human Sexuality.* New York: Holt, Rinehart and Winston.

Kilpatrick, D. G., Veronen, L. J., and Resnick, P. A. (1979). The aftermath of rape: recent empirical findings. *American Journal of Orthopsychiatry 49*: 658–669.

Kinsey, A. C., Pomeroy, W. B., and Martin, C. E. (1948). *Sexual Behavior in the Human Male.* Philadelphia: W. B. Saunders.

Kinsey, A. C., Pomeroy, W. B., Wardell, B., Martin, C. E., and Gebhard, P. H. (1953). *Sexual Behavior in the Human Female.* Philadelphia: Saunders.

Klein, D. F. (1968). Psychiatric diagnosis and a typology of chemical drug effects. *Psychopharmacologia* 13(5):359–386.

Klein, M. (1946). Notes on some schizoid mechanisms. In *Developments in Psychoanalysis*, ed. J. Riviere. London: Hogarth Press.

Kleist, K. (1960). Schizophrenic symptoms and cerebral pathology. *Journal of Mental Science 106*:246–253.

Knupfer, G. (1972). Ex-problem drinkers. In *Life History Research in Psychopathology,* vol. 2, ed. M. Roff, L. N. Robins, and M. Pollack. Minneapolis: University of Minnesota Press.

Kogan, K. L., and Jackson, J. K. (1965). Stress personality and emotional disturbance in wives of alcoholics. *Quarterly Journal of Studies on Alcohol 26*(3): 395–408.

Kraeplin, E. (1919). *Dementia Praecox and Paraphrenia.* Trans. R. M. Barclay, ed. G. M. Robertson. Edinburgh: E. S. Livingstone.

Kringlen, E. (1968). An epidemiological clinical twin study of schizophrenia. In *The Transmission of Schizophrenia*, ed. D. Rosenthal, and S. S. Kety. New York: Pergamon.

―――― (1970). Natural history of obsessional neurosis. *Seminars in Psychiatry* 2:403–419.

Kroger, W. S. (1977). *Clinical and Experimental Hypnosis in Medicine, Dentistry, and Psychology.* 2nd ed. Philadelphia: JB Lippincott.

Krupnick, J. L., and Horowitz, M. J. (1981). Stress response syndromes. *Archives of General Psychiatry 38*:428–436.

Lacey, J. I. (1956). The evaluation of autonomic responses: toward a general solution. *Annals of the New York Academy of Science 67*:123–164.

Lader, M. (1976). Physiological research in anxiety. In *Research in Neurosis,* ed. H. M. Van Praag. Utrecht: Bohn, Scheltema, & Holkema.

Lahti, R. A., and Majchrowicz, E. (1974). Ethanol and acetaldehyde effects on metabolism and binding of biogenic amines. *Quarterly Journal of Studies of Alcohol 35*:1–14.

Laing, R. D. (1960). *The Divided Self*. London: Tavistock.

———— (1964). Is schizophrenia a disease? *International Journal of Social Psychiatry 10*:184–193.

———— (1967). *The Politics of Experience*. New York: Pantheon.

Lang, A. R., Goeckner, D. J., Adesso, V. G., and Marlatt, G. A. (1975). Effects of alcohol on aggression in male social drinkers. *Journal of Abnormal Psychology 84*:508–518.

Lehmann, H. E. (1974). The somatic and pharmacologic treatments of schizophrenia. *Schizophrenia Bulletin 13*:27–45.

Leiblum, S. R., and Rosen, R. C. (1979). The weekend workshop for dysfunctional couples: assets and limitations. *Journal of Sex and Marital Therapy 5*(1): 57–69.

Levy, S. M. (1976). Schizophrenic symptomatology: reaction or strategy? A study of contextual antecedents. *Journal of Abnormal Psychology 85*:435–445.

Lewine, R. R. (1981). Sex differences in schizophrenia: timing or subtypes? *Psychological Bulletin 90*(3):432–444.

Lewinsohn, P. M., Youngren, M. A., and Grosscup, S. J. (1979). Reinforcement and depression. In *The Psychobiology of the Depressive Disorders: Implications for the Effects of Stress*, ed. R. A. Depue. New York: Academic.

Liberman, R. P., and Raskin, D. E. (1971). Depression: a behavioral formulation. *Archives of General Psychiatry 24*(6):515–523.

Liberman, R. P., Wallace, C., Teigan, J., and Davis, J. (1974). Interventions with psychotic behaviors. In *Innovative Treatment Methods in Psychopathology*, ed. K. S. Calhoun, H. E. Adams, and K. M. Mitchell. New York: Wiley.

Lidz, T. (1973). *The Origin and Treatment of Schizophrenic Disorders*. New York: Basic Books.

Liem, J. H. (1974). Effects of verbal communications of parents and children: a comparison of normal and schizophrenic families. *Journal of Consulting and Clinical Psychology 42*:438–450.

Linn, E. L. (1977). Verbal auditory hallucinations: mind, self, and society. *Journal of Nervous and Mental Disease 164*:8–10.

LoPiccolo, J., and Heiman, J. (1977). Cultural values and the therapeutic definition of sexual function and dysfunction. *Journal of Social Issues 33*(2):166–183.

Luby, E. D., Grisell, J. L., Frohman, C. E., et al. (1962). Biochemical, psychological, and behavioral responses to sleep deprivation. *Annals of the New York Academy of Science 96*:71–78.

Lucas, C., Sansbury, P., and Collins, J. G. (1962). A social and clinical study of delusions in schizophrenia. *Journal of Mental Health 108*:747–758.

Mace, D. (1971). The sexual revolution: its impact on pastoral counseling. *Journal of Pastoral Care 25*(4):220–232.

MacKay, J. R. (1961). Clinical observations on adolescent problem drinkers. *Quarterly Journal of Studies in Alcoholism 22*:124–134.

MacKinnon, P. C. (1969). The palmar anhidrotic response to stress in schizophrenic patients and control groups. *Journal of Psychiatric Research* 7(1):1–7.

Magaro, P. A. (1981). The paranoid and the schizophrenic: The case for distinct cognitive style. *Schizophrenia Bulletin* 7:632–661.

Maher, B. A. (1966). *Principles of Psychopathology: An Experimental Approach.* New York: McGraw-Hill.

Mahler, M. S. (1975). *The Psychological Birth of the Human Infant.* New York: Basic Books.

———— (1976). *On Human Symbiosis and the Vicissitudes of Individuation.* New York: Library of Human Behavior.

Malatesta, V. J. (1978). The affects of alcohol on ejaculation latency in human males. Unpublished doctoral dissertation, University of Georgia.

Maletzky, B. M., and Klotter, J. (1974). Smoking and alcoholism. *American Journal of Psychiatry* 131(4):445–447.

Malitz, S., Wikens, B., and Esecover, H. (1962). A comparison of drug-induced hallucinations with those seen in spontaneously occurring psychoses. In *Hallucinations,* ed. L. J. West. New York: Grune & Stratton.

Mandell, A. J., Segal, D. S., Kuczenski, R. T., and Krapp, S. (1972). The search for the schizococcus. *Psychology Today* 6(5):68–72.

Marks, I. M. (1969). *Fears and Phobias.* New York: Academic.

———— (1973). New approaches to the treatment of obsessive-compulsive disorders. *Journal of Nervous and Mental Diseases* 156:420–428.

———— (1976). Neglected factors in neurosis. In *Research in Neurosis,* ed. H. M. Van Praag. Utrecht: Bohn, Scheltema, & Holkema.

Marlatt, G. A. (1974). Modeling influences in social drinking: an experimental analogue. Paper presented at the Association for Advancement of Behavior Therapy, Chicago.

———— (1978). Craving for alcohol, loss of control, and relapse: a cognitive-behavioral analysis. In *Alcoholism: New Directions in Behavioral Research and Treatment,* ed. P. E. Nathan, G. A. Marlatt, and T. Loberg. New York: Plenum.

Marlatt, G. A., Demming, B., and Reid, J. B. (1973). Loss-of-control drinking in alcoholics: an experimental analogue. *Journal of Abnormal Psychology* 81:233–241.

Massie, H. N., and Beels, C. C. (1972). The outcome of the family treatment of schizophrenia. *Schizophrenia Bulletin* 6:24–36.

Masters, W. H., and Johnson, V. E. (1966). *Human Sexual Response.* Boston: Little, Brown.

———— (1970). *Human Sexual Inadequacy.* Boston: Little, Brown.

———— (1976). Principles of the new sex therapy. *American Journal of Psychiatry* 133(5):548–554.

Masterson, J. F. (1972). *Treatment of the Borderline Adolescent.* New York: Wiley.

Mathews, A. M., and Gelder, M. G. (1969). Psychophysiological investigations of brief relaxation training. *Journal of Psychosomatic Research* 13:1–12.

May, P. R. A. (1975). Schizophrenia: Evaluation of treatment methods. In

Comprehensive Textbook of Psychiatry ed. A. M. Freedman, H. I. Kaplan, and B. J. Sadock. Baltimore: Williams & Wilkins.

McCary, J. L. (1973). *Human Sexuality: Physiological, Psychological, and Sociological Factors,* 2nd ed. New York: Van Nostrand.

McClelland, D. C., Davis, W. N., Kalin, R., and Wanner, E. (1972). *The Drinking Man.* New York: The Free Press.

McCord, W., McCord, J., and Gudeman, J. (1960). *Origins of Alcoholism.* Stanford, Calif.: Stanford University Press.

McCord, W., Porta, J., and McCord, J. (1962). The familial genesis of psychoses. *Psychiatry 25*:60–71.

Mednick, S. A. (1958). A learning theory approach to research in schizophrenia. *Psychological Bulletin 70*:681–693.

Mednick, S. A., and Schulsinger, F. (1973). A learning theory of schizophrenia: thirteen years later. In *Psychopathology: Contributions from the Social Behavioral and Biological Sciences,* ed. M. Hammer, K. Salzinger, and S. Sutton. New York: Wiley.

Meehl, P. E. (1962). Schizotaxia, schizotypy, schizophrenia. *American Psychologist 17*:827–838.

Meichenbaum, D. (1974). A self-instructional approach to stress management: a proposal for stress inoculation training. In *Stress and Anxiety,* vol. 1, ed. C. D. Spielberger and I. Sarason. New York: Winston and Sons.

Mello, N. K., and Mendelson, J. H. (1970). Experimentally induced intoxication in alcoholics: a comparison between programmed and spontaneous drinking. *Journal of Pharmacology and Experimental Therapy 173*:101–105.

Meltzer, H. Y., and Stahl, S. M. (1976). The dopamine hypothesis of schizophrenia: a review. *Schizophrenia Bulletin 2*:19–76.

Menninger, K. (1938). *Man Against Himself.* New York: Harcourt Brace.

Metzger, D. (1976). It is always the woman who is raped. *American Journal of Psychiatry 133*(4):405–408.

Miller, P. M. (1976). *Behavioral Treatment of Alcoholism.* New York: Pergamon.

Miller, W. R. (1978). Behavioral treatment of problem drinkers: a comparative outcome study of three controlled drinking therapies. *Journal of Consulting and Clinical Psychology 50*:491–498.

Mills, H. L., Agras, W. S., Barlow, D. H., and Mils, J. R. (1973). Compulsive rituals treated by response intervention: an experimental analysis. *Archives of General Psychiatry 28*:524–534.

Minuchin, S., Rosman, B. L., and Baker, L. (1978). *Psychosomatic Families: Anorexia Nervosa in Context.* Cambridge: Harvard University Press.

Mishler, E., and Waxler, N. (1968). *Interaction in Families: An Experimental Study of Family Processes and Schizophrenia.* New York: Wiley.

Mosher, L. R. (1974). Psychiatric heretics and extra-medical treatment of schizophrenia. In *Strategic Intervention in Schizophrenia: Current Developments in Treatment,* ed. R. Cancro, N. Fox, and L. Shapiro. New York: Behavioral.

Mosher, L. R., and Gunderson, J. G. (1973). Special report: schizophrenia. *Schizophrenia Bulletin 1*:7-9.

Mosher, L. R., Menn, A., and Matthews, S. M. (1975). Soteria: evaluation of a home-based treatment for schizophrenia. *American Journal of Orthopsychiatry* 45:455-467.

Mosher, L. R., Pollin, W., and Stabenau, J. R. (1971). Identical twins discordant for schizophrenia: neurologic findings. *Archives of General Psychiatry 24*:422-430.

Munjack, D. J., and Staples, F. R. (1976). Psychological characteristics of women with sexual inhibition (frigidity) in sex clinics. *Journal of Nervous and Mental Disease 163*:117-129.

Murphy, H. B. (1978). Cultural influences on incidence, course, and treatment response. In *The Nature of Schizophrenia: New Approaches to Research and Treatment,* ed. L. C. Wynne, R. L. Cromwell, and S. Matthyse, pp. 586-594. New York: Wiley.

Nathan, P. E. (1977). An overview of behavioral treatment approaches. In *Behavioral Approaches to Alcoholism,* ed. G. A. Marlatt and P. E. Nathan. New Brunswick, N.J.: Rutgers Center for Alcohol Studies.

Nathan, P. E., and O'Brien, J. S. (1971). An experimental analysis of the behavior of alcoholics and nonalcoholics during prolonged experimental drinking: a necessary precursor of behavior therapy? *Behavior Therapy 2*:455-476.

National Institute of Alcohol Abuse and Alcoholism (1974). DHEW publication no. ADM 75-31. Washington, D.C.

Nelsen, J. (1983). Dealing with resistance in social work practice. In *Handbook*. New York: Adelphi University Press.

Nemiah, J. C. (1967). Obsessive-compulsive reaction. In *Comprehensive Textbook of Psychiatry,* ed. A. M. Freedman and H. I. Kaplan. Baltimore: Williams & Wilkins.

Nowinski, J. K., and LoPiccolo, J. (1979). Assessing sexual behavior in couples. *Journal of Sex and Marital Therapy* 5(3):225-243.

Neucherlein, K. H. (1977). Reaction time and attention in schizophrenia: critical evaluation of the data and theories. *Schizophrenia Bulletin 3*:373-428.

O'Brien, C. P. (1975). Group therapy for schizophrenia: a practical approach. *Schizophrenia Bulletin 13*:119-130.

O'Brien, C. P., Hamm, K. B., Ray, B. A., et al. (1972). Group vs. individual psychotherapy with schizophrenics: a controlled outcome study. *Archives of General Psychiatry 27*:474-485.

Okura, K. P. (1975). Mobilizing in response to a major disaster. *Community Mental Health Journal 2*(2):136-144.

O'Leary, K. D., and Wilson, G. T. (1975). *Behavior Therapy: Application and Outcome*. Englewood Cliffs, N.J.: Prentice-Hall.

Osmond, H., and Smythies, J. (1952). Schizophrenia: a new approach. *Journal of Mental Science 98*:309-315.

Palazzoli, M. S. (1978). *Self-starvation: From Individual to Family Therapy in the Treatment of Anorexia Nervosa.* New York: Jason Aronson.

Park, L. C., Baldessarini, R. J., and Ketty, S. S. (1965). Methionine effects on chronic schizophrenics: patients treated with monomine oxidase inhibitors. *Archives of General Psychiatry 12*:346–351.

Paul, G. L., and Lentz, R. J. (1977). *Psychosocial Treatment of Chronic Mental Patients: Milieu versus Social-Learning Programs.* Cambridge: Harvard University Press.

Pendery, M. L., Maltzman, I. M., and West, L. J. (1982). Controlled drinking by alcoholics? New findings and a reevaluation of a major affirmative study. *Science 217*(9):169–174.

Perlberg, M. (1979). Adapted from trauma at Tenerife: the psychic aftershocks of a jet disaster. *Human Behavior.* April:49–50.

Perlman, H. H. (1962). What is social diagnosis? *Social Science Review* 17–31.

Petzel, T. P., and Johnson, J. E. (1972). Time estimation by process and reactive schizophrenics under crowded and uncrowded conditions. *Journal of Clinical Psychology 28*(3):345–347.

Pihl, R. O., and Spiers, P. (1978). Individual characteristics in the etiology of drug abuse. In *Progress in Experimental Personality Research*, vol. 8, ed. B. A. Maher. New York: Academic.

Polich, J. M., Armor, D. J., and Braiker, H. B. (1980). *The Course of Alcoholism: Four Years After Treatment.* Santa Monica: Rand Corporation.

Post, R. M., Stoddard, F. J., Gillin, C., et al. (1977). Alterations in motor activity, sleep, and biochemistry in cycling manic-depressive patients. *Archives of General Psychiatry 34*:470–481.

President's Commission on Mental Health (1978). *Report to the President.* Washington, D.C.: U.S. Government Printing Office.

Rabkin, J. G., and Struening, E. L. (1976). Life events, stress, and illness. *Science 194*:1013–1019.

Reiss, D. (1974). Competing hypotheses and warring factions: applying knowledge of schizophrenia. *Schizophrenia Bulletin 8*:7–11.

Renshaw, D. C. (1978). Sex and values. *Journal of Clinical Psychiatry 39*(9): 716–719.

Resnick, C. K., Atkeson, B., and Ellis, E. (1981). Social adjustment in victims of sexual assault. *Journal of Consulting and Clinical Psychology 49*(5):705–712.

Rimm, D. C. (1973). Thought stopping and covert assertion in the treatment of phobias. *Journal of Consulting and Clinical Psychology 41*:466–467.

Rimm, D. C., Saunders, W. D., and Westel, W. (1975). Thought stopping and covert assertion in the treatment of snake phobias. *Journal of Consulting and Clinical Psychology 43*:92–93.

Ritchie, P. L. (1975). The effect of the interviewer's presentation on some schizophrenic symptomatology. Unpublished doctoral dissertation, Duke University.

Ritzler, B. A. (1981). Paranoia: prognosis and treatment: A review. *Schizophrenia Bulletin 7*:710–728.

Ritzler, B. A., and Rosenbaum, G. (1974). Proprioception in schizophrenics and normals: effects of stimulus intensity and interstimulus interval. *Journal of Abnormal Psychology 83*(2):106–111.

Robbins, L. N. (1966). *Deviant Children Grown Up.* Baltimore: Williams & Wilkins.

Roe, A., Burks, B. S., and Mittleman, B. (1945). Adult adjustment of foster children of alcoholic and psychotic parentage and influence of the foster home. *Memorial Section on Alcohol Studies.* no. 3. New Haven: Yale University Press.

Rosenfeld, H. A. (1965). *Psychotic States: A Psychoanalytic Approach.* New York: International Universities Press.

Rosenhan, D. L. (1973). On being sane in insane places. *Science 179*:250–258.

Rosenthal, D. (1970). *Genetic Theory and Abnormal Behavior.* New York: McGraw-Hill.

Rosenthal, D., Wender, P. H., Kety, S. S., et al. (1975). Parent–chid relationships and psychopathological disorder in the child. *Archives of General Psychiatry 32*:466–476.

Rosman, B. L., Minuchin, S., and Liebman, R. (1975). Family lunch session: An introduction to family therapy in anorexia nervosa. *American Journal of Orthopsychiatry 45*:846–854.

Ro-Trock, G. K., Wellisch, D. K., and Schodar, J. C. (1977). A family therapy outcome study in an inpatient setting. *American Journal of Orthopsychiatry 47*:514–522.

Sachar, E. J., Kanter, S., Buie, D., et al. (1970). Psycho-endocrinology of ego disintegration. *American Journal of Psychiatry 126*(8):1067–1078.

Salzman, L. (1968). Obsessions and phobias. *International Journal of Psychiatry 6*:451–468.

Sandifer, K. G., Jr., Pettus, C., and Quade, D. (1964). A study of psychiatric diagnosis. *Journal of Nervous and Mental Disease 139*:262–267.

Sahakian, B. J. (1979). *Psychopathology Today,* 2nd ed. Itasca, Ill.: Peacock.

Sank, L. I. (1979). Community disasters: primary prevention and treatment in a health maintenance organization. *American Psychologist 34*:334–338.

Sarbin, T. R., and Mancuso, J. C. (1980). *Schizophrenia: Medical Diagnosis or Moral Verdict.* New York: Pergamon.

Scanlon, P. (1983). Fee and missed appointments as transference issues. In *Handbook.* New York: Adelphi University Press.

Schatzman, M. (1973). *Soul Murder.* New York: Random House.

Scheff, T. J., (1970). Schizophrenia as ideology. *Schizophrenia Bulletin 2*:15–19.

Schildkraut, J. J. (1977). Biochemical research in affective disorders. In *Depression: Clinical, Biological, and Psychological Perspectives,* ed. G. Usdin. New York: Brunner/Mazel.

Schuckit, M. A., and Rayses, V. (1979). Ethanol ingestion: differences in blood acetaldehyde concentrations in relatives of alcoholics and controls. *Science 203*:54–55.

Scott, C. L. (1976). Life events and schizophrenia: comparison of schizophrenics with a community sample. *Archives of General Psychiatry 34:*1238-1241.

Searles, H. (1959). The effort to drive the other person crazy: an element in etiology and psychotherapy of schizophrenia. *British Journal of Medical Psychology 32*:1-19.

Seligman, M. E. (1975). *Helplessness: On Depression, Development, and Death.* San Francisco: W. H. Freeman.

Seligman, M. E., and Hager, M., ed. (1972). *Biological Boundaries of Learning.* New York: Appleton-Century-Crofts.

Sellers, E. M., and Kalant, H. (1976). Drug therapy: alcohol intoxication and withdrawal. *New England Journal of Medicine 294*(4):757-762.

Selye, H. (1976). *The Stress of Life*, rev. ed. New York: McGraw-Hill.

Shimkunas, A. M. (1972). Demand for intimate self-disclosure and pathological verbalizations in schizophrenia. *Journal of Abnormal Psychology 80*:197-205.

Shulman, L. (1979). *The Skills of Helping Individuals and Groups.* Itasca, Ill.: Peacock.

Sidman, M. (1960). Normal sources of pathological behavior. *Science 132*: 61-72.

Siegel, M., Niswander, G. D., Sachs, E., and Stravos, D. (1959). Taraxein: fact or artifact? *American Journal of Psychiatry 115*:819-820.

Sines, O. J. (1959). Reserpine, adrenaline, and avoidance learning. *Psychological Reports 5*:321-324.

Singer, J., and Singer, I. (1972). Types of female orgasms. *Journal of Sex Research 8*: 255-267.

Singer, M. T., Wynne, L. C., and Toohey, M. I. (1978). Communication disorders and the families of schizophrenics. In *The Nature of Schizophrenia: New Approaches to Research and Treatment,* ed. L. C. Wynne, R. L. Cromwell, and S. Matthyse, pp. 499-511. New York: Wiley.

Slater, E. (1968). A review of earlier evidence of genetic factors in schizophrenia. In *The Transmission of Schizophrenia,* ed. D. Rosenthal and S. S. Kety. London: Pergamon.

Snyder, S. H. (1974). *Madness and the Brain.* New York: McGraw-Hill.

Sobel, P. E. (1961). Infant mortality and malformation in children of schizophrenic women. *Psychiatric Quarterly 35*:60-65.

Sobell, M. B., and Sobell, L. C. (1973). Individualized behavior therapy for alcoholics. *Behavior Therapy, 4*:49-72.

Spitz, R. A. (1965). *The First Year of Life: A Psychoanalytic Study of Normal and Deviant Development of Object Relations.* New York: International Universities Press.

Steiner, C. M. (1969). The alcoholic game. *Quarterly Journal of Studies on Alcohol 30*:920-938.

Steinglass, P., Weiner, S., and Mendelson, J. (1971). A systems approach to alcoholism: a model and its clinical application. *Archives of General Psychiatry 24*(5):401-408.

Stephens, J. H. (1970). Long-term course and prognosis in schizophrenia. *Seminars in Psychiatry 2*:464–485.

Stephens, J. A. (1978). *Schizophrenia Bulletin 4*(1):25–47.

Stern, R. S., Lipsedge, M. S. and Marks, I. M. Obsessive ruminations: a controlled trial of thought-stopping technique. *Behavioral Research and Therapy 11*(4):659–662.

Strauss, M. E., Fourema, W. C., and Parwatikar, S. D. (1974). Schizophrenics' size estimation of thematic stimuli. *Journal of Abnormal Psychology 83*(2): 117–123.

Strean, H. S. (1976). A psychosocial view of social deviancy. *Clinical Social Work Journal 4*(3):187–203.

Sullivan, H. S. (1931). The modified psychoanalytic treatment of schizophrenia. *American Journal of Psychiatry 11*:519–527.

_____ (1956). *Clinical Studies in Psychiatry.* New York: Norton.

_____ (1962). *Schizophrenia as a Human Process.* New York: Norton.

Sweeney, D. R., and Maas, J. W. (1979). Stress and noradrenergic function in depression. In *The Psychobiology of the Depressive Disorders: Implications for the Effects of Stress,* ed. R. A. Depue. New York: Academic.

Szasz, T. S. (1976). *Schizophrenia: The Sacred Symbol of Psychiatry.* New York: Basic Books.

Tavel, M. E. (1962). A new look at an old syndrome: delirium tremens. *Archives of Internal Medicine 109*:129–134.

Tollison, C. D., Nasbilt, J. G., and Frey, J. D. (1977). Comparison of attitudes towards sexual intimacy in prostitutes and college coeds. *Journal of Social Psychology 101*(2):319–320.

Torrey, E. F. (1980). Epidemiology. In *Disorders of the Schizophrenic Syndrome,* ed. L. Bellak. New York: Basic Books.

Torrey, E. F., Torrey, B. B., and Burton-Bradley, B. G. (1974). The epidemiology of schizophrenia in Papan, New Guinea. *American Journal of Psychiatry 131*(5):567–573.

Torrey, E. F., Torrey, B. B., and Peterson, M. R. (1977). Seasonality of schizophrenic births in the U.S. *Archives of General Psychiatry 34*:1065–1069.

Turner, S. M., Hersen, M., Bellak, A. S., and Wells, K. C. (1979). Behavioral treatment of obsessive-compulsive neurosis. *Behavior Research and Therapy 17*:95–106.

Uhlenhuth, E. H. (1973). Free therapy said to be helpful to train wreck victims. *Psychiatric News 8*(3):1–27.

Uhlenhuth, E. H., Lipman, R. S., Baltes, M. B., and Stern, M. (1974). Symptom intensity and life stress in the city. *Archives of General Psychiatry 31*:759–763.

Ullman, L. P., and Kransner, L. (1975). *Psychological Approach to Abnormal Behavior* 2nd ed. Englewood Cliffs, N.J.: Prentice-Hall.

Ungerstedt, U. (1971). Stereotaxic mapping of the monoamine pathways in the rat brain. *Acta Physiologica Scandinavica 367*:1–48.

Ursin, H., Baade, E., and Levine, S. (1978). *Psychobiology of Stress.* New

York: Academic.

Van Buskirk, S. S. (1977). A two-phase perspective on the treatment of ano-rexia nervosa. *Psychological Bulletin 84*:529–547.

Vandereycken, W. (1982). Paradoxical strategies in a blocked sex therapy. *American Journal of Psychotherapy* 36(1):103–108.

Vaughn, C. E., and Leff, J. P. (1976). The influence of family and social fac-tors on the course of psychiatric illness: a comparison of schizophrenic and de-pressed neurotic patients. *British Journal of Psychiatry 129*:125–137.

——— (1981). Patterns of emotional response in relatives of schizophrenic pa-tients. *Schizophrenic Bulletin* 7:43–44.

Veronen, L. J., Kilpatrick, D. G., and Resnick, P. A. (1979). Treating fear and anxiety in rape victims: implications for the criminal justice system. In *Perspec-tives on Victimology,* ed. W. H. Parsonage. Beverly Hills: Russell Sage.

Victor, M., and Adams, R. (1953). The effects of alcohol on the nervous sys-tem. *Research Publication Association of Nervous Mental Disorders 32*:526–573.

Von Domarus, E. (1944). The specific laws of logic in schizophrenia. In *Lan-guage and Thought in Schizophrenia: Collected Papers,* ed. J. S. Kasanin, pp. 104–114. Berkeley: University of California Press.

Wagner, G., and Metz, P. (1980). Impotence (erectile dysfunction) due to vas-cular disorders: an overview. *Journal of Sex and Marital Therapy 6*(4):223–233.

Walsh, T. B. The endocrinology of anorexia nervosa. *Psychiatric Clinics of North America 3*(2):299–312.

Ward, C. H., Beck, A. T., Mendelson, M., et al. (1962). The psychiatric no-menclature: reasons for diagnostic disagreement. *Archives of General Psychiatry 9*: 27–39.

Waring, M., and Ricks, D. F. (1965). Family patterns of children who became adult schizophrenics. *Journal of Nervous and Mental Disease 140*:351–364.

Waxler, N. E. (1974). Culture and mental illness: a social labeling perspective. *Journal of Nervous and Mental Disease 159*(6):379–395.

Webb, S. D., and Collette, J. (1975). Urban ecological and household corre-lates of stress-alleviate drug use. *American Behavioral Scientist 18*:750–769.

Weiss, J. M., Glazer, H. I., Pohecky, L. A., et al. (1979). Coping behavior and stress-induced behavioral depression: studies of the role of brain catecholamines. In *The Psychobiology of the Depressive Disorders: Implications for the Effects of Stress,* ed. R. A. Depue. New York: Academic.

Weissman, M. M., and Klerman, G. L. (1977). Sex differences and the epidemi-ology of depression. *Archives of General Psychiatry 34*:98–111.

Wender, P. H., Rosenthal, D., Kety, S. S., et al. (1974). Cross-fostering: a re-search strategy for clarifying the role of genetic and experiential factors in the etiol-ogy of schizophrenia. *Archives of General Psychiatry 30*(1):121–128.

White, R. W., and Watt, N. F. (1973). *The Abnormal Personality*. New York: Ronald.

Williams, A. F. (1966). Social drinking, anxiety, and depression. *Journal of Personality and Social Psychology 3*:689–695.

Wilsnack, S. (1973). Femininity by the bottle. *Psychology Today 6*.39–42.

Wilsnack, W. (1983). Handling resistance in social case work. In *Handbook*. New York: Adelphi University Press.

Wilson, G. T. (1978). Booze, beliefs, and behavior: cognitive process in alcohol use and abuse. In *Alcoholism: New Directions in Behavioral Research Treatment,* ed. P. E. Nathan, G. A. Marlatt, and T. Loberg. New York: Plenum.

Wilson, G. T., and Lawson, D. M. (1976). Expectancies, alcohol, and sexual arousal in male social drinkers. *Journal of Abnormal Psychology 85*:587–594.

Wincze, J. P. (1982). Assessment of sexual disorders. *Behavioral Assessment* 4(3):257–271.

Winnicott, D. W. (1958). *Collected Papers*. London: Tavistock.

Winokur, G., Reich, T., Rimmer, J., and Pitts, F. N. (1970). Alcoholism III: diagnosis and familial psychiatric illness in 259 alcoholic probands. *Archives of General Psychiatry 23*:104–113.

Wolberg, L. R. (1954). *The Technique of Psychotherapy*. New York: Grune & Stratton.

Wolpe, J. (1952). Experimental neuroses as learned behavior. *British Journal of Psychology 43*:243–252.

———— (1953). Learning theory and "abnormal fixations." *Psychological Review 60*:111–123.

———— (1958). *Psychotherapy by Reciprocal Inhibition*. Stanford, Calif.: Stanford University Press.

———— (1969). Basic principles and practices of behavior therapy of neuroses. *American Journal of Psychiatry* 125(9):1242–1247.

Wood, H., and Duffy, E. (1966). Psychology factors in alcoholic women. *American Journal of Psychiatry 123*(3):341–345.

Yates, A. J. (1966). Psychological deficit. In *Annual Review of Psychology,* ed. P. R. Farnsworth. Palo Alto, Calif.: Annual Review.

Yolles, S. F., and Kramer, M. (1969). Vital statistics of schizophrenia. In *The Schizophrenia Syndrome*, ed. L. Bellak and L. Loeb, pp. 66–113. New York: Grune & Stratton.

Zigler, E., and Levine, J. (1981). Premorbid competence in schizophrenia: what is being measured? *Journal of Consulting and Clinical Psychology* 49(1): 96–105.

Zilbergeld, B. (1980). Alternatives to couple counseling for sex problems: group and individual therapy. *Journal of Sex and Marital Therapy* 6(1):3–18.

Zubin, J., and Spring, B. (1977). Vulnerability: a new view of schizophrenia. *Journal of Abnormal Psychology 86*:103–126.

Index